SCRIPT ANALYSIS FOR THEATRE

RELATED TITLES FROM BLOOMSBURY PUBLISHING:

The Art of Rehearsal: Conversations with Contemporary Theatre-Makers
edited by Barbara Simonsen, Isabelle Reynaud and Deborah Vlaeymans
ISBN 978-1-4742-9201-6

A Critical Companion to the American Stage Musical
by Elizabeth L. Wollman
ISBN 978-1-4725-1325-0

Directing: A Handbook for Emerging Theatre Directors
by Rob Swain
ISBN 978-1-4081-2765-0

The Disney Musical on Stage and Screen: Critical Approaches from 'Snow White' to 'Frozen'
edited by George Rodosthenous
ISBN 978-1-4742-3416-0

Reader in Comedy: An Anthology of Theory and Criticism
edited by Magda Romanska and Alan Ackerman
ISBN 978-1-4742-4788-7

Scenography Expanded: An Introduction to Contemporary Performance Design
edited by Joslin McKinney and Scott Palmer
ISBN 978-1-4742-4439-8

Studying Plays
by Simon Shepherd and Mick Wallis
ISBN 978-0-3409-8514-4

The Story of Drama: Tragedy, Comedy and Sacrifice from the Greeks to the Present
by Gary Day
ISBN 978-1-4081-8312-0

SCRIPT ANALYSIS FOR THEATRE

TOOLS FOR INTERPRETATION, COLLABORATION AND PRODUCTION

Robert Knopf

methuen | drama

LONDON • NEW YORK • OXFORD • NEW DELHI • SYDNEY

METHUEN DRAMA
Bloomsbury Publishing Plc
50 Bedford Square, London, WC1B 3DP, UK

BLOOMSBURY, METHUEN DRAMA and the Methuen Drama logo are trademarks
of Bloomsbury Publishing Plc

First published in Great Britain 2017
Reprinted 2018, 2019

Cover Photograph © Geraint Lewis. *Twelfth Night* by William Shakespeare,
A Royal Shakespeare Company Production directed by David Farr.

A catalogue record for this book is available from the British Library.

ISBN: HB: 978-1-4081-8382-3
PB: 978-1-4081-8430-1
ePDF: 978-1-4081-8530-8
ePub: 978-1-4081-8518-6

A catalog record for this book is available from the Library of Congress.

Typeset by Integra Software Services Pvt. Ltd.
Printed and bound in Great Britain

To find out more about our authors and books visit www.bloomsbury.com
and sign up for our newsletters.

To Katie

CONTENTS

PREFACE

A History of Action-Based Approaches to Dramatic Structure

KATIE KNOPF

This book proceeds from the assumption that every play contains a series of peaks, or key moments, of different sizes; one of the principal tasks of script analysis is to identify these moments and define the characters' actions that lead to them. This approach works equally well for almost any play, whether it employs a predominantly climactic dramatic structure or an episodic one, a masculine structure or a feminine one. The search for the most significant and powerful key moments helps us chart a course through the otherwise undefined landscape of the dramatic action; modulating these moments creates the shape of the drama; and translating this shape into acting, directing, and design choices is our ultimate goal. Even in a purely climactic dramatic structure, smaller key moments lead to the final key moment, or climax, which represent turns in the road and keep audiences guessing. Defining the moment-to-moment journey is an art; as such, each theatre artist must make strong artistic choices to distinguish his or her interpretation from others. Only by recognizing the actions that create the journey, and by learning the language with which to communicate and collaborate on shaping it, can theatre artists turn script analysis into compelling theatre.

For well over 2,000 years, philosophers, scholars, and theatre artists have devised methods to analyse and understand scripts. Aristotle wrote the earliest surviving work of dramatic theory, *Poetics*, circa 335 BCE. As written, *Poetics* addressed both comic and tragic plays; after the work was divided into two parts, each written on a separate roll of papyrus, the section devoted to comedy was lost. What remains – Aristotle's description of the elements of a good tragedy – has served as the foundation for most methods of play analysis, allowing theatre scholars and practitioners to adapt, develop, and apply script analysis to the more varied dramatic forms conceived in later eras.

Aristotle applies his theory of imitation, on which humans rely from infancy as a means of learning, to the construction of the drama. He argues that imitation is a natural function through which humans derive pleasure. In drama, imitation involves more than a simple copy, or mimicry, of an action; it is a representation of human life created through the imagination of the dramatist.[1] Drama imitates the ideal reality – one that, through the movement and gestures of the actors, takes its form in the imagination of the spectator. The dramatist and spectator must imagine this alternate reality jointly. With the freedom to create this reality, the dramatist presents embodied stories of humanity to help audience members learn about themselves.

Aristotle believed that tragedy could stimulate *catharsis* – a release of emotions – thus providing audiences with pleasure. The ancient Greeks believed that humans harboured four humours, or vital fluids, in the bloodstream: yellow bile, black bile, blood, and phlegm; a balance of all four indicated optimal health, whereas an excess or deficiency showed malaise. Excess emotion likewise signalled illness, but through the catharsis created by tragedy, the human body and soul could be purged of excess fear and pity, restoring the amounts of each humour to healthy levels.

In *Poetics*, Aristotle defined tragedy, consisting of six elements in order of importance – plot, character, thought, diction, melody, and spectacle – as follows:

> A process of imitating an action which has serious implications, is complete, and possesses magnitude; by means of language which has been made sensuously attractive, with each of its varieties found separately in the parts; enacted by the persons themselves and not presented through narrative; through a course of pity and fear completing the purification of tragic acts which have those emotional characteristics. (25)

In Aristotle's opinion, plot, the structure of events, is the 'heart and soul' of tragedy; without it, tragic art could not exist. Think of a plot as a chain of

---

[1] In his *Poetics*, Aristotle refers to playwrights as 'poets', in keeping with his practice of referring to comedy and tragedy, along with lyric and epic poetry, as 'poetry'. For clarity, we have chosen to use 'dramatist' when referring to Aristotle's *Poetics*.

incidents building from beginning to middle (climax) to end (resolution). A simple plot focuses on a singular, continuous chain of events that does not involve Aristotle's key tragic concepts of reversal, or *peripeteia* – a change in situation, relationship, fortune, or intention that brings the action of the play full circle – and recognition, or *anagnorisis* – the change from ignorance to awareness when the protagonist discovers his own predicament or the true identity of another character.

Complex plots include events caused by *hamartia*, 'a mistake of great weight and consequence' by the hero (Else 38), often translated inaccurately as a tragic flaw. The hamartia leads to complications, further intensified by the main character's recognition of his or her mistake and, in turn, anticipates the character's tragic end, the *catastrophe*. The catastrophe – from the Greek *katastrophe*, meaning 'an overturning' or 'a sudden end' (*etymonline.com*) – comes after the reversal. Thus, the plot progresses from hamartia through recognition and reversal to catastrophe; by contrast, a simple plot involves only a catastrophe. Aristotle favoured complex plots through which fear and pity could be aroused, driven by a sense of causality that gives the plot its internal logic.

Character, the second most important component in an Aristotelian tragedy, provides the moral fibre of the story. The hero should be a good person, as Aristotle assumed that audience members are of good moral character themselves and would therefore rather see a noble character, instead of one less virtuous, receive good fortune at the end. Aristotle notes that if the hero comes into trouble by way of a tragic accident, as a result of hamartia, the play will engage the audience's emotions to a higher degree. The hero should be given qualities appropriate to his makeup (wise if he is aged, for example) and consistent with his mannerisms and conduct. If there is a good reason for a sudden shift in behaviour or morals, the dramatist should explain it to avoid confusing the audience.

The third essential element is thought – the spoken reasoning of characters – which helps the audience understand the character's rationale for his or her actions and provides necessary details that fill the plot. The dramatist's rhetoric should express moral virtue and demonstrate the rational processes through which characters come to conclusions. Diction, the fourth element, refers to how the actors express the moral qualities of their characters, bringing them to life through expert delivery of the play's metrical language. Melody, the fifth element, describes the play's most significant embellishment on stage, accomplished through music. Aristotle highlights the significance of the chorus as an integral part of the cast, contributing to the action, unifying the plot, and contributing to the performance's melody (through chanting) and spectacle (through dance). The final element of tragedy, spectacle refers to anything visual in the play that helps bring the story to life, including the set, costumes, and props, as well as the choreographed movement of the chorus. Aristotle argues that spectacle is the least important element because 'the force of tragedy can be felt even without benefit of public performance and actors, while for the production of the visual effect the property man's art is even more decisive than that of the poets' (29).

Aristotle's three-act dramatic structure – introduction (beginning), climax (middle), and resolution (end) – inspired theatre scholars, including the German writer Dr. Gustav Freytag, to develop similar models for drama. In 1863, Freytag published his essential and oft-quoted *The Technique of the Drama: An Exposition of Dramatic Composition and Art*, in which he proposed a five-part model for dramatic structure, commonly known as Freytag's pyramid. Scholars and playwrights found Freytag's model particularly useful in interpreting Shakespearean drama and ancient Greek plays. Freytag's pyramid best captures the shape of most 'well-made plays', such as Henrik Ibsen's *A Doll's House*, some classical dramas, and plays that employ a predominantly climactic structure, such as the works of Sophocles or Molière. Though his theories may fail to adequately account for the dramaturgical workings and shape of many episodic and experimental plays, Freytag's pyramid still serves as a valuable introduction to dramatic form.

Freytag's model delineates five types of action: introduction, rise, climax, return, and catastrophe. Between these five, he marks three smaller, but no less significant, moments in the structure of a play – the exciting moment, the tragic moment, and the moment of the last suspense. The opening, the introduction, launches the audience into the world of the play, establishing the context for the ensuing action and revealing any knowledge the audience needs to understand the rest of the action. The audience might learn about the hero's background, including his nationality and social and personal relations, as well as the locale and period of the action, and the play's environment. The introduction should introduce characters involved in the plot's counter-play, the opposing force that initiates conflict with the hero. Freytag suggests that 'the time with which the action moves forward', which we might call the tempo of the piece, might also be noted here (118). A solid introduction includes a decisive keynote (central idea or theme) within a finished scene and provides a brief transition into the first moment of the excited action, also known as the complication. An exciting force or moment, triggered by an action or event, sets the central action of the play in motion. The force can come about slowly or abruptly, depending upon the emotional and mental constitutions of the characters; it can arise from the soul of the hero, by way of his adversary, or through an entirely different form. Regardless of its origin, it must serve as the transition from the introduction to the ascending action that follows. Freytag argues that the exciting moment must not detract from the action that follows or determine the hero's fate but hold its own place in the anatomy of the play.

The middle of the play builds upon the exciting moment, moving the action towards the climax, or point of highest tension. The ascent can involve one or many stages to the climax, best structured in scene groups, including a 'unified chief scene, subordinate scene, and connecting scene' (126). By arranging scenes into groups, divided among multiple stages, Freytag allows for a detailed dramatic construction, providing the playwright with the opportunity to control the pace of the play's rising action. Each scene should pique the audience's interest progressively.

The climax takes place at the top of Freytag's pyramid, as the play's action, launched by the exciting moment, escalates and reaches its peak. The hero's fate changes, marking a turning point in the plot. What follows is falling action, in which the conflict's solution is played out. Freytag contends that the strongest climaxes occur in dramas in which the hero drives the rising action, in contrast to dramas that reach their peak through the skill and mischief of the counter-players. The climax most often takes place in the third act of Freytag's structure. In certain instances, the climax can take the form of a double apex, in which the close connection of the climax and tragic force – the event or force that starts the downwards movement of the play – widens the middle segment.

Freytag considers the return, or falling action, the most challenging sequence to construct because the playwright must continue to arouse the audience's interest and heighten suspense after the major action of the climactic moment. To do so effectively, Freytag suggests keeping the number of characters to a minimum and including dynamic artistic and dramatic effects, powerfully placed in well-structured scenes. In the falling action, 'the essence of the whole, [the] idea and conduct of the action, comes forward powerfully; the audience understands the connection of events, [and] sees the ultimate purpose of the poet' (134).

The moment of final suspense must carry considerable weight, for it prepares the audience for the hero's demise in the play's last moments. The faint possibility of a happy ending calls into question the presumed final outcome, offering relief for the audience. Unfortunately for the hero, this prospect is short lived; in the closing action of the play – the catastrophe – the audience experiences catharsis as the conflicts are settled once and for all. Freytag calls for minimal dialogue, to allow the hero's downfall to reveal the true nature of the characters; scenes should be spirited, direct, and concise. The catastrophe most often includes the death, or moral destruction, of at least one character. The hero's life should not be spared, as there is nothing to be gained by doing so; the audience's satisfaction is greatest when the action comes to a definitive conclusion, and the hero comes to a definitive end.

When attempting to apply Freytag's model to the analysis of an episodic play with a non-linear structure, such as the works of contemporary playwrights Annie Baker, Suzan-Lori Parks, Paula Vogel, and Mac Wellman, the transgressions of these plays come into stark contrast. Seen this way, Freytag's model might be used as a lens through which we can better discern innovations in dramatic form. The five-part model fails to completely account for the dramatic structure of some of the very works Freytag based his model on, including the late sixteenth- and early seventeenth-century works of Christopher Marlowe and William Shakespeare, whose plays are so often episodic, with parallel plots played out by many characters in multiple locations. As we will see in the coming chapters, the structure of many plays might not always be symmetrical and simple: the exceptions to Freytag's model may be as significant as the rules.

Some see the emergence of women playwrights in the twentieth century as creating a movement towards 'feminine structure'. In contrast to the step-by-step build to a single climax of Freytag's 'masculine structure', plays that use a predominantly feminine structure consist of multiple peaks, placing the emphasis on the journey instead of a single explosive climax.[2] There is a cumulative effect to the scenes, each one playing an equally important part in the overall experience of the play, affecting and propelling the action that follows. This approach to analysing structure produces a more vivid and detailed reading of any play, one that provides endless options for actors, directors, and dramaturges collaborating on a production. By accepting that the dramatic structure of a play can be seen on a continuum from masculine to feminine – all plays have several key moments, whether they build to a single climax or not – we can apply this approach to plays across all genres, dramatic movements, and time periods.

Because Freytag created his pyramid for the analysis of tragedies, specifically ancient Greek and Shakespearean drama, his language no longer fits the way in which we, as contemporary theatre artists and scholars, read and see most plays. The contemporary colloquial meaning of the word 'climax', for example, has changed greatly since the nineteenth century. According to the Online Etymology Dictionary, the word 'climax' derived in the 1580s from the late Latin *climax*, 'a chain of reasoning in graduating steps from weaker to stronger'. Similarly, the definition of the Greek *klimax* refers to 'propositions rising in effectiveness', literally 'ladder' from the root of *klinein,* 'to slope', from the Proto-Indo-European root *klei,* meaning 'to lean'. The rhetorical meaning evolved in English from a 'series of steps by which a goal is achieved', to 'escalating steps', to 'high point of intensity or development' in 1789, a puritanical usage credited by the Oxford English Dictionary to 'popular ignorance'. The definition of climax as a 'sexual orgasm' was first recorded by

---

[2]See Leroy Clark, *Writing for the Stage: A Practical Playwriting Guide*, Boston: Pearson/Allyn and Bacon, 2006: 89–97.

1880 and is said to have been chosen around 1900 by birth control pioneer and campaigner Marie Stopes as a more accessible word than 'orgasm'. Because we equate the word 'climax' to sensations experienced at the very peak of sexual excitation, we tend to place the climax closer to the end of a play, as opposed to Freytag, who placed the climax at the centre – Act 3 within his five-act structure.

American theatre theorist and playwright John Howard Lawson takes issue with Freytag's five-act structure in *Theory and Technique of Playwriting and Screenwriting* (1949). Calling Freytag's influence on dramatic theory 'unfortunate', Lawson moves away from the work of the theorists who preceded him. His notation for his vision of a play's anatomy is 'AbcdefGH' – 'A' being the exposition, 'b', 'c', 'd', 'e', and 'f' the cycles of the rising action, 'G' the obligatory scene, and 'H' the climax. Defining an action as a 'unit of movement', Lawson insists that cycles of action can appear in any of these subdivisions. If a play is a system of action and each subdivision potentially contains multiple cycles of action, it is possible to reach multiple climaxes. By positioning the large climax, 'H', at the very end of the play, Lawson makes room for the rise and fall of smaller ones that might surface earlier. 'For example, c reaches a climax which is the culmination of a system of action of which the exposition, rising action, and obligatory scene may be traced' (246). Lawson's contributions to the study of dramatic action are indicative of a movement towards working with alternative dramatic structures, following more than fifty years of avant-garde dramatic experimentation.

Lawson also criticized his contemporary, playwright and scholar George Pierce Baker, whose influential *Dramatic Technique* (1919) conceived of a technique for play analysis adapted for young playwrights in the early stages of their development and education.[3] The first textbook to examine the construction of plays as a whole, *Dramatic Technique* offers the up-and-coming dramatist 'not mere theories of playwriting but the practice of dramatists of the past, so that what they have shared in common, and where their practice has differed, shall be clear' (iv).

Although he mostly retains the shape of Aristotle's tragic plot structure, Baker establishes principles for the construction of a well-made play, noted for its compact plot and late climax. He discusses the importance of plotting and

---

[3]Baker yearned for an American theatre with a pool of skilled young dramatists. Founder of the Yale School of Drama, he was the first academic to teach playwriting, having attempted to institute a playwriting programme at his alma mater, Harvard. His attempts there were ridiculed, for at that time, playwrights learned the theory and practice of theatre through first-hand experience in the profession. At Yale, he taught the famed English 47 class (whose students included a young Eugene O'Neill) that began as an experiment at Harvard's all-woman counterpart, Radcliffe College. *Dramatic Technique* is a compilation of lectures that Baker gave at the Lowell Institute in Boston, beginning in 1913 (2).

stresses the significance of given circumstances that the playwright embeds in the script for the actor. A play should be divided into an appropriate number of acts, of suitable length, each playing a significant role in forwarding the narrative. Compelling dramatic narrative involves the progression of what Baker calls 'situations', or what we might call conflicts, discoveries, or events. Because the arrangement of the events is the key to the narrative's success, playwrights should spend time revising for clarity and interest. The play's dialogue must be witty, propel the narrative, and consistently develop characterization. The first draft should focus on clarity, construction, and proper emphasis; each subsequent draft should improve the dialogue and characterization.

Baker refers to dramatic action as 'illustrative action' and believes it should be constructed to convey emotion accurately. He specifies that action should be physical or mental, so long as it stirs an emotional response, a point that Lawson disputes:

> This is of very little value unless we know what constitutes an emotional response. Since what moves us in any action is the spectacle of a change of equilibrium between the individual and the environment, we cannot speak of any action as being exclusively mental or exclusively physical; the change must affect *both* the individual's mind and the objective reality with which he is in contact. Such a change need not involve bustle or violence, but it must involve *doing something*, because if nothing is done the equilibrium would remain static. (167)

Although Baker applied his method to a wide range of plays, it is most useful as a guide to the writing and analysis of well-made, realistic drama. Almost 100 years later, many playwriting and screenwriting teachers still promote some form of Baker's pragmatic advice for developing writers.

In comparison, contemporary playwright Annie Baker (no relation) writes plays that experiment with quite different forms of dramatic action, including ones that some would argue contain little or no action at all. Her 2012 Pulitzer Prize-winning play, *The Flick*, uses a non-linear, predominantly feminine dramatic structure distinguished by long stretches of inaction, as the characters – underpaid employees in a dilapidated movie theatre that is about to be converted from film to digital projection – go about their daily work of sweeping the debris left behind by the theatre's dwindling audiences. Through random banter about classic movies, and with an insider's eye for the daily grind of theatre workers, Baker's characters confess their 'star-crossed' loves, their friendships ebb and flow, and the theatre that has become a vital part of the fabric of their lives undergoes a radical transformation.

The play centres on Sam, a 35-year-old movie theatre veteran, and Avery, a 20-year-old newcomer with an obsession for the theatre's 35-millimetre projector, one of only eight left in Massachusetts, as large chains such as AMC, Regal, and Cinemark have swallowed up old theatres and converted them to digital projection. Rose, the object of Sam's affections, holds the most coveted job at the theatre, running the projector. The beauty of *The Flick* lies in Baker's gentle, affectionate handling of these ordinary people as they become tangled in each other's lives and problems, mixing personal affairs with their jobs and conceiving of no way to extract themselves from their dead-end situations.

Though the play takes place in a single setting, the structure of the dramatic action is chronological, yet non-linear. A typical, linear well-made play moves forward in time, occasionally compressing the action into a shorter period, as in classical Greek drama. Non-linear plays do not move forward in a straight line but skip whenever necessary, sometimes jumping backwards in time. The hallmark of a non-linear plot is its lack of causality; one event does not lead inextricably to the next. The action in *The Flick*, for example, takes place over a few months. Instead of a single climax, the action has several small peaks lacking all but the most rudimentary causality: Rose's attempt to perform sexual acts on Avery; the changeover of the movie house from film to digital; Sam and Rose's quarrel about their relationship, or lack thereof; and Avery's firing by the theatre's new owner after he discovers the trio's minor embezzlement. Each of these moments is surrounded by stretches with no dialogue, filled by the characters' slow, laborious cleaning of the theatre, instead of the emotions that fill the silences in a traditional well-made play. In comparison to a well-made play, *The Flick* creates a relatively flat landscape.

Even though *The Flick* represents an illustrative example of a predominantly feminine dramatic structure, Sally Potter's 1992 film *Orlando*, adapted from Virginia Woolf's *Orlando: A Biography* (1929), is one of the most noted examples of feminine structure in film. Woolf identified herself as a feminist and penned *Orlando* as a biography of sorts, based on the life of her friend and lover, Vita Sackville-West. Potter's film spotlights gender roles and sexual identity in both Elizabethan and modern society (the film ends with Lady Orlando in 1992, the year the film was made). The story concerns an androgynous young nobleman, Orlando (Tilda Swinton), as he evades time and ageing after making a promise to the dying Queen Elizabeth I to watch over her castle and land for all time. Centuries later, after dabbling in poetry and, more seriously, in love, Orlando is appointed British ambassador to the Turks and almost loses his life during a diplomatic brawl. After spending days in a trance-like state, he awakens to find himself physically transformed into a woman. Upon returning to England, Lady Orlando faces the threat of legal action by her detractors, who cannot believe that such a transformation could take place. If they can prove Orlando was a woman to begin with, he will lose his land and royal inheritance. And then there is the small matter of Orlando's eternal existence: If indeed Lady Orlando was born male more than 200 years ago, he should be long dead.

Orlando's narrative structure is made up of several sequences, each one skipping ahead about fifty years, announced by intertitles highlighting the major events about to affect Orlando's life: Death, Love, Poetry, Politics, Society, Sex, and Birth. Instead of building to one major climax, Potter's adaptation employs several smaller climaxes to create a predominantly feminine, episodic dramatic structure – a beautifully crafted, witty investigation of what it means to be born as a woman or a man. From these examples and others, we can see how contemporary dramatic and cinematic scripts may vary greatly from the structures of their predecessors.

In the development of action analysis – somewhere between the traditional structure of the well-made play and the transgressive compositions of avant-garde, experimental, and feminist plays – enters the master acting teacher Constantin Stanislavski, whose search for techniques that actors could use to rehearse and perform a wide range of plays led him to develop a method of script analysis based on the actions and objectives of the characters. Although Freytag, Lawson, and Baker laid the foundation for action analysis, Stanislavski's approach became the cornerstone of modern and contemporary theatre practice. In the introduction that follows the author will explore the ideas presented in the preface in greater detail, linked more directly to Stanislavski's advances.

ACKNOWLEDGEMENTS

I would like to offer most sincere thanks to all the people who were instrumental in the development of this book. My editor at Bloomsbury Methuen Drama, Mark Dudgeon, helped me focus the topics and broaden the book's appeal. Art Borreca, Jim Volz, and Kristine Holtvedt helped me further develop the book's structure and content. Last but never least, Mike Gauger always reminds me to write succinctly and persuasively.

Special thanks go to my wife and partner, Katie, for believing in me in good times and bad. I don't know how I would do it without you – and I don't intend to find out.

Introduction

During the first decade or so of my career in theatre, I trained as a director, dramaturg, and scholar. I directed productions at several professional theatres in New York, wrote and edited books about silent film comedy, avant-garde theatre, and directing, taught and directed at Purdue University and the University of Michigan, Ann Arbor, and went on to produce six seasons of theatre and dance at the University at Buffalo/SUNY as chair and producing director. I am grateful to have worked with so many generous and creative collaborators who genuinely contributed their very best work to every production. Yet for all my training and experience, the frequent miscommunication among areas of specialization – acting, directing, design and technology, technical direction, stage management, and dramaturgy – never ceases to surprise me. As theatre teachers and practitioners, we all seek to develop a collaborative art form that requires each area to work closely with the others towards a unified vision, yet we do not always speak the same language.

As producing director of a large university theatre and dance department, my broader perspective on production practices allowed me to finally observe how these issues unfold from each area's point of view. Sitting in on design and production meetings, I began to see just how frequently we, as theatre artists – students, professors, and guest artists – talk past each other: describing ideas in the specialized language of our areas, or attempting to use language with which we may not feel completely comfortable. Because I saw the big picture of each production season more clearly as producing director than I had in the past as director or dramaturg for a single production, I began to think about how better communication about plays among actors, directors, designers and technical directors, stage managers, and dramaturges might create stronger collaborations. I sought to find and articulate a set of terms and concepts that all members of a creative ensemble might employ to share their ideas about a play, argue for different interpretations, and eventually come together to explore a single vision as a team of equals, not rivals.

It was not my goal to develop a new system for working on theatre, but to synthesize the dominant practices in professional and university theatres into a comprehensive approach to analyse, discuss, and envision scripts for production. Despite my personal interest in the innovations of experimental and avant-garde theatre practice, I appreciated that almost all theatre artists ground their understanding of a script in terms of action – what the characters do to each other to get what they want from each other – and that the language for discussing what happens on stage among characters has been shaped, for over eighty years, by the work of the Russian master acting teacher Konstantin Stanislavski. He was the first to articulate a system for analysing and describing reciprocal action: the give and take among characters as they pursue and revise their actions in response to a wide variety of challenging obstacles, hostile environments, and interpersonal conflicts.

To be sure, there are plays that do not seem to rely upon this kind of direct action. The Symbolist plays of Maurice Maeterlinck, such as *The Blind*, *Interior*, and *Intruder*, appear 'static' to the casual observer and reader, more concerned with establishing mood than forwarding action. Samuel Beckett's plays frequently appear to lack action or, at the very least, feature characters who seem to travel in circuitous routes that cover very short distances. More recently, the plays of Annie Baker seem to move forward in short, sporadic spurts of action, with few sustained moments of high stakes between them. Yet at their core, all these plays and playwrights still create and embrace characters who do things to each other, no matter how ineffectually, even if other elements of drama and production are more prominent. If we understand how action shapes most plays, we might, when confronted by a less action-dominant script, more easily discover the elements that become more essential than action to the shape of the play in performance.

Stanislavski was already an established professional theatre director, actor, and artistic director when he began to develop the ideas that would form the foundation of his acting technique.[1] As an actor, he had gone through several frustrating periods – the actor's equivalent of writer's block – during which he felt that his performances had gone dry or become stale. To be fair, these dry spells arose in response to new production conditions that Stanislavski had encountered – long runs of a single play, for which he had to perform the same role night after night for months – compelling a radical change from past rehearsal and performance practices.

---

[1]Stanislavski co-founded the Moscow Art Theatre with playwright and director Vladimir Nemirovich-Danchenko in 1898, but he did not experiment with the first elements of what became known as Stanislavski Technique or the Stanislavski System until 1911–18. He did not develop his 'method of physical actions' until 1934–38.

In the Elizabethan theatre for which William Shakespeare wrote, for example, theatre companies performed plays in repertory: each company had a large core of plays that it was ready to perform on a moment's notice, and each night of the week, the company performed a different play. A large number of companies competed for a relatively small number of potential audience members; to attract audiences night after night, each company varied its offerings nightly. To be able to handle such a wide range and number of plays, actors were typecast. Acting companies developed 'lines of business', and each actor specialized in a type of role or a narrow range of roles – the roles for a light comedian, an old man, a clown, a young woman (played by boy actors), or a romantic lead. These were called lines of business because each actor learned his role by interning for a more experienced actor; thus, the roles were passed down the line from one generation to the next. Actors learned the physical 'business' associated with these roles in this way, and the business could be easily applied to a similar role in a new play with a limited amount of rehearsal. Given the constant turnover in a company's offerings, the company had very little time for rehearsal – perhaps a day for a new play or a few hours to brush up a play that the company had not performed recently. And though the company would select props and costumes from its stock for each play, there was no director in the modern sense and no designers specifically charged with deciding how these elements would be deployed.

In the early twentieth century, the artistic and critical success of the Moscow Art Theatre led the company to perform the same plays for extended runs and international tours that sometimes lasted many months. As an actor, Stanislavski found that his performances would lose their freshness over the course of these long runs. His performances became erratic, and he constantly complained about the elusiveness of his inspiration as an actor. Although he no longer followed the formulas and stock business associated with Elizabethan lines of roles, Stanislavski felt that he settled into patterns of physical and psychological behaviour with his roles, and over the long haul of an international tour, these became static and dead for him. He simply could not retain the inner impulse and creativity that had led him to create each role in a particular way in the first place. He began to search for a way to reinvigorate a role without losing the core of the character or upsetting the overall sense of the production.

During his first period of experimentation (c. 1911–16), Stanislavski explored **emotional memory** (also known as affective memory or emotional recall) as a technique for actors to create genuine, truthful emotions on stage by recalling or reliving moments from an actor's past so that they may recreate similar emotions when needed in rehearsal and performance. This would become one of the earliest cornerstones of American Method acting, developed and popularized by Lee Strasberg. Later, Stanislavski and his disciples, most prominently Vsevolod Meyerhold, Yevgeny Vahktangov, Michael Chekhov, and Richard Boleslavsky, experimented with approaches to training actors that worked from the 'inside out' – from the actor's inner psychology to his or her exterior physical behaviour – and from the 'outside in' (Meyerhold, in particular, was known for his system of **biomechanics**, a technique that focused first on developing the physical gifts of the actor, then employing them to influence the actor's psychology.). Stanislavski's final approach to actor training, according to Sonja Moore, one of the last theatre teachers to assist and work closely with him, focused on teaching actors to control the smallest muscles in their backs, which he believed could be used to trigger different emotional responses.

During the 1930s and 1940s, several American acting teachers worked with Stanislavski and his disciples, either during their American tours or, in the case of Stella Adler, by travelling to Paris to work with the master himself. Each of his American disciples acquired and focused primarily on whatever new approach Stanislavski was developing. For this reason, Strasberg worked obsessively on emotional memory and sense memory with his students, whereas Adler rejected emotional memory in favour of more extensive research for roles. Stanislavski rejected Strasberg's single-minded focus on memory-based acting work, as did later proponents of other Method acting approaches, such as Sanford Meisner, the originator of Meisner Technique, who refocused attention on the truthfulness of the interaction between actors in the moment.

Yet ultimately, most of Stanislavski's Russian disciples and the American Method teachers he inspired shared one technique: the actor's choice of playable actions. This approach starts in the form of a question, although the question can be phrased differently from teacher to teacher: What are you doing? What do you want? What do you need? What are you playing? The acceptable answers should always boil down to some variation of this basic formula: a character does something (a playable verb, or *action*) to someone (the other character in the scene, or *receiver*) to get something (a desired response from the other character, or *objective*).[2] Actors use this 'action analysis' to break down a scene into several units or chunks of dialogue, each defined by a change in the characters' subject matter and the objectives of one or both of the characters. An actor can then see the arc of the role as a series of unit-by-unit objectives, further shaped by moment-to-moment changes in the actions the actor uses to achieve his or her character's objectives. By focusing on what a character needs or wants and what the character does to obtain it, action analysis helps an actor uncover the truth of the moment – what is really at stake beneath the dialogue.

---

[2]See William Ball, *A Sense of Direction: Some Observations on the Art of Directing,* New York: Drama Books, 1983.

Action analysis has also became a central tool for directors, owing to the preponderance of mid- to late twentieth-century directors who had been trained by Strasberg, Adler, Meisner, and their students, as well as the directors' need for clear communication with actors who have been trained in the Stanislavski System, American Method Acting, and their variants. For directors, action analysis provides a straightforward way of breaking down a script into rehearsal units that actors intuitively understand as units of action. It offers directors a way of figuring out their own interpretation of a play's central conflicts and then provides them with the language to communicate with actors and collaborate on further developing and fine-tuning these choices in rehearsal.

For designers, action analysis helps them better understand the director-actor collaboration and share in shaping the action. Of course, designers have a great deal of other concerns: the period, style, and environment of the play; the rhythm of the world created; its colours, textures, and sounds. All of these have a place in action analysis, though designers might translate the action into different forms and elements than do actors. But the fundamental impulse behind action analysis – to discover and interpret what the characters do to each other, moment to moment – is extremely valuable for designers attempting to create a stage world in which these actions occur. Seeing the play in terms of units of action allows designers the opportunity to influence what will happen within each unit and help shape the arc of the action from unit to unit. Acquiring the *lingua franca* of action analysis provides designers with a foundation for collaborating on an interpretation of the action with each other, with directors, and, in more ensemble-based rehearsal environments, with actors. Being able to communicate their vision in terms of concrete actions and objectives helps designers shape the ensemble's decisions and make the production more dynamic, both visually and aurally.

Last but not least, dramaturges benefit from action analysis because their research into the many contexts of the play will affect the ensemble's action choices. Action analysis and dramaturgical research should guide the dramaturge's contribution to the choice of a translation or adaptation of a play for a production. The better that dramaturges understand action, the more effective they can be as researchers and translators as well as literary managers, selecting material for development and guiding playwrights' revisions of plays in what might be lengthy and convoluted development.

WHAT IS A PLAYABLE ACTION, AND WHY IS ACTION SO CENTRAL?

A **playable action** is a verb that captures or expresses what one character is doing to another. It must be a verb because it must capture an action: something that is being done in a specific time and place. In grammatical terms, actors search for transitive verbs – verbs followed by a direct object (a noun), which is almost always, for the actor, one of the other characters on stage at that time. In its most complete form, adding a third part, the **objective**, completes the character's action. An objective is best thought of as a **desired response** – what one character hopes to get the other character to do. The desired response needs to be something that the character could achieve during a particular scene. We will look more closely at how to choose playable actions in Chapter Two, but for now, I would like to explain why action is the most essential part of script analysis for realistic plays, and for the vast majority of plays overall.

Imagine, for a moment, that you are eavesdropping on two people in the midst of a heated discussion. Each person appears to be invested in the conversation. Each is doing something to the other. And each appears to have something at stake: for people to get into this kind of conflict, they must want or need something from each other. Even if other people were involved in the conversation, we could tell who was acting on whom. We can infer what they are doing to each other or what their actions are. One might try to dominate the other in various forms: badger, force, overwhelm, and annihilate. The other one might, in response, try to placate the first one in several ways: soothe, confirm, praise, and surrender. When the two change their actions in response to each other, we speak of the action as being **reciprocal**. And if we watched them for a few minutes, we might see a narrow or wide range of **tactics**: different actions chosen in the heat of the moment as ways of responding to new information, adapting to new realizations, and countering the other person's tactics.

Yet we might have a much tougher time figuring out what each person wants from the other one. In some cases, this 'need' or 'objective' might be overt; it might be the subject matter of the conversation. But this is not always the case. Think about the times you have gotten into a fight with someone about something insignificant, only to realize afterwards that you were actually upset about something else; you were seeking a different response from what the conversation seemed to indicate. In this way, the objective or desired response of any conversation, scene, or unit can be elusive, whereas the action – what the people, characters, or actors are doing to each other – is frequently something more easily observed and described by a transitive verb.

In a sense, what we are talking about is subtext, from the actor's point of view. Things happen below the surface of the literal meaning of the words, when characters pursue objectives that are not the obvious subject matter of the dialogue, or when a character or actor chooses to play an action that seems to vary from what the text means in the most literal sense. This means that **subtext**, although frequently implied by the playwright, remains open to interpretation by the actors through their selection of actions and objectives. And these choices, particularly when pursued over the long haul of a play and reinforced by the director's and designers' choices, can add great depth to a production by layering a complex set of motivations, needs, want, and desires beneath the text. Analysis of the actions and objectives of a play can explore a wide range of interpretations for production, from the most literal to the most innovative or obscure. Both action and objective can be used to shift the emphasis of a scene, individually or in combination. Frequently, the most unusual or unexpected combinations of action and objective prove the most striking and revelatory in performance.

One way for you to find strong playable choices of action is to examine what is *literally* going on in a scene and then search for actions that differ from the literal. When we search for something beyond the literal, we frequently find what lurks beneath the surface, and as we might find with an iceberg, the mass beneath the surface can lead to the most dramatic consequences. Consider a scene with relatively low stakes, early in the action of a fairly traditional realistic play. At the start of Act 1 of Henrik Ibsen's *Hedda Gabler*, Hedda and her husband, George Tesman, have returned from a six-month honeymoon across Europe to their new home. Tesman's Aunt Julie, also known as 'Miss Tesman' in many translations, raised him as a child and mortgaged her pension to help pay for furnishing the couple's new home. She has stopped by the morning after their ship landed to check on the couple and see whether they are pleased with the furnishings. After Miss Tesman speaks with her nephew and reminds him of the sacrifices she has made for him, Hedda joins them. Let us look at the actions in this scene, which I see as the third major unit in Act 1 (lines 212–295).[3] After Miss Tesman greets Hedda in a somewhat uncomfortable exchange that will prove to be typical of their relationship, the dialogue centres on three concerns, the first two of which the characters expose within otherwise ordinary, commonplace topics of conversation. Miss Tesman gives Tesman his old bedroom slippers, which his dying Aunt Rena, Miss Tesman's sister, has embroidered for him. Hedda insults both Tesman and his aunt by complaining about their new maid, Berta (the aunts' long-time maid), who she says has left her old hat on a chair. Finally, Tesman points out to his aunt how much Hedda has 'filled out' during their honeymoon.

In the first chunk of this scene, Miss Tesman and Hedda are, in a literal sense, greeting each other. 'To greet' is an action, a playable verb (we will examine

---

[3]Throughout the book, I will use the line numbers from the *Norton Anthology of Drama* whenever possible. I will also describe the scenes in enough detail for you to locate them without the line numbers.

what makes an action 'playable' in Chapter Two; you will find a comprehensive list of playable verbs in Appendix A), though a scene that begins with each character greeting each other, although perfectly playable, might be a bit flat or formal. I would immediately look for evidence in the text of what might be going on beneath the surface of the greetings. In this scene, I see clues in the second and third lines of dialogue:

> HEDDA [Holds out her hand]   Good morning, dear Miss Tesman. What an early hour to call. So kind of you.
> MISS TESMAN [Seems somewhat embarrassed]   And has the young bride slept well in her new home?

Hedda's lines, together with the stage direction for Miss Tesman suggest that Hedda has embarrassed Miss Tesman by bringing attention to her visiting rather early in the morning. Is Hedda's slight of Miss Tesman purposeful or inadvertent? If it is inadvertent, then perhaps the action is a positive one: to approve, respect, or praise. If, however, Hedda is criticizing the early hour of Miss Tesman's visit, then perhaps Hedda means to undermine Miss Tesman: to provoke, fluster, or belittle. Or perhaps she is trying to have some fun with Miss Tesman: to tease. In response, Miss Tesman immediately brings attention to the newlyweds' being in their new home. What is Miss Tesman's reciprocal action? To remind Hedda that she helped secure the home for them? To distract Hedda with a new topic, one that she hopes will please her? To shame or embarrass her, for criticizing her in front of her beloved nephew?

Just as Miss Tesman is about to leave – after she declines Hedda's invitation to sit down with them – she hands George a package containing his old bedroom slippers. On the literal level, she offers the slippers, and he accepts them and shows them to Hedda, who declines to look at them. But Miss Tesman might intend to remind George of the comfort and warmth she gave him while she was raising him, or to entice him to encourage her to visit more frequently. George might, in turn, try to invite, coax, or perhaps even, in his own absurd way, electrify Hedda into sharing his delight over his precious slippers ('Here, Hedda, take a look.'). Hedda, before rejecting George's entreaty, might tease, mock, or humiliate him (perhaps she is being sarcastic when she replies, 'I remember you kept talking about them on our honeymoon.'). Each of these possibilities offers different ways for the actors and characters to trace paths of action through the scene.

In response to this somewhat uncomfortable interchange, Hedda suggests that Berta, who has been with Miss Tesman and George since his early childhood, will not be sufficient for them, because she has left her old hat on a chair – a hat that Miss Tesman had told George in the previous scene she had bought to impress Hedda:

HEDDA [Interrupts]   Tesman, we really can't go on keeping this maid.
MISS TESMAN   Not keep Bertha?
TESMAN   What makes you say that, dear? What?
HEDDA [Points]   Look at that! She's left her old hat lying on the chair.
TESMAN [Appalled, drops his slippers on the floor]   But, Hedda – !
HEDDA   Suppose someone came in and saw it?
TESMAN   But Hedda – that's Auntie Juju's hat!
HEDDA   Oh?
MISS TESMAN [Picks up the hat]   Indeed it's mine. And it doesn't happen
   to be old, Hedda dear.

From Miss Tesman's and George's reactions, we can infer that Hedda has
offended both of them; in a later scene with Judge Brack at the start of Act 2,
Hedda admits that she pretended to think it was the maid's hat, though we
should never blindly trust that characters are always telling the truth, even in
what might seem to be a confession. Yet even if we accept Hedda's statement
as truth, we must still decide how an actress might play her action. In a literal
sense, when Hedda points to the hat, she is disapproving of it. But what is
she doing to Tesman by bringing this up? Is she pressuring him to fire Berta?
Deceive, needle, pester, devastate, embarrass – all are possible tactics (short-
term actions) for Hedda. In response, Tesman is shocked and tries his best to
subdue or suppress her, while Miss Tesman takes offence, and scolds, chastises,
or tries to silence Hedda.

All of which leads us to the final bit of this scene, in which Tesman observes
'how plump and buxom' Hedda has gotten during the trip. The implication,
which generations of theatre critics have noted, is that Hedda is pregnant.
Tesman is a clueless husband, but it is safe to assume that he means this as a
compliment; I doubt that he would call his newlywed wife fat on their first
full day in their new home. In response, Miss Tesman immediately changes the
quality of her attention to Hedda:

MISS TESMAN [Has folded her hands and is gazing at her]   She's
   beautiful – beautiful – Hedda is beautiful [Goes over to Hedda, takes her
   head between her hands, draws it down and kisses her hair]. God bless
   and keep you, Hedda Tesman. For George's sake.
HEDDA [Frees herself politely]   Oh – let me go, please.
MISS TESMAN [Quietly, emotionally]   I shall come and see you both every
   day.

In the first lines of this exchange, when Miss Tesman kisses Hedda's hair, is she,
in a sense, worshipping Hedda, or is she suffocating her? When she promises to
visit every day, is Miss Tesman protecting her or threatening her? What action

lies beneath the literal surface of the dialogue when Miss Tesman uses Hedda's married name, Hedda Tesman?

Each of the actions we have discussed in this scene could be a tactic, or what we will call a **shift.** In his book *How Life Imitates Chess*, former World Chess Champion and political activist Garry Kasparov distinguishes between strategy (long term) and tactics (short term). For our purposes, it is useful to think of shifts as intended for the short term and therefore tactical, as opposed to objectives, which are intended for the long term and therefore strategic. A shift is a type of (tactical) action: a playable verb adopted by a character in the moment, usually in response to new information, a change in circumstances, a realization, or an obstacle (see Chapter Two). As much as moment-by-moment shifts will shape the rhythm, tempo, and intention of a scene, the guiding principle for making these choices should still be based on what the characters want from each other. And that, in turn, will make it possible for us to find an overall, predominant action for each character in the scene.

From the range of possible actions detailed above, we can make choices that will establish a pattern of actions, and that pattern plays a major part in beginning to shape the action. Although you will learn to choose an overall action for each character in each unit of a play that we analyse, the pattern of actions might be described in greater detail through the moment-to-moment shifts. During the short scene in Act 1 of *Hedda* that we have been examining, one theatre artist might see Hedda as a subtle manipulator, one who uses a range of actions such as praise, tease, and needle to get what she wants. Another might see her as a more heavy-handed bully, preferring to embarrass, humiliate, and deceive. Yet another might see her as volatile, switching among subtle and heavy-handed actions with ease.

The other half of the action formula, the objective, offers a chance to further define the subtext of the scene. An objective should always be articulated as a **desired response** from another character in the scene, and it must be something that could be achieved in that place and time. Hedda has just woken up to her new life and might simply want Miss Tesman to leave the house. To raise the stakes a bit, Hedda might be looking to embarrass Miss Tesman so she will know her place in this house and limit the frequency and duration of future visits. Hedda might pursue her objective more aggressively to hide or postpone Miss Tesman's discovery of her pregnancy. Miss Tesman, for her part, appears to be focusing her attentions first on her nephew, George. She might want George to persuade Hedda to welcome her into their home as a member of the family, a thought that Hedda might find unsettling, to say the least. But once Hedda insults her, she might want Hedda to apologize. In the wake of this conflict between his wife and his aunt, George might imply that Hedda is pregnant so the two most important women in his life will declare a truce. Exploring the choices among the three characters allows us to find the dynamics of the action in this scene. Even though it is a low-stakes scene with a great deal of exposition, strong, clear choices about action and objective help us define the shape of the action to better capture and retain an audience's attention.

A higher-stakes scene often offers the opportunity to make a more surprising choice of objective. In Act 2 of Oscar Wilde's *The Importance of Being Earnest*, Gwendolen Fairfax pays a surprise visit to the country home of her fiancé, Jack Worthing, where she is invited to afternoon tea by Jack's ward, Cecily Cardew, who has just become engaged to Algernon Moncrief (lines 498–640). Because each of their fiancés is living a double life by adopting the assumed name 'Mr. Ernest Worthing' – Jack does so in town, Algernon does so in the country – both women mistakenly conclude that they are engaged to the same man. Once they discover this, the women talk about the differences between living in town and the country as Cecily serves tea for the two of them, and the butler, Merriman, looks on. Barely containing her jealousy of and fury at Gwendolen, Cecily sabotages Gwendolen's tea:

> GWENDOLEN   You have filled my tea with lumps of sugar, and though I asked most distinctly for bread and butter, you have given me cake. I am known for the gentleness of my disposition, and the extraordinary sweetness of my nature, but I warn you, Miss Cardew, you may go too far.
> CECILY [Rising] To save my poor, innocent, trusting boy from the machinations of any other girl there are no lengths to which I would not go.
> GWENDOLEN   From the moment I saw you I distrusted you. I felt that you were false and deceitful. I am never deceived in such matters. My first impressions of people are invariably right.
> CECILY   It seems to me, Miss Fairfax, that I am trespassing upon your valuable time. No doubt you have many other calls of a similar nature to make in the neighborhood.

> *Enter JACK*

Jack enters at the height of the conflict between the two women. It is evident that beneath the veneer of upper-class manners, the two women are attacking each other aggressively. But what do they want or need from each other? What responses do they desire? Does Cecily want Gwendolen to leave, does she want her to back off, or does she literally want to make her sick? Does Gwendolen want Cecily to back off, or to fear her? The choice of objective will give the scene a sense of purpose, underlying stakes, and a goal towards which the actions in the scene will lead.[4]

---

[4]See Chapter Two and Appendix B for a more detailed analysis of this scene.

Stanislavski believed that by revisiting and revising the actions and objectives, an actor could keep his or her performance fresh over a longer run. Each character's overall goal for a play or production – the **super-objective** – does not change, but actors might change or tweak the actions, objectives, and shifts to refresh themselves, find new energy, and encourage the production to grow over the course of a longer run. To return to the tea scene in *Earnest*, let us say the actress playing Cecily developed the following action/objective for this scene during rehearsals: *Cecily wants to humiliate Gwendolen so she will be embarrassed.* After several weeks of performances, the scene feels as though it is going stale for the actors. The actress might raise the stakes by changing her objective slightly: *Cecily wants to humiliate Gwendolen so she will be sickened.* Or she might change the action to find a new route to the original objective: *Cecily wants to taunt Gwendolen so she will be embarrassed.* Or she might change both action and objective: *Cecily wants to taunt Gwendolen so she will be sickened.* As long as the overall objective remains essentially the same for both actors, the scene will stay true to the director and designers' conception of the production. But by changing the dynamics slightly – pursuing a slightly more or less aggressive action or objective for a chunk of a scene – an actor can reinvigorate the scene and find new life in a role.

If we realize this going into our first script analyses, we might feel somewhat freer to make strong choices and yet not become preoccupied with doing it 'perfectly'. After all, our analyses will be a starting point for discussing the play with directors, designers, and actors. During rehearsal and even, as we have seen, during the run of a production, these actions and objectives will evolve. Script analysis is not intended to set the production in stone, but to empower the entire ensemble to sculpt it together. For this reason, we need to focus on finding the major actions and objectives to articulate the big picture of a play or production, rather than micromanage our view of the action to control every moment.

When we do 'zoom in' on the action and analyse smaller moments, we must remain conscious of the many other artists who can influence the action during rehearsals and production. All collaborative theatre artists benefit from focusing their attention on what is vital to an agreed-upon point of view for the production, rather than fighting over minutiae. There is a moment in the film *Saving Mr. Banks* when Mrs. Travers, the author of the *Mary Poppins* book series, insists that Mr. Banks must be clean-shaven in the film, and the young lyricist, Bob Sherman, looks her in the eye and asks, 'Does it matter?' It matters to Mrs. Travers greatly because of her personal connection to the people who served as models for the characters (in this case, her father, who was clean-shaven in real life). But as theatre artists, occasionally caught up in the heat of the moment, we should continually ask ourselves this question about contested choices: does it matter? As long as a choice stays true to the core of the production's interpretation and action, minor differences in opinion very rarely matter so much that it is worth sacrificing the collegial environment of the collaboration. The open discussion of potential choices is what matters most; by considering various options, the ensemble explores different routes to the same core.

This book will teach students to break down a play into playable units of action and then express the dynamics by assigning the characters playable verbs (actions) and desired responses (objectives). The ultimate goals of this analysis are to find the unifying action of any play, discover the impulses that shape its action, and acquire a shared vocabulary for collaborating with other theatre artists in making these interpretive decisions. We will be working to create a written analysis of a play that is easy to refer to in rehearsal and production, so as to best prepare us for collaboration. Such an analysis needs to be neat and compelling, so that the most important elements are simple to find. You will need to photocopy or scan each page of the script so that the text is surrounded by enough empty space to allow for your notations in the margins. You will learn to use a series of symbols designed to help you 'score' a script, condense your notations to their essence, and render them so that they stand out on the page. I will provide you with a series of 'blueprints' to help you analyse text and organize your observations and interpretations of given circumstances, character, relationship, structure, and environment. And we will use all this analysis as the foundation for writing and presenting the guiding light of a good theatre production: what Harold Clurman referred to as the 'spine' – a statement of the **core action** of a play.

The fundamental questions we will ask of all scripts will be, 'What is the action of the play, and how can we shape it? What do the characters want from each other, and what are they doing to each other to get it?' Action is the touchstone of this approach, because all plays – whether traditional or experimental, realistic or abstract – involve actions that occur through time. By focusing on action, artists from all theatre disciplines can develop a language to attack and shape the movement of action.

To figure out how to shape the action in rehearsal and production, students will learn to analyse the structure of a play practically, by breaking down the action into playable units, usually one to five pages each. Within the overall arc of the action, we will examine significant characters not only for their actions and objectives but also for their relationships with each other and the ways in which they alter each other's status, based on the work of Keith Johnstone.[5] Finally, students will learn how to uncover and imagine shifts in tempo and rhythm to help create dynamic pacing in performance.

---

[5]See *Impro: Improvisation and the Theatre*, New York: Theatre Arts, 1979, and *Impro for Storytellers*, London: Faber and Faber, 1999.

Unlike many books on script analysis, this book will devote early attention to helping students develop crucial dramaturgical skills, the oft-neglected groundwork for making informed choices in theatre. In particular, the book will focus on researching the history of the writing of the play and its productions, to better understand the choices the playwright has made and the range of choices that significant productions have explored. The book will also examine concerns involved in the translation of a play originally written in a foreign language, to better understand the selection or commission of a translation as part of interpreting the original script.

Our case studies will focus on how particular canonical, experimental, and contemporary plays can be approached through this system of analysis and communication. We will use nine plays as case studies: Sophocles's *Oedipus the King*, Shakespeare's *Twelfth Night*, Georg Büchner's *Woyzeck*, Ibsen's *Hedda Gabler*, Wilde's *The Importance of Being Earnest*, Tennessee Williams's *A Streetcar Named Desire*, Griselda Gambaro's *Information for Foreigners*, August Wilson's *Fences*, and Paula Vogel's *How I Learned to Drive*. For each analytical skill or element that we cover, I will use examples from at least two of the case study plays. I will offer some backstory for each example, so that you should be able to follow it without having read the play. This will allow you to work through the book in at least three different ways: (1) by pairing the reading with one of the case study plays used as an example for the technique or skill being studied; (2) by pairing the reading to another case study play, and working through it in greater detail; and (3) by using the reading to analyse a play of your choice – for a final project for a class, or to prepare a script for rehearsal and production, as actor, director, designer, or dramaturge.

CHAPTER ONE

The World of the Play

Before embarking upon the major task of analysing the action of a play, we must understand as much as possible within the time constraints of a particular project about the larger contexts within which the action occurs. We need to comprehend the world surrounding the play's characters to make compelling decisions about their actions within the play, supported by the text. We start by gathering information about the given circumstances of the play; the historical context for the setting and the writing of the play; and the history of the writing of the play and its production. On this foundation, we analyse the characters and environment of the play before interpreting the characters' actions, objectives, and tactics.

It might seem tedious to start by gathering information from the text and conducting research; after all, the context for the action can seem a good deal less exciting than the action itself. But without understanding the context, a theatre artist can easily misunderstand the action, particularly when working on a play set and/or written in an earlier period or a culture with which the artist is unfamiliar. Conversely, the closer the artist is to the setting of a play, the easier it is to understand the context. Think about how much you know about the communities with which you are most familiar. If I asked you to tell me the values and hierarchy of your academic department, your company, or your circle of friends, you would probably be able to tell me a great deal. If I asked you to do the same for a neighbouring department or competing company, you would probably provide less detail, even if you had some contact or familiarity with it. The further you stray from the circles that you frequent – to include the surrounding communities, or the entire geographic region, for example – the less you would know without more inquiry. In context, characters' actions might have vastly different consequences. Most plays take place in contexts that are not within our comfort zone; we should not assume we understand the implications of their actions.

Any time we go to a new place, we immediately begin to size up the values, hierarchy, and customs prevalent there. As we do so, we can alter our actions and behaviour – the tone of our voices, the degree to which we assert ourselves, the way in which we dress, move, and gesture – so they are most likely to help us achieve our goals. This process is 'assimilation', which for some implies giving up our sense of individuality or cultural heritage – but most of us assimilate to some extent. Before analysing the actions in a play, we need to assimilate as theatre artists; we must acknowledge and absorb the values and customs of the world of the play. We don't have to agree with them, but we do need to be aware of them so we do not miss the significance of the action.

A classic story about former President Richard Nixon is illustrative. Travelling to Brazil on a diplomatic mission in the 1950s, Nixon exited the aeroplane and greeted the crowds that had gathered to see him with his trademark gesture from that era: He raised both arms high above his head, each hand in what Americans know as the 'OK sign' – thumb and forefinger forming a circle, with the other three fingers outstretched. There was only one problem: In Latin America, this sign means something completely different; it is an obscene gesture, equivalent to giving someone the middle finger in America, Canada, or the United Kingdom.[1]

When we gather information about the world of the play, we are doing our best to read the signs correctly. To understand these signs, we start by looking at the given circumstances revealed in the text of the play, as well as the circumstances suggested by the previous action divulged in its dialogue. In Chapter Two, Dramaturgy, we develop the research tools to uncover information about the historical setting for the play's action, the history of the writing and production of the play, and its criticism. We limit our analysis of the first element, given circumstances, to the facts contained within or implied by the play's text, whereas the latter three elements will involve some research to flesh out what we might already know about the play and playwright from our previous work and studies of theatre.

GIVEN CIRCUMSTANCES

The special world of the play's environment and the characters' situation, which the playwright suggests explicitly and implicitly, provides the most meaningful context for the characters' actions. We can look at six different types of **given circumstances**: setting; date and time; class structure; government and laws;

---

[1]Needless to say, this was not the best way for Nixon to kick off his tour, and it may have had something to do with his decision to adopt another gesture during his presidency: both arms raised high above his head with each forefinger and middle finger in the 'V' sign for victory (or peace).

social circles; and religious institutions and beliefs. The first two will almost always be stated in the script, whereas the others might be explicit, implicit, or of relatively minor importance. Be prepared to examine the text closely for clues, but do not feel obligated to complete your analysis of each element with the same quantity of information. For given circumstances, we will use *A Streetcar Named Desire*, *How I Learned to Drive*, and *Information for Foreigners* as our primary case studies, though I refer to other case study plays in passing.

Any play will naturally emphasize some of these categories of given circumstances more than others, and that, in and of itself, is significant. For example, law and government are significant to the action in *Oedipus the King*, which involves a murder, incest, and the governance of a kingdom. In *A Streetcar Named Desire*, Stanley Kowalski explicitly mentions the Napoleonic Code when berating his sister-in-law, Blanche DuBois, about his shared interest in her home, Belle Reve. Laws are also important to the action of *How I Learned to Drive*, in which the legal age of consent and the legal definition of incest figure prominently. Yet there is very little mention of laws or government in *Twelfth Night*.

We start by looking at setting, which some refer to as place. I like to visualize the setting in the largest scope possible and then zero in on the most specific location. Thus, we start (for most plays) with a continent or country on Earth, then zero in on the city or town, the neighbourhood, and the actual residence or locations in that area, including details of the public and private sites (buildings, homes, public squares, forests, etc.) and their purposes. From this vantage point, you should also note any and all environmental issues, such as the weather and the quality and quantity of light, to be further adjusted for the time of year, which we examine in the next given circumstance.

Consider a play with which most of us are unfamiliar, originally written in Spanish: Griselda Gambaro's *Information for Foreigners* (With all of the plays we study, if you do not have access to the text, feel free to consult a plot summary for basic facts.). In a play such as this, most of us will be on equally uncertain footing, and the need to be specific and detailed about the setting will be self-evident. To develop a shared language for analysing and discussing a play that is foreign to us, we need to do a bit of research – at the very least enough for us to understand the circumstances within which the action takes place.

Gambaro wrote the play from 1971 to 1972 and set it in her native Argentina, just before the country's 'Dirty War', a period of state terrorism marked by the abductions, torture, and murder – 'disappearances' – of tens of thousands of left-wing activists. We begin by noting that the play takes place in the South American country and next observe that the playwright offers no further geographic details. Before we look more closely at the environment within which the action takes place, we should pause to consider why Gambaro, writing a play that embodies the political terrorism of her country at that time, would not locate the setting more specifically, in a particular city, for example. Our first assumption with accomplished playwrights should always be that the absence of detail is a purposeful choice, which means that what a playwright does not tell us can be just as important as what a playwright does tell us.

In this case, I would infer that Gambaro wants the first Argentine audiences to see the events in the play as taking place in their own city, so they cannot distance themselves from the events they will witness. This raises significant issues for productions outside Argentina, which might not be able to reproduce this effect in another country and political environment. To be as specific as possible in our analysis, we would note that the city or town is not noted, but that it could be seen as any town or 'Everytown' in Argentina. And we would note that the playwright has set the play in Argentina in 1971, contemporaneous with the first performances of the play, and includes brief excerpts from Argentine newspapers of that period.

We would then look more closely at the setting for the action, zooming in from the city to the physical areas within which the action takes place. In the stage directions, Gambaro states that the action should transpire 'in a two story residential house with empty rooms, some of which interconnect, and passageways, some dark and some crudely lit'. The audience will be separated into several groups, each led by a guide through a series of twenty scenes of torture and abductions, some of which are based on events from that period, ones that the first Argentine audiences would have recognized. Each group will, by necessity, see the scenes in a different order, until the groups reassemble for the last scene. Some of the scenes are intended to be extremely realistic, but others are more stylized.

Gambaro's setting the play in a real house, rather than a theatre, and the lack of information about the city or neighbourhood lead me to believe that she wants the audience to see the action as taking place in the here and now, wherever the audience is watching the performance. This seems to be one of the most powerful decisions that a director could make – to bring the action as close as possible to the audience. Dividing into groups, audience members experience the action more intimately. When each group is guided from scene to scene in a different order, the shape of the action is further personalized. Only at the end of the play will the audience members share a final scene and then, perhaps, share information that they have acquired throughout their tour of the residence, as no two groups will have seen the same scenes in the same order. Indeed, no two groups will have seen the identical scenes, as each group sees a different performance of each scene – a variation amplified by the many contexts within which each group sees each scene. We should also note that all the action takes place indoors, in rooms and corridors that are dark or crudely lit. Critic Selena Burns has called the overall effect that of 'a horror house of torture' (38).

One of the most important and yet underappreciated qualities of a strong and effective script analysis is concision. We need to be comprehensive yet succinct, so that when we glance down at our notations on a script, we can quickly and easily recognize the essence of our point of view. For this reason, I have created a series of charts, or 'blueprints', that allow you to organize and present some parts of your analysis, such as given circumstances, so they can be easily grasped at a glance. For setting, for example, the first part of the given circumstances blueprint for *Information for Foreigners* might look something like this:

Setting	
Continent, country, city	South America, Argentina, city unknown ('Everytown')
Physical area(s)	'A spacious, residential house, preferably two stories, with corridors and empty rooms, some of which interconnect' (Gambaro 69)
Environment	'A horror house of torture' (Burns 38)
Climate and light	'Some of the corridors are dark, while others, in obvious contrast, are crudely lit' (Gambaro 69)

For each play that we examine and analyse, different aspects of the setting will be significant. For *A Streetcar Named Desire*, by setting the action in the French Quarter of New Orleans, at the end of the line (literally) for a streetcar named 'Desire', Tennessee Williams suggests not only a metaphorical environment for Blanche's final descent into madness but also climate and light. I would note the repeated mentions of heat, coloured lights, and Blanche's desire to always cover the lights in the Kowalskis' apartment so that her age and condition are less apparent to Mitch. For Paula Vogel's *How I Learned to Drive*, it is important to observe that all the action takes place on a stage, as a story told by L'il Bit, the narrator, at times directly to the audience, with other locations visited in flashback as she tells her story. Like *Information for Foreigners*, Vogel's play takes place in the actual theatre that serves as the venue for each performance, but Vogel uses the setting as a way of distancing the narrator and the audience from action in the flashbacks, making up more than 80 per cent of the play. By contrast, Gambaro uses the venue to bring the audience as close as possible to the action.

Vogel's use of direct address to the audience and storytelling in flashback are among the most significant structural elements of the play, calling attention to the second category of given circumstances: time. When we speak of 'time' in a play, we must analyse not only the period when the action takes place but also the playwright's use of time – how the action moves through time, and how compressed or spread out the scope of time might be. The period helps us understand the world of the play, its norms, beliefs, and values. The writer's use of time reveals a lot about how the action will unfold. Films such as Quentin Tarantino's *Pulp Fiction* (1994), Woody Allen's *Annie Hall* (1977), and Christopher Nolan's movies, most notably *Memento* (2002) and *Inception* (2010), employ time fluidly, moving backwards and forwards in the service of the writer/director's storytelling logic. *How I Learned to Drive* employs a similar approach. L'il Bit addresses the audience directly, telling the story of her relationship with her Uncle Peck, from her perspective in her thirties or forties looking back to her teen years. The setting is the stage where the performance takes place (for the narration), with flashbacks to suburban Maryland, Uncle Peck's car and studio, L'il Bit's home and college dorm, a restaurant by the Maryland shore, and a fishing hole, all suggested by a few minimal props.

How I Learned to Drive covers a large amount of time through its flashbacks, and an even greater amount of time through narration. The story – which we define as including the entire scope of the events told both through narration and enactment chronologically – begins in 1951 with L'il Bit's birth and ends in the present day, or in whatever year the narration occurs, perhaps 1997, the year of the play's premiere. Most of the enacted and narrated action takes place from 1964, when L'il Bit was 13 and first made a deal with Uncle Peck to meet him once a week for driving lessons, to 1969, when she turned 18, the age of majority and consent. Most of the story is used in the plot, contributing to its primarily episodic structure. We would also note that many of the scenes take place on significant dates in L'il Bit's life: the day she got her driver's licence, her high school graduation, and her eighteenth birthday. All these dates are also significant to the shape of the action, as one of the primary journeys in the play, particularly from Uncle Peck's perspective within the flashbacks, is towards L'il Bit turning 18, when he can and will legally attempt to seduce her and propose to her.

The timeline for the action, scene by scene, looks roughly like this:

1. 1997 or present
2. June 1969
3. 1951
4. 1969
5. 1970
6. 1968
7. 1968
8. 1960s
9. 1960s
10. 1979
11. 1966
12. 1967

13. 1966
14. 1966
15. 1966
16. 1965
17. 1969
18. 1964
19. September 1969
20. December 1969
21. December 1969
22. 1997 or present
23. 1962
24. 1997 or present

Searching for a pattern, we can see that the play moves backwards and forwards in time from scenes 1–5, until gaining a bit of traction and moving more steadily back from scenes 6 and 7, when L'il Bit gets her driver's licence (1968), to scene 18, when she struck her original deal with Uncle Peck (1964). Once that happens and the audience members think they understand how the relationship started, the action jumps forward to 1969, leading to Peck's meeting L'il Bit in a hotel on her eighteenth birthday. When L'il Bit rejects Peck's advances, their most shocking and significant secret is finally revealed in a climactic flashback scene from 1962, when Peck first molested L'il Bit at age 11.

For time, then, the blueprint for *How I Learned to Drive* might look something like this:

Time	
Year, season, time of day	Narration: 1997 or present
	Enacted scenes: 1962–69
Length of time period	Many scenes take place on important days (birthday, graduation, driver's licence)
	Most scenes take place at night
Logic of movement of time	Story: 1951–97/present
	Enacted scenes: 7 most significant years of the story
	Episodic structure with some direct address scenes and monologues
	Action moves from 1997/present narration to 1968 (her driver's licence) jumps around backwards to 1964 (her first driving lesson) then fast-forwards to 1969 (her eighteenth birthday), before jumping back to climactic scene in 1962 (Peck molesting L'il Bit at age 11), concluding in 1997/present.

From this part of the blueprint, we have become well aware of the need to understand how the action moves from scene to scene in the absence of a chronological progression of events. Why does L'il Bit tell this story in this way? Why are the scenes in this order? And what is the relationship between the direct address narration scenes in the present and the enacted flashbacks? All these concerns will help us approach later elements of script analysis, such as the unit breakdown and the unit actions/objectives, with greater sensitivity to how the playwright uses time. We have also established the time for most of the enacted scenes (1962–69), which will allow us to research the period more precisely for design as well as dramaturgical purposes.

In *Streetcar*, time moves purely chronologically. We should note that Williams wrote the play in the 1940s, and it opened on Broadway in 1947. The Desire Street streetcar line ran through New Orleans's French Quarter until 1948, when a bus line replaced it. Although Williams does not specify a year in his script, it is safe to assume that the action takes place in the 1940s, contemporaneous with the writing and first production of the play. Williams also reveals, through dialogue, that Stanley Kowalski was a Master Sergeant in the Army Engineer Corps (see scene 1), and served in Salerno, Italy, during World War II (see scene 11), further narrowing the action to 1945–47.[2]

Of the eleven scenes in *Streetcar*, the first six take place over the course of two days in early May, after the arrival of Stella's sister, Blanche DuBois. Scenes 7 through 10 occur over a late afternoon and evening in mid-September, on Blanche's birthday, the night when Stella gives birth and Stanley rapes Blanche. The final scene, in which Stanley has Blanche taken away to a sanatorium, is set several weeks later. In the original Broadway production, the intermission was taken between scenes 6 and 7. For this reason, we can examine the first six scenes as a clean chronological progression of events in May 1946 or 1947, ending with Blanche and Mitch coming together as a couple. After the intermission, the action jumps forward four months for four scenes that unfold chronologically, at which time Stanley has uncovered Blanche's secret past, using it to escalate his attacks in a more concerted effort to push her out of their home – first buying her a bus ticket home, then telling Mitch about Blanche's past, and finally raping her (the climax or most significant **key moment** in the play). Several weeks later, the final scene in October depicts Blanche's removal from the premises by a sanatorium doctor and staff. We can see a clear arc in early May for the first six scenes, a second arc in mid-September for the next four scenes, leading to the climactic rape scene; and a final concluding scene in October in which Stanley finally disposes of Blanche.

---

[2]The Allied forces invaded Sicily at Salerno in 1943. I'm assuming that Stanley and Stella have been together for at least a year. There are no indications that the action takes place during wartime, so we can probably narrow the action even further, to 1946–47.

The contrast in how time functions or moves in these three plays could not be greater. To fully grasp the action of each play, we must start from this understanding of time – not simply the period within which the action is set but the ways in which time functions as the action unfolds: how time moves backwards and forwards in *How I Learned to Drive*; how the use of real time and a flexible order of scenes creates a unique experience for each group of audience members in *Information for Foreigners*; and how scenes 1–6 and 7–10 in *A Streetcar Named Desire* build two crescendos, the first coming just before the intermission (a key moment) and the second at the final key moment/climax of the play.

The conflicts in *Streetcar* are fuelled by class differences, the third set of given circumstances that will be analysed. When we examine class structure, we are looking for the range of economic classes represented in a play, the overall economic health and range of wealth seen in the world of the play, and the placement of each character within that range. In *Streetcar*, Stanley, the son of a Polish immigrant, is working class, as are all of the characters with whom he associates: the upstairs neighbours, Eunice and Steve, as well as the other men from Stanley's poker game, Mitch and Pablo. Similarly, the minor characters from the first ten scenes are lower class, such as the Mexican woman who sells flowers for the dead and the young man who comes to the door collecting money for the newspaper. In contrast, Stella and Blanche were raised in a declining upper-class family.

Stella appears to have made a smooth transition to her new life in the French Quarter with Stanley, but Blanche clings closely to her more affluent roots in Laurel, Mississippi, where the family owned Belle Reve (in French, 'beautiful dream'). According to Blanche, Belle Reve has been 'lost', one of the central reasons why Blanche has come to stay with Stella and Stanley. Her fall in status – from a member of an established Southern plantation family to a desperate and near destitute teacher, fired for sleeping with a seventeen-year-old student and forced to stay with her sister, Stella, and her gruff, uneducated working-class husband – is central to the action of the play. The first six scenes build the conflict between Blanche and Stanley, and culminate in her subtle seduction of Stanley's best friend, Mitch, an awkward, somewhat shy man who still lives with his mother. The next four scenes capture the full range of Stanley's attacks on Stella.

For class structure, our blueprint for *Streetcar* might look like this:

Class structure	
Classes	A collapsing Southern aristocracy; a working-class melting pot
Economic health	Stable after World War II, with increased class mobility
Characters within each class	Destitute former aristocracy (Blanche); former aristocracy, now working class (Stella); working class (Stanley, Mitch, Steve, Eunice, Pablo, minor characters)

The implications of this class division of characters are profound. The actors playing Stella and Blanche will hold themselves and speak differently from the working-class characters, most obviously Stanley, the contrast reflected in the give and take in the dialogue as well as in the characters' regional dialects. Blanche's costumes capture the faded glory of her past, most palpable when Stanley tears through Blanche's trunk in scene 2, manhandling her few remaining fake fur pieces and costume jewellery, stand-ins for the trappings of wealth that Blanche can no longer afford to maintain. Only in the dim light upon which Blanche insists, with a few cheap props and costume pieces to suggest her faded past, can she cast a spell on Mitch in the hopes of marrying out of her misfortunes. If Stanley can dispel these myths of class and bring her down to his level, then he can destroy her future with Mitch and rid himself of Blanche forever.

Keep in mind that not all types of given circumstances will be significant for every play. Moreover, uniform circumstances might be as significant as diverse ones. In *How I Learned to Drive*, for example, all the characters are lower middle class, with very little to distinguish among them. Yet in many of our other case study plays, class differences play a significant part in the action and conflicts: the contrast between a family with an aristocratic name but little money (the Moncriefs-Bracknells) versus a family with no name and an uncertain lineage (the Worthings) in *The Importance of Being Earnest*; the class differences among royalty, shepherds, and the blind seer, Tiresias, in *Oedipus the King*. Look closely for signs of class structure and class differences, but do not impose these distinctions when they are not significant to the action.

The given circumstances regarding government and laws in a play can be explicit or implicit, so it is important to give some thought to these circumstances and search for clues in the text. *How I Learned to Drive* and *A Streetcar Named Desire* are both set in America during the twentieth century; American theatre artists can assume that they understand the government and legal system because they are familiar with it. Remember to look beyond the overall system and examine more closely the details that might directly affect the action of the play. In *How I Learned to Drive*, the laws on incest and the age of consent in Maryland at that time (18) are essential to understanding the action. Because Uncle Peck and L'il Bit are not blood relatives, legally he could divorce his wife and marry L'il Bit, so although his interest in his niece is extremely disturbing and likely delusional, his plan to marry her after she turns 18 is not illegal or impossible. This appears to be part of a strategy by Vogel to keep Uncle Peck from being seen as abhorrent until the final scenes of the play. We might also observe that the rules of driving are repeatedly used to introduce scenes and structure the play.

In scene 2 of *Streetcar*, Stanley lectures his wife, Stella, about the fate of Belle Reve, over which he argues he has a legal claim to ownership: 'In the state of Louisiana we have the Napoleonic Code according to which what belongs to the wife belongs to the husband and vice versa' (lines 59–60). To better understand the action of the play, we would also want to examine the laws in Mississippi, where Blanche grew up; the legal status of homosexuality (Blanche's husband commits suicide after she discovers him with another man); the definition of statutory rape (Blanche slept with a high school student); and the laws of bankruptcy (how did she 'lose' Belle Reve?). We do not need to do more than obtain a passing knowledge of these ideas, but if we neglect to do so, or assume that we understand what these terms mean, we risk missing not only the literal meanings but also the range of actions and subtexts open to the ensemble in rehearsal and production.

A play set in a foreign country, such as *Information for Foreigners*, requires even greater attention to the government and laws under which the action takes place. To understand the action, we need to investigate the political situation in Argentina in the early 1970s, when the country descended into state terrorism that accelerated over the next decade. The world of the play is based on the acts and environment of terrorism; without knowledge of these events, it would be virtually impossible to make sense of the action and impact of the play. Our notations might look something like this, though I caution that this would merely be a starting point for further research about this aspect of *Information for Foreigners*:

Government and laws	
System	Military coup in 1966 led to the appointment of successive presidents by the military and the installation of an authoritarian-bureaucratic state.
Relevant laws	Government suspended collective bargaining and workers' right to strike.
Restrictions/freedoms	Political speech and congregation risk violent retribution and terrorism, including abductions, torture, and 'disappearances'.
Participation/ environment	Widespread news coverage and awareness of terrorism daily for all citizens.

Perhaps no category of given circumstances is as consistently relevant to the action of most plays as the social circles that surround the characters. It might be most useful to think of them as a series of circles that overlap with each other: family, friends, neighbourhood/community, work, school, and media. The last of these, media, can help shape the beliefs and therefore the actions of characters in modern plays, and will only become increasingly influential in contemporary plays with the rise of social media such as Facebook, YouTube, Twitter, Instagram, Tumblr, Snapchat, and Vine. In the past few years, social media have expanded the range of many people's social circles exponentially, speeded the transmission of information within circles, and opened lives to more snooping, as seen in the National Security Agency scandal that erupted in 2013.

By examining a play such as *A Streetcar Named Desire*, we can start to see how social circles help shape action. Stanley and Stella are husband and wife; Stella's older sister, Blanche, dejected after her humiliation back home in Laurel, Mississippi, overstays her welcome as their guest. Surrounding this core family unit, we find a group of friends (Stanley's poker/bowling buddies) and neighbours (Eunice and Steve, who live above the Kowalskis). The poker buddies form a male bastion of drinking, gambling, and testosterone, from which Mitch, Stanley's best friend, emerges as the most sympathetic to Blanche's plight. The neighbours form a backdrop to the passionate love/hate relationship of Stanley and Stella, normalizing the men's drinking and the couple's fighting within the context of this neighbourhood. In contrast to Blanche's former middle-class position as a schoolteacher, most of the other characters are working class, epitomized by Stanley's job as a factory worker.

Media play a simpler role in the action of *Streetcar*. Stanley has to make several phone calls to uncover Blanche's sordid past, and Blanche claims she has received a last-minute, imagined or hallucinated telegram from her college boyfriend, Shep Huntleigh, inviting her to join him on a Caribbean cruise. In a contemporary setting, all of Blanche's transgressions most likely would have been broadcast to the world on traditional and social media long before her arrival at the Kowalskis' apartment. But because of the absence of this publicity, Blanche has the opportunity to reinvent herself when she moves in with Stanley and Stella. The male-dominated, working class, macho world of Stanley and his buddies forms a bubble that Blanche finds nearly impossible to enter. No amount of paper lanterns and soft lighting will protect her from the harsh glare of Stanley's world, and for most of the play she will try to dance around the edges of this world to attract Mitch, her only realistic opportunity to achieve salvation. Blanche is thinly protected by her sister's oversight, as Stella tries to manage Stanley and keep him at bay. Once Stella goes into labour and leaves the apartment for the hospital, however, Blanche is left vulnerable to Stanley's aggressive impulses. We might condense this analysis into a chart thusly:

Social circles	
Family and friends	Stanley and Stella (husband and wife); Stella and Blanche (sisters, from a wealthier family than Stanley and his friends); Stanley's poker buddies (macho male bastion); Eunice and Steve (neighbours).
Community	Working class New Orleans neighbourhood. Noisy, male dominated.

Media	News travels slowly. Pre-social media. Dominant forms are telephone, newspaper, and telegraph. Gossip from person to person is the most intrusive form of communication.
Restrictions/privileges	Men congregate in groups, go out when they want, enjoy all-male activities. Women are expected to provide comfort, satisfaction, and sustenance to men: home, sex, and food.

The social circles in *Streetcar* have major implications for the play's action, character development, and conflict, as well as its design. Stella straddles the Southern aristocracy within which she and Blanche grew up and her newly adopted working-class life with Stanley. In the first act, Mitch is drawn to the remaining traces of Blanche's upbringing, whereas Stanley tries to challenge Blanche's claim of poverty, hoping to inherit a piece of the DuBois estate. Once Stanley realizes that Blanche is broke, he investigates her past and exploits the reports of her scandalous behaviour to destroy her relationship with Mitch.

The final category of given circumstances, religious institutions and beliefs, can be the easiest to overlook. For liturgical drama and plays with an explicit religious context, such as T.S. Eliot's *Murder in the Cathedral* or John Patrick Shanley's *Doubt*, the religious implications are evident – but religion also motivates much of the action of classic Greek tragedies such as *Oedipus the King* and lays a foundation for the action of modern classics such as *Miss Julie*. We must train ourselves to look more deeply for the religious underpinnings of the beliefs that are central to the sexual and cultural restrictions in plays. In *How I Learned to Drive*, there are the obvious taboos around paedophilia and incest, raised by Uncle Peck's long cultivation of his relationship with L'il Bit. In this case, the prohibitions against paedophilia and incest are legal as well as religious. Uncle Peck uses the law of consent to rationalize that a relationship with L'il Bit will be acceptable after she turns 18. One way to view his rationalization is that he is looking for any authority to justify his interest in her. Vogel situates Peck in a grey area: she is his niece, but not by blood; she turns 18; he claims he would divorce his wife before marrying her. L'il Bit again raises the spectre of the age of consent in a monologue, when she tells the audience how she seduced a high school boy she met on a bus when she was in her twenties.

The chart for religious institutions and beliefs in *How I Learned to Drive* might look like this:

Religion	
Institutions	Christian, perhaps Catholic.
Beliefs	There is no explicit mention of religious beliefs.
Restrictions/privileges	Prohibition against incest and paedophilia.

PREVIOUS ACTION

With rare exception, playwrights reveal the previous actions of their characters through their dialogue to help fuel the current action and stakes. We consider 'previous action' to include not only characters' actions before the plot but also action that takes place off stage and is recounted by a character on stage. In *Oedipus the King*, for example, not only would we consider Oedipus's history with his mother and father to be previous action, but we would also include Jocasta's hanging herself and Oedipus's blinding himself, as these occur off stage during the play and are then described on stage by witnesses. Previous action and off-stage action challenge the theatre artist in similar ways: The actor and director must find a way to activate the telling of the past in the present. Playwrights use previous action to develop character and to create a more fully imagined past for their characters, yet they must do so in a way that furthers the action in the present. If the actors are not doing something to each other in the present when retelling the past, then the exposition of the past will seem clunky, making the playwright's hand far too obvious. The best playwrights will introduce previous action seamlessly; regardless of the playwright's success at doing so, the ensemble must find a way to make the retelling of the past live in the present.

Previous action can fuel script analysis in several ways. First, previous action provides context, by establishing the norms of behaviour within the world of the play. In *Twelfth Night*, we should observe that this is a world in which elites hold on to their passion and grief for extraordinary lengths of time; Olivia has been in mourning for her father and brother for seven years, while Orsino has pined for Olivia for almost as long. Second, previous action reveals aspects of character, by showing us how the character has behaved in previous circumstances. Oedipus's ability to solve riddles, rashness in the face of conflict, and frequent desperate attempts to avoid the fate predicted for him by the oracle help us better understand him. Finally, previous action must always be played as present action. When retelling the past, the director and actor must discover what one character is doing to another, or the exposition will seem clunky – exposing not just the character's past, but also the playwright's craft.

When examining previous action as given circumstances, we need to look at what the details of the characters' previous actions tell us about the world of the play (We will return to the other aspects of previous action in the chapters on character and action later in the book.). What do the characters' previous actions tell us about the values, hierarchy, and customs of this world? In one column, we list the significant previous actions revealed in the dialogue; in another column, we list at least one conclusion we can draw from the previous action.

In *Streetcar*, Blanche DuBois left her hometown of Laurel, Mississippi, in disgrace after losing her job, her husband, and the family estate in a mortgage foreclosure. Stanley investigates Blanche's past and uncovers the rumours about her in her hometown, which he passes on to Stella and then Mitch, to undercut Mitch's feelings for Blanche and stop him from proposing to her. Owing to Blanche's emotional reaction to the charges, we are never clear about the truth of each rumour, but she appears to confirm most of the rumours. The previous action chart for given circumstances might look something like this:

Previous action	This is a world in which ...
Blanche's family estate, Belle Reve, was lost in a foreclosure, due to her family's 'epic fornications' (scene 1).	Fortunes can decline quickly.
After Blanche discovered her husband, Allan, with a male lover, Allan shot himself (scene 6).	Desire can be dangerous to oneself and to others.
Blanche was forced to leave her job as a high school English teacher after sleeping with a seventeen-year-old student (scene 7).	There are serious consequences for violating society's norms of behaviour.
Blanche might have worked as a prostitute (scene 7); she has slept with multiple partners (soldiers) on the same night (scene 9).	Loneliness and emotional emptiness can drive people to behave in ways they might not otherwise consider.

Given the title of Williams's play, it is not surprising that desire has such a key part in this world. In scene 1, Blanche tells Eunice, 'They told me to take a street-car named Desire, and then transfer to one called Cemeteries and ride six blocks and get off at – Elysian Fields!' This journey, from desire to death to afterlife, appears to be an endless cycle for Blanche, starting with the deaths of her mother and husband, leading her to sexual encounters with a high school student and various strangers, and culminating in her rape in scene 10 and institutionalization. In contrast, Stanley and Stella's desire takes them on a journey to a new life, represented by the birth of their child on the anniversary of Blanche's birth, diverting Stella's love from older sister to infant child, and ultimately displacing Blanche from their home.

DRAMATURGY

Dramaturgy is 'the art or technique of dramatic composition and theatrical representation', according to Merriam-Webster's Dictionary. To those of you who think of theatre research as the province of scholars, I submit that dramaturgy is practical scholarship – research to help theatre artists make informed artistic choices. An oft-overlooked element of script analysis, dramaturgy has a two-century history in Germany but a scant few decades in America. With the establishment of resident professional theatres across the United States starting in the 1960s, a need arose for professional theatre artists who could help translate the significance of plays for each region and venue. Dramaturges, usually in their capacities as resident dramaturges or literary managers, help with play selection, translate or commission translations of foreign language plays, and help shepherd the development of new plays through readings and workshops. Play workshops, such as the National Playwrights Conference at the Eugene O'Neill Theater Center in Waterford, Connecticut, the Actors Theatre of Louisville's Humana Festival of New Play, and the Sundance Institute Theatre Programme, help playwrights see their work in its embryonic stages and get feedback from a wide range of actors, directors, fellow playwrights, and dramaturges. Only a handful of American universities, most notably Yale, Harvard, Columbia, Massachusetts-Amherst, and Iowa, offer a Master of Fine Arts (M.F.A.) degree in dramaturgy, but many others incorporate dramaturgy coursework and production work into their bachelor's, master's, and doctoral programmes.

Most contemporary American dramaturges have been trained in the dramaturgy methodology developed and popularized at Yale, the only American university that offers both an M.F.A. and Doctor of Fine Arts in Dramaturgy. The Yale method centres on the creation of a 'Dramaturg's Protocol' for the play being studied or produced, which includes four main sections, as described in *Dramaturgy in American Theater* by Leon Katz:

(1) relevant historical, cultural, social, or other pertinent background of the play,

(2) relevant biographical information concerning the playwright,

(3) a critical and descriptive production history of the play,

(4) a critical analysis and breakdown of the play (115).

This approach does not require or even encourage the director or production team to create a historically accurate production, but it enables the director and collaborators to make artistic choices with full knowledge of the context in which the playwright wrote, whatever their take on the play or the period or country in which they set the action. Each of the first three elements helps provide a critical context for understanding the action of the play and its significance at the time the playwright wrote it. The fourth element, in my view, combines the type of script analysis in which we engage and a review, cursory or thorough, of published criticism of the play. By and large, the more distant the play's writing and setting from the culture and time of a new production, the greater the need for research into the original period, playwright, and production history.

For our purposes, dramaturgical research into the period of the setting as well as the period when the play was written might help clarify the significance of the given circumstances of the script. The playwright's period can reveal a great deal about what his or her concerns might be when tackling particular subject matter. Also, it might help us better understand the actions and stakes of the characters. For example, theatre scholars often note that Hedda Gabler is likely to be pregnant at the start of the play bearing her name, yet a bit of dramaturgical digging into Norway's views and laws on abortion during Ibsen's time would reveal that from 1842 to 1902, abortion was a criminal offence. Given that the play was written in 1890 (only eight years after women were granted the right to attend the University of Oslo, and six years after the founding of the official women's rights organization in Norway), the legal status of abortion tells us a lot about the range of actions Hedda might consider if she is pregnant. The repeated mentions of her fear of scandal might have as much to do with her fear of discovery of a back-alley abortion as with her other fears.

In addition, dramaturgical research into the history of the playwright's writing (different drafts or versions, translations, play development) and into previous productions might uncover a wider range of potential approaches for a new production. Most of Shakespeare's plays were based on written histories or the plots of previously produced plays that he combined and crafted for his own purposes; going back to look at these sources can help clarify his choices. Oscar Wilde originally wrote *The Importance of Being Earnest* as a four-act play focused more on Algernon than Jack, but during rehearsals for the first production, actor-manager George Alexander asked Wilde to shorten the play to three acts, with a greater focus on Jack, the role he himself played (Raby 163). The four-act version is still in print and would be a valuable asset for a curious theatre company to explore, if only in rehearsal or design meetings.

In the context of script analysis, we can use dramaturgy to isolate some key avenues of research, which I illustrate with examples from one of our case study plays, Georg Büchner's *Woyzeck*. The table of contents for a dramaturge's protocol for *Woyzeck* might look something like this:

1. Biography of playwright Georg Büchner
2. Büchner's other work: *Danton's Death, Leonce and Lena, Lenz*
3. Historical sources for *Woyzeck*
4. History of the writing and publication: four fragments
5. Production history
6. Critical history
7. Major editions, adaptations, and translations
8. Criticism
9. History and structure of the early nineteenth-century German military

For a professional dramaturge, a comprehensive protocol might easily be 200–300 pages long, including summaries or excerpts from noteworthy critical articles, historical sources, and reviews from major productions. For a working actor, director, or designer under the pressure of production deadlines, even a brief summary of significant findings will help create a solid context for action and production choices.

THE WRITING OF THE PLAY AND ORDER OF SCENES

Woyzeck is an unfinished play; the playwright died from typhus before he was able to complete it. In fact, some scholars believe that Büchner was dying while he was working on the last draft. People dying of typhus often hallucinate – perhaps a contributing factor to the hallucinatory feeling of some scenes. None of Büchner's other plays display this hallucinatory quality, though *Leonce and Lena* is whimsical and *Danton's Death*, like *Woyzeck*, is based on a historical figure.

A medical doctor and professor, Büchner based the play on the case of a man who was executed for the murder of his lover in Büchner's time, as well as two similar cases, so the playwright viewed the source material through the lens of the medical knowledge of the early nineteenth century. Scholars have established that Büchner read the medical reports on all three murderers; his interest was therefore medical (as a doctor), personal (as a dramatist), and political (he was a proto-socialist who believed that all men were equal, even the most downtrodden, Richards 8). Upon his death, the playwright left four partial drafts of the play, which his brother hid for four decades, embarrassed by the content. The play was finally uncovered and published by Karl Emil Franzos in several publications from 1875 to 1879, but the original manuscript was heavily damaged by the use of chemicals in an ill-fated attempt by Franzos to preserve the faded handwriting (Richards 2). The first draft has twenty-one scenes, the second draft has nine, the third draft has two, and the fourth draft contains seventeen that revise many of the scenes from the first three drafts. Büchner left no instructions as to how the drafts fit together, and writers and directors have created translations and adaptations with free rein to change the order of scenes. The episodic nature of the play, multiple plot lines, lack of clear linear causality in much of the plot, and the absence of copyright protection have allowed the play to become a Rorschach test from which each writer and director might see and construct his or her own version.

Some scenes appear to be revisions of scenes from earlier drafts. The first draft has a scene that might be the intended ending, but it is not included in the subsequent drafts; whether this means that Büchner was happy with this ending is a matter of conjecture. The fourth draft goes about two-thirds of the way through the plot, then drops off, unfinished; most versions of the play rely on several scenes from the first two drafts to complete the play. The names of several characters change from draft to draft, and at least a dozen different arrangements of the scenes have been published and produced, as well as Alban Berg's opera version, *Wozzeck*.[3] The chart below captures the vast variety of scene orders in a few representative versions of *Woyzeck*.

---

[3] The spelling of Berg's opera derives from the corruption of Büchner's handwriting by the chemicals used in an attempt to preserve it, which made the title character's name illegible.

Draft, scene	Characters	A	B	C	D	E	F
4.1	Woyzeck, Andres	2	2	2	1	1	1
4.2	Marie, Margret, Drum Major	3	3	3	2	2	2
4.3	Marie, Woyzeck, Carnival Barker, Drum Major, Sargent	4/5	4/5	4	3	3	3
4.4	Woyzeck, Marie	8	6	5	4	4	
4.5	Woyzeck, Captain	1	1	1	5	5	5
4.6	Marie, Drum Major	6	8	7	6	7	6
4.7	Woyzeck, Marie	14	10	9	7	10	7
4.8	Woyzeck, Doctor	7	7	6	8	6	8
4.9	Captain, Doctor		9		9		9
4.10	Woyzeck, Andres	10	11	10	10	11	10
4.11	Inn	11	12	11	11	12	11
4.12	Woyzeck	12	13	12	12	13	12
4.13	Woyzeck, Andres	13	14	13	13	14	13
4.14	Inn	17	18	16	14	15	14
4.15	Woyzeck, Jew	19	19	17	15	17	15
4.16	Marie, Karl the idiot, Child	20	20	18	16	18	16
4.17	Woyzeck, Andres	18	22	19	17	19	17
1.14	Grandmother, Children	21	23	20	18	20	18
1.15	Woyzeck, Marie	22	24	21	19	21	19
1.16	Two people	25.3		23.3	20	23.1	20
1.17	Inn: Woyzeck, Katey, others	23	25	22	22	22	21
1.18	Children	26	27		23		22
1.19	Woyzeck	25.1	26	23.1	24	23.2	23
1.20	Woyzeck	25.2		23.2	25		24
1.21	Unattributed speech	27	29				25
3.1	Professor, students, Woyzeck	15	15	14		8	+
3.2	Woyzeck, Karl, Children	24	28		21		+
1.8	Woyzeck, Andres	16	17	15		16	

Note: Woyzeck is named Louis and Marie is named Magreth in the first two drafts.

+ = optional scene in this version

Key. A = Geoffrey Dunlop (1927); B = Carl Richard Mueller (1962); C = Michael Hamburger (1972); D = David G. Richards (1977); E = John Mackendrick (1979); F = Henry J. Schmidt (1986)

From this chart, an innovative theatre company, director, adaptor, or translator could easily construct a version of the play in yet another new sequence of scenes. Any thoughtful company would recognize that for this play perhaps more than any other, the choice of an existing translation/version/adaptation would be a crucial artistic decision.

Woyzeck contains four central plotlines:

1. Woyzeck, a low-level soldier, works for a Captain and a Doctor, each of whom abuses him. Woyzeck shaves his Captain, who talks to him about philosophy and asks him questions that he does not have the ability to answer. The Doctor pays him money to eat nothing but peas for an experiment, berates him for not being able to control his bladder (he needs Woyzeck's urine specimen for the experiment), and suddenly turns ecstatic when Woyzeck describes one of his hallucinations to him. Later the Captain and Doctor perform a vaudeville routine together. In the first scene of the third draft, a Professor (whom several translations see as the same character as the Doctor of the fourth draft) implores Woyzeck to demonstrate to his class how he can wiggle his ears like a donkey.

2. Woyzeck has five scenes with his fellow soldier, Andres, to whom he confesses his hallucinations and paranoid delusions. In one scene, Woyzeck gives Andres some of his most prized possessions, foreshadowing his intention to take the life of his common-law wife, Marie, and perhaps his own.

3. Marie appears to realize that Woyzeck is troubled and distracted. He notices that Marie is wearing new shiny earrings but appears to believe her when she says she found them. In another scene, he accuses her of being a sinner and implies she might have syphilis. He claims he has seen her with a man, which she admits somewhat defiantly. He sees her dancing with the Drum Major. He tells her he needs to take her someplace but will not reveal where. She goes with him, and he slits her throat, seemingly in the midst of a hallucination. He throws the knife in a pond.

4. Marie and the Drum Major have an affair. Marie sees the Drum Major marching, and her neighbour accuses her of being a slut. When she goes to the carnival with Woyzeck, the Drum Major and a friend ogle her and talk about her looks in blatantly sexual terms. The Drum Major helps Marie onto the carnival stage, but they do not talk to each other. Marie invites him to her house and asks him to march for her, but when he propositions her, she appears to reject him. At an inn or dance hall, the Drum Major picks a fight with Woyzeck and beats him badly.

Several other scenes do not relate directly to the action of the four main plotlines:

1. A grandmother tells a dark fairy tale about an orphan's disappointing journey to the moon (1.14).
2. Two people hear an eerie sound and go to investigate (1.16).
3. Woyzeck plays hobbyhorse with his son and an unexplained character, Karl the idiot (3.2).
4. Woyzeck buys a knife (4.15).
5. Woyzeck dances with Katey at an inn, and she sees blood on his hand and elbow (1.17).
6. Two children go to see a dead body (1.18).
7. An unidentified character speaks of a beautiful murder (1.21).

Any or all of these scenes might be selected to help shape the action and rhythm of a particular adaptation of the script, as there is no definitive version of *Woyzeck*.

Translations and versions

Another aspect of dramaturgical research for any play originally written in a foreign language would be the selection of a translation. Any translation of a play is to some extent a rewriting of it, but in the case of *Woyzeck*, the variety and range of translations are enormous. Translators usually aim to fit the translation to the time and culture of the intended production; the same idea applies to selecting a translation. Let us compare a couple of lines of dialogue from the dated 1927 Dunlop translation to John MacKendricks's British-inflected 1979 translation. In scene 4.6, the Drum Major attempts to seduce Marie:

DUNLOP: And you're a fine bit of skirt! By Gad – shall we lay out a breed of drum majors?
MACKENDRICK: And you're a real woman. Christ, I'm going to fill your belly full of drum-majors, sire a whole damn stable of them.

In just one line of dialogue, we see the freedom a translator enjoys to create his or her own voice in a translation, particularly with a play such as *Woyzeck*, which is in the public domain.

And consider scene 4.14, in which the Drum Major beats up Woyzeck:

DUNLOP: Keep off, whoever isn't a soused God Almighty.... I'll pommel 'is nose into 'is — for 'im .... You son of a —. Shall I pull your tongue

from your mouth for you and twist it round your middle? Shall I leave as
much breath in your carcass as an old woman's —.
MACKENDRICK: If y're not 's pissed 's creeping Jesus keep away from me.
I'll ram y'r nose up your arse!…Bastard; rat turd. I'm going to knock the
breath out'v you alright. You won't have enough f'r an old woman's fart.

In this dialogue, we get a taste of the British-ness of Mackendricks's translation,
as well as the difference in what types of profanity the translators believed
was acceptable in their times. Simply by examining each translator's use of
language, a director and ensemble could select a translation that most closely
matches their needs and vision for a production.

Imagine that we are creating an adaptation or translation for a production
of *Woyzeck*. How might the research above inform our choices? Start by
considering our expected audience. A young university audience at a liberal arts
college or university might favour a translation with more profanity and grit; a
more conservative or older audience might prompt us to select or commission
a translation with less aggressive language. In either case, we would need to
carefully examine the order of scenes to see how the shape of the action differs
from one version of the play to another.

For example, Berg's opera version, *Wozzeck*, employs a fairly logical and
causal selection and arrangement of scenes, whereas many other adaptations
and translations have arranged the scenes to disrupt causality, leading to a
structure that opens possibilities for more avant-garde productions. Several
versions of the play open with scene 1.5, in which Woyzeck shaves the Captain,
even though there is no proof that Büchner intended this to be the first scene.
What happens to the shape of the action in these versions? I suggest that putting
scene 1.5 first foregrounds the effects of Woyzeck's abuse or teasing at the
hands of one of his authority figures as one source of his mental decline. It also
establishes his place in the military, as well as his lowly rank.

Several versions skip scene 4.9, the vaudeville-style scene involving the
Captain and the Doctor. One of the most stylized scenes that Büchner wrote,
it therefore pulls the overall play away from a more naturalistic or realistic
style. Büchner left the scene in his final draft, so my educated guess is that
he wanted to keep it. If we include it, where would we place it, and what
could it add? What kind of production might successfully use a variety of acting
styles, including vaudeville? What sort of stage environment or space allows for
eclectic performance styles? What sort of play has characters whose voices and
acting styles vary among scenes?

Production history

A thorough production history allows theatre artists who are contemplating
a new production a glimpse at the potential interpretations already explored.

This helps avoid repeating the mistakes (or successes) of the past and can open up a play to new interpretations in production. Always read production reviews and history with a critical, almost sceptical eye, as the critic or scholar's point of view will have been heavily influenced by his or her time and personal aesthetic preferences. In part because of the fragmented quality of the text, and in part because of the style of Büchner's writing, *Woyzeck* has an extremely long and wide-ranging production history. Here is just a sample of the play's production history, culled from William Reeve's 1979 study, *Georg Büchner*, and updated with newspaper reviews of more recent productions:

1913 Premiere performance, Residenz Theatre, Munich. Use of revolving stage helped create smooth transitions and maintain the pacing.

1920 Berlin Lessingtheater. Expressionistic sets with naturalistic acting style 'failed to provide a consistent point of view' (141).

1921 Deutsche Theatre, Berlin. Directed by Max Reinhardt. Realistic sets on a revolving stage. Emphasis on gesture and mime. Avoided political implications. Long, but considered aesthetically successful.

1925 Alban Berg's opera *Wozzeck* premieres, Berlin.

1937 On the 100th anniversary of Büchner's death, the Nazis allowed the only production of *Woyzeck* during their reign. Realistic, with emphasis on Woyzeck as 'a universal symbol of human suffering' (144).

1967 Polish Stary Teatr, Cracow. The director 'transformed the tragedy into a ballad set in the folk-song tradition of Polish Galicia at the beginning of the nineteenth century' (147).

1969 La MaMa, New York. Ignored social and political aspects of the play. Costumes did not distinguish between class and rank. Production stressed 'athletic elegance' (150).

1971 Teatro Stabile, Turin, Italy. Presented all four drafts of the play in the order they were written: the first one at breakneck speed, and each successive draft progressively slower.

1972 Zurich Schausspielhaus, Switzerland. Directed by playwright Friedrich Dürrenmatt. His version ended with the barber scene from the first draft, with the Barber's role, usually played by the Captain, played by the Drum Major.

Krefelf-Monchengladback, Germany. Double-bill production of play and opera.

Frankfurt, Germany. Staged as a play within a play. Frame play as a fair.

1973 Open Space, London. Directed by Charles Marowitz, who 'changed the tragedy into a trial, in which each member of the cast eventually arrived at his or own verdict' (155).

1974 Bremen, Germany. Combined stylized staging (Captain and Doctor scene had them on stilts) with ultra-realistic acting in other scenes.

1975 Classic Stage Company, New York. Realistic production with a fence dividing the audience from the actors for most of the production.

Hannover Schauspielhaus, Germany. One-act curtain raiser was a circus act in which a professor oversees Woyzeck in a cage.

1990 Hartford Stage, CT. Adaptation, written and directed by Richard Foreman, entitled *Lights Blotted Out – Woyzeck*. Minimalist production punctuated by 'ear-piercing buzzers and hot lights' (Gussow 1990).

1992 Public Theatre, New York. Directed by Joanne Akalaitis, with score by Philip Glass. The use of 'alternate scenes and extracts from early drafts of the play' gave the production more momentum and a 'greater centricity to the role of Marie' (Gussow 1992).

2000 Betty Nansen Theater, Copenhagen, Denmark. Adapted and directed by Robert Wilson. Music and lyrics by Tom Waits and Kathleen Brennan. English premiere at Brooklyn Academy of Music, 2002. Rock musical version, with Wilson's trademark slow-moving, dream-like stage tableaus and grotesque performance style (Pareles).

2013 Adaptation by Punchdrunk, London, entitled *The Drowned Man*. Set in a fictional movie studio, this site-specific production invites the audience to wander through four floors of the 200,000 square foot theatre installation wearing white masks. The adaptation follows two narratives – first, a couple within the studio; second, a couple living on the edge of town – loosely based on *Woyzeck* (Healy).

From *Woyzeck*'s production history, we might gather a range of directorial approaches to the play, focusing on different elements of the play in production: dramatic structure; design, space, and stage configurations; acting styles; tempo; music and sound. Each of these elements is a vital part of any interpretation of *Woyzeck*; a familiarity with the decisions that past theatre artists have made about any of these elements may dissuade us from exploring some of these avenues in favour of others. Dramatic structure, for example, will be a crucial element of any production of *Woyzeck*. Its unfinished nature and multiple drafts offer theatre artists unparalleled freedom to construct their own versions of the play. Our dramaturgical research reveals the range of approaches to dramatic structure already explored. Many productions start the play with the scene in which Woyzeck shaves the Captain, from which we might conclude that these productions emphasized military rank and authority. At least three versions of the script skip the scene between the Captain and the Doctor, in spite of the knowledge that Büchner included this scene in his fourth and final draft. We might conclude that dropping the scene, in which Woyzeck does not appear, may help the play focus more fully on its central character, or that including the scene, which comes off as almost vaudevillian in its over-the-top comic style, might be useful for a production interested in exploring the different stylistic voices Büchner employs throughout the play. Several versions and productions of the play use the scene from the third draft in which the Professor, whom some see as the same character as the doctor, demonstrates to his students how he has trained Woyzeck, a scene that compliments the shaving scene's focus on how authority figures manipulate Woyzeck.

In selecting the scenes and scene order for a production of *Woyzeck*, we are forced to make strong choices about what we would include and emphasize, leading us to construct different core actions for the play. This is true of any play, but never more so than with *Woyzeck*, because it is an unfinished script with several scenes revised in four drafts, with only traces of causal action among the scenes to guide our choices.

Criticism

Used carefully, criticism of the play and playwright can open up a wide range of interpretations of the play and help place the play within the playwright's oeuvre. Yet most criticism reveals as much about its author and his or her place and times as it does about the play it purports to analyse. For example, in the 1880s, when *Woyzeck* was first published, the play's fragmentary and incomplete nature – the very element that has made it so popular with directors over the past 100 years – was considered evidence of its shortcomings. In the midst of the economic depression of the 1930s, many critics saw *Woyzeck* as a 'proletarian tragedy':

> [Woyzeck] has a problem, but because Germany has not yet developed beyond the contradiction of poor and rich to the new contradiction of proletarian and capitalist, he can find no solution except death – and death will not solve the problem of the proletariat, for, as Woyzeck says, 'even if we went to heaven, we would have to help make the thunder' (Kresh).

In later criticism, critics and scholars will see in the play all manner of styles, from naturalism to realism to the grotesque and the Theatre of the Absurd. By the 1970s, theatre critic John Simon will have credited Büchner's work as the precursor of many of the twentieth century's theatrical inventions:

> [*Danton's Death*], along with its sister masterpiece *Woyzeck*, anticipates … the essential elements of realism, poetic realism, naturalism, impressionism, expressionism, Sachlichkeit and magic realism. And to these we might add black humor and the theater of the absurd.

For this reason, it remains the responsibility of each theatre artist to examine the action of any play closely and evaluate criticism on the basis of his or her reading of the play in the dual context of the place and time it was written and the place and time of the intended production. No single interpretation, scholar, or critic will fit every production context.

CHARACTER

Character analysis is part of the big picture: a foundation for choices about actions and objectives. For this reason, it is an early element of script analysis. To recap, first we analysed the script for the world of the play, looking for the playwright's given circumstances. Next we analyse a major character from two of our case study plays, examining the script for explicit indications of character that will serve as the basis for interpreting each character's actions. You should stick to the script and, for the time being, refrain from embellishing what the playwright has provided. This does not mean that the playwright's physical description of the character controls how any production may be cast – but at the very least, a director or ensemble should recognize what the playwright has suggested before moving in a different direction. To simplify this part of your analysis and make it easy to digest in a glance, we use a character blueprint, and I again encourage you to be succinct.

Start by focusing on the characteristics that the playwright describes in stage directions, and then search for statements that characters make about themselves and that other characters make about them. Be careful: characters are not always honest with themselves about who they are, and others might not have accurate perceptions about them. Take these statements with a grain of salt – note discrepancies between what a character says and does, and between what characters say about themselves and what others say about them.

As we begin to analyse character, remember that the most complete test of character is what a character does – their actions. Our initial character analysis will mine the script for character traits or characteristics that establish the foundation for the analysis of actions in Chapter Two. For now, look for six basic types of characteristics, formulated as questions:

Physical: What does the playwright tell us about the physicality of the character, if anything?

Psychological: What is the character's mental state? Is the character in any way balanced, neurotic, psychotic, or deluded?

Intellectual: In what ways has the character's mind developed (schooling, environment, self-teaching, street smarts)?

Social class and job: In what class was the character raised, what class is he or she in throughout the play, and how would you describe his or her job or career path?

Family and friends: Where was the character born and raised, and how has this shaped his or her identity? How did family and upbringing influence his or her religious, political, and ethical beliefs? To what degree is he or she surrounded by friends and family or isolated?

Wants and morals: What does the character want most and what is he or she willing to do to get it?

To demonstrate how this works in practice, I will focus on lead characters in two of our case study plays: a Greek tragedy, *Oedipus the King* (Oedipus), and a modern drama, *A Streetcar Named Desire* (Blanche). Oedipus presents an interesting challenge, as many of us first heard of this character as part of a term used in Freudian psychology: the Oedipus complex. It is a very good example for that reason, because Freud's use of the term sharply contrasts with the way in which Sophocles thought about his character. Freud's concept of the Oedipus complex theorized that all children secretly wanted to have sex with their opposite-sex parent. Sophocles based his play on a Greek myth in which Oedipus devotes the formative years of his adult life to trying to avoid a prophecy that he would kill his father and marry his mother. Freud understood that he was taking poetic liberties with the myth and Sophocles's play, but his theory became such a famous part of modern psychology that contemporary audiences know it better than the myth from which he drew it. Again, a little dramaturgical research will prevent us from seeing the character in the wrong context.

Physical traits

What, if anything, does Sophocles tell us about Oedipus's physical traits? To start with, we have the central character's name, Oedipus. Of course, this is Greek to us, both figuratively and literally, so we must research the meaning of his name in Greek. When analysing the work of any accomplished playwright – particularly with a play that is still considered one of the best tragedies ever written, more than 2,400 years after its premiere – we should always assume that the playwright's choices are significant, rather than accidental, and thus might contain important information. For the roots of a word or name, the best place to start is a dictionary of etymology, a reference book that explains the origins and historical development of words. In this case, we will be using the most easily accessible compilation of etymological information, the Online Etymology Dictionary (www.etymonline.com), which brings together several dozen reference sources from a variety of nations. The listing, which includes three modern uses of the name Oedipus, among them Freud's Oedipus complex, first provides the roots of the original Greek name: 'literally "swollen-foot", from *oidan* "to swell" ... + *pous* ... "foot'". Oedipus's name, therefore, refers to an injury from when he was a baby and his mother, upon hearing an earlier prophecy that her son would kill his father, pinned his ankles together and ordered his servant to abandon the baby to certain death. The servant, feeling pity for the boy, instead passed him on to a shepherd from a neighbouring land, who brought him back to his king, Polybus of Corinth, where he was raised as if he were Polybus's own son.

Much can be made from good dramaturgical research into Oedipus's name, but we will concentrate on what it reveals about his physicality: we can infer that he has a distinctive limp, despite his royal bearing – as a child born of royalty in one land and raised as royalty in another, he would have been trained in physical combat and sports. Here it might be useful as well to refresh our theatre history and recall that Sophocles wrote when the lead actors wore masks larger than their heads, which enlarged their stage presence, and *cothurni*, thick-soled boots that made them taller than the chorus members. Therefore, Sophocles created his version of Oedipus knowing that the actor playing this role would be the largest figure on stage, whose ability to communicate physical characteristics would be both enhanced and limited by the mask and shoes he wore. A limp would be a strong distinguishing characteristic, made all the more meaningful when its significance is revealed at the end of the play. Yet other mentions of Oedipus's physical appearance are almost non-existent, particularly given that Sophocles included scarce stage directions, none of which describe physicality in detail, as modern and contemporary playwrights, freed from the conventions and limitations of masks and *cothurni*, frequently do.

There is, however, one more significant mention of Oedipus's appearance. Jocasta, Oedipus's birth mother and wife, relates how her first husband, Laius, was murdered during a chance encounter at a crossroads. When Oedipus, haunted by his own memory of such an encounter, asks what Laius looked like, she replies, 'He was swarthy, and the gray had just begun to streak his temples, and his build ... wasn't far from yours' (816–818). One of a number of revelations that accumulate until Jocasta and then Oedipus realize who he is and what he has done, it is also a physical description: Oedipus looks like his birth father, Laius, the slain king. For all that can be written about the play and Oedipus's character from these discoveries, we need to limit ourselves to the simplest expression of his physicality, which might look like this on our character blueprint:

Physical	
What does the playwright tell us about the physicality of the character, if anything?	Oedipus limps (origin of his name), stands taller than his peers (*corthuni*), and is built like his birth father, Laius, himself a king. From this semblance, as well as Oedipus's royal upbringing, we can infer he has a royal bearing.

I would also note the lack of descriptions and comments about Oedipus's physical characteristics by other characters. This is in part because Sophocles was writing with full knowledge of the theatrical conventions of his time; the use of masks and simple, standardized costumes limited his palate for physical characterization.

For *A Streetcar Named Desire* (1947), playwright Tennessee Williams knew that the first production was likely to be produced on Broadway with a large budget, given the Broadway success of his previous play, *The Glass Menagerie* (1944), which won the New York Drama Critics Circle Award for Best Play in 1945. Although Williams's stage directions for *Streetcar* contain some dream-like flashback sequences in which the sound and lighting express Blanche DuBois's inner turmoil and past, Williams knew that Elia Kazan, with whom he had established a bond while working on *Glass Menagerie*, would direct the premiere. As a member of the Group Theater and co-founder of the Actors Studio, Kazan was one of the major proponents of Method acting and psychological realism for stage and film acting; Williams thus had a good sense of the acting style and type of actors that Kazan was likely to cast in *Streetcar*. Yet Williams, in his production notes to *Glass Menagerie*, had already made it clear that he was looking to replace realistic conventions with 'a new, plastic theatre' – one that used 'expressionist and poetic devices [to allow] fuller access to the truth'. With that in mind, let us examine the female lead role in *Streetcar*, Blanche DuBois, for information about her physical characteristics.

Once again, we will start by looking at her name. According to the Online Etymology Dictionary, Blanche is a feminine proper name, 'from French *Blanche*, from Old French *blanc* "white", of Germanic origin....A fairly popular name for girls born in the U.S. from about 1880 to 1900'. I would also note that according to the Oxford Dictionary, 'blanch' (without the 'e') means 'grow pale from shock or fear'. Her name, therefore, might be a sign of both her physical appearance – pale white, in contrast to the vast majority of people in New Orleans's melting plot, the colours of the city, and the overall atmosphere of decay that Williams describes in his initial stage direction – and its figurative source: her husband's suicide, which shocked her and left her fearful for her future. She blanched when she discovered her husband was with a man, he shot himself immediately afterwards, and through the course of the play, she blanches in fear of Stanley and his brusque (in her mind), brutish manners and friends. Of Stanley's group, only sheltered 'momma's boy' Mitch offers Blanche a possible escape from the future she fears.

In Williams's first description of Blanche's entrance into the world of the play, he emphasizes how out of place she seems:

> Her appearance is incongruous to this setting. She is daintily dressed in a white suit with a fluffy bodice, necklace and earrings of pearl, white

gloves and hat, looking as if she were arriving at a summer tea or cocktail party....Her delicate beauty must avoid strong light. There is something about her uncertain manner, as well as her white clothes, that suggests a moth. (I, 1, 16)

In her first scene with the Kowalskis's neighbour, Eunice, Williams immediately establishes Blanche's connection with her family's recently 'lost' plantation, Belle Reve. Eunice boils down the plantation to its essence, 'A great big place with white columns', in stark contrast to the Kowalskis's tiny, rundown apartment. Eunice lets her into the apartment and Blanche sits stiffly, 'clutching her purse as if she were quite cold', and is easily startled by the sound of a cat.

Once her sister, Stella, arrives, Blanche immediately asks her to turn off the ceiling light so she can avoid its 'merciless glare', the start of Blanche's repeated attempts to control the lighting so she can create the right look for herself. She is afraid of the strong light of day because it might reveal her age, her 'blanched' and frightened appearance, and her vulnerability. In scene 2, Stanley tears through Blanche's wardrobe trunk, convinced that the fake furs and rhinestone tiara that Blanche brought with her prove that she is withholding her family's fortune from the Kowalskis; in scene 10, having uncovered Blanche's sordid past and the truth about the family's squandered fortune, he sees her furs and tiara for what they are: worthless costume jewellery, part of Blanche's feeble attempt to keep up appearances. We might therefore capture Blanche's most significant physical traits in this way:

Physical	
What does the playwright tell us about the physicality of the character, if anything?	Blanche's name means 'white' or 'pale from fear'. She is beautiful yet delicate. She dresses to mask her vulnerability and age, attempting to keep up the appearance of wealth and good breeding upon which she prides herself. She avoids strong, direct lighting at all times, in a vain effort to hide the effects of her life on her appearance.

Psychological traits

In examining Oedipus's character traits, I would observe first that because there are no stage directions in the play, there are no character descriptions from the playwright. Yet Sophocles reveals several significant characteristics to us, both through reports of Oedipus's previous actions by other characters and through his actions during the play. Oedipus has followed a convoluted journey to his station in life, king of Thebes. Having been raised as a Corinthian prince and heir to the throne, he fled the city after a drunken man told him that he was not the son of his father, Polybus. From there, he travelled to Delphi to ask the god Apollo whether this rumour was true, only to hear Apollo's pronouncement of his fate: to kill his father, marry his mother, and sire children from this incestuous coupling (872–874). He fled Corinth, murdered a man on the road (who turned out to be his birth father, Laius), and solved the riddle of the Sphinx, thus freeing Thebes from the Sphinx's torture. For this act of heroism, Thebes rewarded Oedipus with the hand of the queen, Jocasta (his birth mother), and the Theban throne.

We need to boil down these facts into two or three essential psychological qualities. We might observe that Oedipus is paranoid, running away from a drunk's rumour and an outlandish prophecy with no hard evidence. Yet he is not truly paranoid, because his greatest fears turn out to be true. Furthermore, we need to consider Oedipus's behaviour in the context of his world, one in which prophecies come true and humans, even royalty, believe in what the gods and prophets foretell. Still, his actions, past and present, tell us much about his character. Rather than confront his fate, he tries to run away from it. Despite his attempts to avoid his fate by fleeing his homeland, he murders a man on the road in a fit of rage; he lacks self-control. Finally, during the play, he loses his temper and bullies everyone who tries to help him: his brother-in-law, Creon; his wife, Jocasta; the blind seer, Tiresias; and the shepherds. So we might capture the essence of his psychology in this way:

Psychological	
What is the character's mental state? Is the character in any way balanced, neurotic, psychotic, or deluded?	Oedipus is strong willed but rash. He lacks self-control, particularly when under pressure. He might seem paranoid, but his fears turn out to be justified. In this world, he deludes himself into believing he can run away from his fate.

Returning to Blanche in *A Streetcar Named Desire*, we again find ourselves in more familiar territory: a realistic character in a predominantly realistic play. In his stage directions, Williams immediately brings attention to Blanche's fragile psychological state. The minute she walks on stage and sees where Stella lives, she reacts strongly, 'Her expression is one of shocked disbelief' (16). Her clothing, 'daintily dressed...looking as if she were arriving at a summer tea', identifies her as an outsider in this setting. Williams goes to great lengths to describe her essential vulnerability: 'Her delicate beauty must avoid strong light. There is something about her uncertain manner, as well as her white clothes, that suggests a moth.' Blanche is skittish, easily startled by a cat's screech, and reaches for a drink whenever her vulnerability is exposed, displaying surprising ease when downing straight whiskey without water or a chaser (scene 1, 69).

Haunted by her past, she hears music and voices. She makes up stories about wealthy suitors, such as Shep Huntleigh, who call to court her. By the end of the play, Stanley arranges for her to be taken to a sanatorium after what appears to be a nervous breakdown, and Blanche, finally, accepts the doctor's hand and 'the kindness of strangers' (scene 11, 162–3). Putting all this together, we might describe her extreme vulnerability and her fragile psychological state in this way:

Psychological	
What is the character's mental state? Is the character in any way balanced, neurotic, psychotic, or deluded?	Blanche is fragile, vulnerable, neurotic, and possibly borderline psychotic. She hears voices and music. When her vulnerability is exposed, she creates a fantasy world as a defence. How strongly does she believe in her fantasies? That may be a question for casting and rehearsal.

Intellectual traits

Playwrights always offer some clues to a character's intellectual traits, though they might be implicit in the character's actions, use of language, or station in life. It is essential for us to look beyond our initial assumptions about a character's intelligence. A highly educated character might lack other intellectual traits, such as ingenuity or even curiosity, whereas a street-smart character might still be extremely well read, despite a lack of formal schooling. Two characters might be highly educated, but they might not have the same intellectual traits. In *Hedda Gabler*, for example, both Tesman and Løvborg have earned doctorates in the same field, yet Tesman, a researcher whose strengths are in digging through archives and organizing other people's thoughts, prefers to write about the past, whereas Løvborg applies his intellectual gifts to innovation and imagination and feels compelled to write about the future.

Oedipus appears to have many intellectual gifts; his shortcomings are less apparent. As the adopted son of a king of Corinth in ancient Greece, he would have received the best formal education available in his day. We also discover that Oedipus became king of Thebes by solving the riddle of the Sphinx, a riddle that had stumped all the best minds of Thebes. This appears to indicate that Oedipus has tremendous logical abilities. Yet despite many clues to his own identity, it takes Oedipus almost the entire play to figure out that he is the son of Laius and Jocasta, and that by running away from his adopted parents to avoid his fate, he has inadvertently fulfilled it by killing Laius and marrying

Jocasta. For this reason, I might observe that Oedipus lacks self-awareness. His judgement seems to be further clouded by overconfidence in his intellectual abilities: certain that he will find the killer of Laius and that he is innocent, he promises to banish the killer from Thebes. What would otherwise be considered a strength – his intellectual curiosity and drive to find out the truth – leads to his public humiliation and punishment. Our analysis of his intellectual traits could be summarized like this:

Intellectual	
In what ways has the character's mind developed (schooling, environment, self-teaching, street smarts)?	Raised as a prince, Oedipus is highly educated. He is highly logical (solved the riddle of the Sphinx). His overconfidence in his intellectual abilities and lack of self-awareness blind him to his own identity; his hunger for truth pushes him to discover and suffer the consequences of his own crime.

By contrast, Blanche's intellectual ability might be a little less apparent because of her fragile psychological state, yet Williams provides a wealth of information about it. We might assume that Blanche had some education beyond high school because we know that she is a high school teacher who is either on a leave of absence, if we believe her (scene 1, line 117–128), or, more likely, was fired, according to Stanley's sources (scene 7, lines 84–88). Certainly her parents had the financial ability to send her to college, and during the 1940s, teaching was one of the professions that women, for societal reasons even more prevalent in the South, could readily pursue. Given her ability to make up stories about herself and her suitors, it is fair to say that she has a strong imagination. She is far sharper than Mitch, whom she is able to manipulate rather easily, but meets her match when pitted against Stanley's street smarts and tenacity. Her blueprint might look like this:

Intellectual	
In what ways has the character's mind developed (schooling, environment, self-teaching, street smarts)?	Blanche is likely college educated, perhaps with a degree in education. She is imaginative and loves to make up stories. She is more than intelligent enough to handle the expectations of a naïve man such as Mitch, but not strong enough to withstand the inquisitive and aggressive street smarts of Stanley.

Social class and job

When we examine Oedipus and Blanche for their social class and jobs, we see quite divergent paths. Oedipus, a Theban prince by birth, was adopted and raised as a prince in Corinth. Yet in an attempt to escape his fate, he gave up his position and homeland to make his way in the world alone. He then solved the riddle of the Sphinx, for which he was rewarded with Jocasta's hand in marriage, thus making him king of Thebes. His job is king, a job that, unlike many who inherit the position, he earned by solving the riddle. Thus he sees himself as a self-made man. As he does not know that he is also king by birthright, he might try to overcompensate for his belief that he is a foreigner in Thebes. He feels he must prove himself repeatedly, which only brings out the truth of his crime and the execution of his self-inflicted punishment. Thus, his blueprint for social class and job might look like this:

Social class and job	
In what class was the character raised, what class is her or she throughout the play, and how would you describe his or her job or career path?	Oedipus is a king by birth and by deed. He believes he has become king thanks to his cleverness. Because he feels certain that he is a foreigner in Thebes, he constantly tries to prove himself. In the end, his strength proves his downfall, as he proves his own crime and serves his own sentence.

Blanche was raised in Southern aristocracy, part of a long line of wealthy owners of Belle Reve. But the family squandered its fortune, and she was forced to give up Belle Reve. After her husband committed suicide and she had an affair with one of her high school students, she was fired from her job as a teacher and fled town to stay with her sister and Stanley in New Orleans. She believes Mitch is her last hope of regaining her respectability. He might be of a lower class, but at least she would be a married woman with a steady home and income. Her blueprint might look like this:

Social class and job	
In what class was the character raised, what class is he or she throughout the play, and how would you describe his or her job or career path?	Aristocratic by birth, Blanche has fallen on bad times. Her husband committed suicide. After having an affair with a student, she was fired from her job as a high school teacher. She desperately wants to regain some measure of respect by marrying working-class Mitch.

Family and friends

Family and friends shape a character's identity and offer clues to a myriad of character traits, including religious, political, and ethical beliefs. To assess the character's degree of isolation, we can also look for the presence or absence of friends and family during the play. Oedipus provides particularly fertile ground for these questions, as he discovers that his relationships with Jocasta and Creon are quite different from what he believed at the start of the play. We would therefore note that Oedipus was the offspring of the king and queen of Thebes, Laius and Jocasta, but was adopted and raised as their own by the king and queen of the neighbouring city-state, Corinth. Obviously, it is significant that he kills his birth father, Laius, and marries his birth mother, Jocasta. We should also note that his brother-in-law, Creon, is also his uncle, and that his children are also his half-siblings, as they are the children of his wife and mother, Jocasta. Finally, I would observe that although his closest blood relations surround him – Jocasta and their daughters, Antigone and Ismene – the situation becomes more and more problematic for him, as the action of the play reveals the latent duplicity of these relationships. He has no friends within the action of the play and makes no mention of friends. In this way, the play focuses on his complex relationships with his family.

As the dominant religion of ancient Greece was polytheistic, Oedipus believes in multiple gods; most prominent in the play is the god Apollo, who prophesized his fate. Yet he tries to avoid his fate, which suggests that he overestimates his ability to defy the gods. Politically, he is a monarch but appears to be quite responsive to the will of the people, who call on him at the start of the play to find Laius's killer and stop the plague in Thebes. His ethics are those of his time and culture; he believes that the killer of the king should be brought to justice, and he accepts his own punishment when he discovers that he is the killer. Yet he thinks nothing of killing Laius when he has a confrontation with him at a crossroads. We might summarize these findings on our blueprint as follows:

Family and friends	
Where was the character born and raised, and how has this shaped his or her identity? How did family and upbringing influence his or her religious, political, and ethical beliefs? To what degree is he or she surrounded by friends and family or isolated?	Son of the king and queen of Thebes, Laius and Jocasta. Adopted son of the king and queen of Corinth, Polybus and Merope. Married to Jocasta, his birth mother. Two daughters appear in the play, Antigone and Ismene – both the products of incest. Believes in multiple gods. Believes in prophecy but tries to avoid his fate. Willing to murder but also believes in justice for the murderer of Laius, even when it turns out to be him. Part of a monarchy, but as king, he is responsive to the plight of the people. The closer he comes to realizing that his wife is also his mother, the more isolated he feels.

I would also note that the considerable quantity of information in this section of the character blueprint for Oedipus, which reveals the significance of family to the action, an obvious, though easily overlooked element of the play's given circumstances.

Placed in a more realistic setting, Blanche's family relationships are more traditional, though no less significant. She was raised in an aristocratic family and is used to being waited on, but after the suicide of her husband, when she discovered him in a sexual liaison with a man, and the death of the last of her relatives, she is evicted from the family estate, Belle Reve. Thus her manners and way of life have outlived their utility. Her only living relative is Stella, who is, by Blanche's standards, 'slumming it' with Stanley, the uneducated, working-class son of Polish immigrants. She has no friends left in her hometown, and the only friend she makes in New Orleans is her intended suitor, Mitch. When Stanley succeeds in poisoning Mitch's affections with reports of her scandalous sexual history, she is completely isolated from everyone but her sister. And after Stanley rapes her in scene 10, she faces an unseen dilemma before scene 11: does she tell Stella what Stanley did and risk being called a liar (for she has lied many times already), or does she hide the terrible truth? She tells the truth, but Stella, as much from self-preservation as anything, does not believe her, as she tells Eunice: 'I couldn't believe her story and go on living with Stanley' (scene 11, line 36).[4] For these reasons, Blanche ends the play with no family and no friends, as captured in her most-quoted line, spoken to the doctor who comes to take her away to a sanatorium, 'I've always depended upon the kindness of strangers' (lines 162–163). Finally, we might note that although she was raised to be a Southern aristocratic lady, circumstances have forced her to revise her morality to survive – she sleeps with strangers, fabricates stories about long-lost lovers returning to woo her, and breaks a bottle in a last-ditch effort to defend herself from Stanley's advances. Our character blueprint for Blanche might condense this information like this:

Family and friends	
Where was the character born and raised, and how has this shaped his or her identity? How did family and upbringing influence his or her religious, political, and ethical beliefs? To what degree is he or she surrounded by friends and family or isolated?	Daughter of a wealthy Southern family, Blanche was raised to be a lady. She married a young man who committed suicide when she discovered him with another man. Aside from her younger sister, Stella, all her relatives died and the family estate was lost. Faced with these circumstances, she was willing to do anything to save herself: sleep with strangers, woo a man she would have deemed beneath her (Mitch), and break a bottle to ward off Stanley's advances. After Stanley's rape, she has lost everything – even her sister.

[4]For the film version of *Streetcar*, Williams revised the ending to imply that Stella may leave Stanley.

So Blanche, like Oedipus, finds herself isolated and banished by the end of the play, though she loses even her sister's belief in her, whereas Oedipus's daughters take pity on him and lead him into the palace after his blinding and before his banishment.

Wants and morals

Having established a character's core characteristics, we next turn to the most revealing type of character analysis, asking 'What does the character want, and what is he or she willing to do to get it?' The answer will guide our analysis of the character's actions and objectives throughout the play, as we establish, unit by unit, how the character pursues his or her wants or desires. We should remain open to revising a character's wants following our more detailed action analysis, but our initial attempt to define his or her wants will establish a starting point for our more detailed, moment-to-moment choices.

Oedipus has several wants:

- To save Thebes from the plague
- To find the killer of the late Theban king, Laius
- To discover his true identity
- To escape the prophecy that he is fated to kill his father and marry his mother.

Any of these could serve as the central objective – or **super–objective** – that fuels his actions throughout the play. He is willing to investigate, to dominate others, and to murder.

Blanche wants to survive, to save herself from the indiscretions of her past, to secure a fresh start on life, to build a new life. In the past, she was willing to sleep with her student and also with strangers in order to survive. She is willing to move to New Orleans, to give up her privacy, to seduce Mitch (a man she may consider beneath her), to lie about her past, and to break a bottle to defend herself. By compiling all our findings, we might generate the following two sample blueprints:

Character Blueprint for Oedipus from *Oedipus the King*

Physical	
What does the playwright tell us about the physicality of his character, if anything?	Oedipus limps (origin of his name) stands taller than his peers (*corthuni*) and is built like his birth father, Laius, himself a king. From this semblance, as well as Oedipus's royal upbringing, we can infer he has a royal bearing.

Physical	
What is the character's mental state? Is the character in any way balanced, neurotic, psychotic, or deluded?	Oedipus is strong willed but rash. He lacks self-control, particularly when under pressure. He might seem paranoid, but his fears are justified. In this world, he deludes himself into believing he can run away from his fate.
Intellectual	
In what ways has the character's mind developed (schooling, environment, self-teaching, street smarts)?	Raised as a prince, Oedipus is highly educated. He is highly logical (solved the riddle of the Sphinx). His overconfidence in his intellectual abilities and lack of self-awareness blind him to his own identity; his hunger for truth pushes him to discover and suffer the consequences of his own crime.
Social class and job	
In what class was the character raised, what class is he or she in throughout the play, and how would you describe his or her job or career path?	Oedipus is a king by birth and by deed. He believes he has become king thanks to his cleverness. Because he feels certain that he is a foreigner in Thebes, he constantly tries to prove himself. In the end, his strength proves his downfall, as he proves his own crime and serves his own sentence.
Family and friends	
Where was the character born and raised, and how has this shaped his or her identity? How did family and upbringing influence his or her religious, political, and ethical beliefs? To what degree is he or she surrounded by friends and family or isolated?	Son of the king and queen of Thebes, Laius and Jocasta. Adopted son of the king and queen of Corinth, Polybus and Merope. Married to Jocasta, his birth mother. Two daughters present in the play, Antigone and Ismene – both the products of incest. Believes in multiple gods. Believes in prophecy but tries to avoid his fate. Willing to murder but also believes in justice for the murderer of Laius, even when it turns out to be him. Part of a monarchy, but as king, he is responsive to the plight of the people. The closer he comes to realizing that his wife is also his mother, the more isolated he feels.
Wants and morals	
What does the character want, and what is he or she willing to do to get it?	Oedipus wants to save Thebes from the plague, to find the killer or Laius, to discover his true identity, and to escape his fate. In the past, he has been willing to run away from home and also to murder; during the play, he relentlessly investigates the murder of Laius and dominates others to get the answers he seeks.

Character Blueprint for Blanche from *A Streetcar Named Desire*

Physical *What does the playwright tell us about the physicality of the character, if anything?*	Blanche's name means 'white' or 'pale from fear'. She is beautiful yet delicate. She dresses to mask her vulnerability and age, attempting to keep up the appearance of wealth and good breeding upon which she prides herself. She avoids strong, direct lighting at all times, in a vain effort to hide the effects of her life on her appearance.
Psychological *What is the character's mental state? Is the character in any way balanced, neurotic, psychotic, or deluded?*	Blanche is fragile, vulnerable, neurotic, and possibly borderline psychotic. She hears voices and music. When her vulnerability is exposed, she creates a fantasy world as a defence. How strongly does she believe in her fantasies?
Intellectual *In what ways has the character's mind developed (schooling, environment, self-teaching, street smarts)?*	Blanche is likely college educated, probably with a degree in education. She is imaginative and loves to make up stories. She is more than intelligent enough to handle the expectations of a naïve man such as Mitch, but not enough to withstand the inquisitive and aggressive street smarts of Stanley.
Social class and job *In what class was the character raised, what class is he or she in throughout the play, and how would you describe his or her job or career path?*	Aristocratic by birth, Blanche has fallen on bad times. Her husband committed suicide. After having an affair with a student, she was fired from her job as a high school teacher. She desperately wants to regain some measure of respect by marrying working-class Mitch.
Family and friends *Where was the character born and raised, and how has this shaped his or her identity? How did family and upbringing influence his or her religious, political, and ethical beliefs? To what degree is he or she surrounded by friends and family or isolated?*	Daughter of a wealthy Southern family, Blanche was raised to be a lady. She married a young man who committed suicide when she discovered him with another man. Aside from her younger sister, Stella, all her relatives died and the family estate was lost.
Wants and morals *What does the character want, and what is he or she willing to do to get it?*	Blanche wants to survive. In the past, she was willing to sleep with one of her high school students and also with strangers. During the play, she moves to New Orleans, lies about her past, gives up her privacy, woos a man she would have deemed beneath her (Mitch), and breaks a bottle to ward off Stanley's advances.

ENVIRONMENT

The characters' environment will be a vital part of the core action statement and discussions with designers, but only after we have fully analysed the characters' actions and objectives throughout the play. For now, we begin our analysis of environment with the playwright's description of place, supplemented by our analysis of the characters who inhabit the place. After we have broken down the structure of a play into units and analysed each unit in greater detail in Chapter Two, we will use all of our findings to develop an approach to the play's environment within a core action statement. For now, we will look at what the playwright has given us in terms of environment, without further interpretation.

We must first look at the playwright's description of place, and then ask ourselves, whose space is it? In *Oedipus the King*, the entire action takes place in a mythic past, in a single public space, in front of the Theban palace in ancient Greece, in front of a chorus of citizens. Oedipus is the king and therefore the most powerful person in this space, but he mistakenly believes he is an immigrant, born in Corinth rather than Thebes. At the very moment he realizes he is a Theban, he is subject to banishment for the crime of killing his father, the late king.

In *Hedda Gabler*, by contrast, the entire action takes place around 1890, in a single private place, the home of Hedda and her newlywed husband, George Tesman. It is an upscale home in the fashionable part of Christiana, Norway (now the nation's capital, Oslo), far north and therefore with much less sunlight in the winter than the summer; the action takes place in September. George bought the house for Hedda because she had told him she loved it, but actually hates the house. She only told George she loved the house because she was desperate for something to talk about with him. And because Brack arranged for the loan with which George purchased the house, and George's Aunt Julie put up her pension as collateral for all of the furnishings, the house actually belongs to Aunt Julie more than George or Hedda – a constant reminder of Hedda's debt to the Tesmans, whom she sees as beneath her.

In *Fences*, August Wilson sets the entire play in Pittsburgh, in the yard and porch of the Maxson family. Under the watchful eye of his wife, Rose, the father, Troy, occupies the yard for most of the play, ignoring his wife's continual requests for him to build a fence around the yard to protect their family. At the height of the conflict between Troy and his son, Cory, in Act 2, scene 4, Troy kicks his son out of the house. When Cory tells Troy he'll be back for his things, Troy replies, 'They'll be on the other side of that fence' (line 172). In this way, the fence that was supposed to protect the family becomes a barrier between father and son – one that Cory will not cross again until his father's funeral towards the end of the play.

In all three plays, we can define the ways in which the environment serves as a single disputed territory. Similarly, in *Streetcar* the action takes place in Stanley and Stella's noisy one-bedroom basement apartment, in a noisy, steamy section of New Orleans. As Stanley himself observes, in Louisiana, still legally under the Napoleonic Code, what belongs to a husband belongs to his wife and vice versa. For this reason, although Stanley is the breadwinner, Stella has the power, both legally and within their marriage, to invite her sister to stay with them for several months, whereas Stanley has the right to invite his buddies over to the house for poker. With only a curtain to shield Blanche, in the front room, from Stanley and Stella, in the back room, Blanche wonders whether the living arrangements are proper for her visit. She puts a paper lantern on the bare light bulb in the front room to make it more 'her space', and to help conceal any traces of her actual age from potential suitors, such as Mitch, so he will not ask why she is unmarried. The play can be seen as a battle for territory: Only after Stanley lifts Blanche and carries her into his inner sanctum can he rape her, at which point Blanche is hard pressed to hold on to any territory in the apartment, aside from the bathroom and tub, where she hides until the doctor and nurse come to take her away to a sanatorium.

In *Earnest*, the first act takes place in town, and the next two acts take place in the country. Once again, these environments indicate territory: Jack is 'Ernest' in town and Jack in the country. In town, he has the freedom to do and be whatever he wants, whereas in the country, he has added stature and responsibility as a landowner and as Cecily's guardian. Conversely, Algernon is 'Ernest' in the country, where he might court Cecily, but Algernon in town, where he must live up to family obligations, playing piano for his aunt, Lady Bracknell, when she entertains, and entertaining married women at social functions. We get an even stronger sense of these aspects of environment from the two men's costumes: Algernon wears his 'Bunburying' suits in the country to flirt with Cecily, while Jack chooses to wear all black when she returns to his country estate, in mourning for his profligate 'brother', Ernest, as part of a futile attempt to rid Cecily of her obsession with Jack's reports of Ernest's troubles.

In both Paula Vogel's *How I Learned to Drive* and Griselda Gambaro's *Information for Foreigners*, the action takes place in a number of different spaces, but the playwrights describe the use of these environments in vastly different ways. Gambaro explicitly calls for the play to take place in an actual residence with separate rooms and hallways for each scene. The many scenes all take place inside one real building, and the audience, split into several small groups, visits each space in a different order, with each scene performed simultaneously, so that while one group sees a particular scene, they may hear another scene in the background. In this way, the environment for *Information for Foreigners* might increase the audience's sense that the events taking place on stage are real. Vogel also contains all of the locations within a single space – the theatre at which the play is performed. Because *How I Learned to Drive* takes place in a theatre with most of the action portrayed in flashback, the environment increases the distance between the audience and the performers by supplying minimal realistic detail, bringing attention to the space as place for performance rather than one that might convey the illusion of reality. Vogel further emphasizes the quality of distance in the penultimate scene, when the central character, L'il Bit, is literally split in two: Peck molests the body of the older actress playing L'il Bit in her thirties, while the younger female chorus member speaks her lines from somewhere else on stage – a non-realistic staging of the most emotionally devastating flashback in the play.

We can also examine a play for how the environment might affect the play's relationships. In *Oedipus*, for example, the setting of the action at the front door of the Theban palace lends Oedipus increased power at the start of the play, when he is strong, and looms large over his crumpled form at the end of the play, when he has fallen. In *Hedda*, as Brack gains power over Hedda in Act 4, we might begin to see how his arrangement of the loan for the home prior to the start of the play transforms into his power over both home and future mistress at the end. In *Earnest*, location changes identity and status; whoever is home might have more power, but they have less freedom to reinvent themselves. In *How I Learned to Drive*, the physical confines of the automobile within which Peck gives L'il Bit driving lessons most frequently increases his power over her because he owns the car: not only is the car his territory, but once inside it, L'il Bit has much less physical space to evade Peck's advances. Outside of the car – in L'il Bit's college room on her eighteenth birthday, for example – Peck is nearly powerless to prevent L'il Bit's rejection of him.

The environment might also further define the pattern created by the structure of scenes. In *Information for Foreigners*, Gambaro insists upon having small groups of audience travel from room to room with a guide, thus reinforcing the sense that audience members are strangers in a strange land, their movements controlled by a guide. In *Streetcar* and *Hedda*, the central characters each try to progressively change their environment to make it more their own: Hedda moves her piano; Blanche puts up her paper lantern. Thus, even in a simple single setting, we should look for ways in which the playwright suggests the mutability of the environment. Likewise, in a predominantly episodic play, such as *How I Learned to Drive*, we should carefully examine the progression of spaces from one scene to the next, looking for a pattern that we might further define in production. In a play with a single setting, such as *Oedipus*, the entrances and exits of the characters Oedipus summons define the scenes, which are further delineated by choral odes between scenes.

At last, we might ask of any play, how can the environment raise the stakes of the action? In *Oedipus*, the domineering pillars upstage might increase our awareness of how much power is at stake, and reveal, through scale and possibly symmetry, how small Oedipus becomes in light of powers higher than his – Creon and the gods. In *Streetcar*, the flimsiness of the curtain that separates Blanche from the Kowalskis might be further expanded to include the thin walls between the Kowalskis and their neighbours (whom Williams suggests we hear bickering) and from the neighbourhood (whose sounds and lights Williams implies invade the space).

The blueprint for the environment for *Oedipus the King* might look something like this:

Whose space is it?	A palace belonging to the king (Oedipus), but only for as long as he rules. It is a sign of his strength at the start of the play in contrast to his weakness and fall at the end. The action takes place outside the palace, in front of many witnesses of all classes – royal (Creon and Jocasta), priests and seers (Tiresias), shepherds and citizens (chorus).
How does the environment affect relationships?	Set in front of the Theban palace, with large stone doors and pillars (likely symmetrical). The space lends power to the Theban ruler – Oedipus at the start of the play, Creon at the end – and looms large over whomever the king summons. By the end of the play, Oedipus is blind and miserable; he depends upon Creon for permission to enter the palace before he is banished from Thebes forever – a crumpled form before the all-too-solid pillars of power.
How does the environment define the pattern created by the structure of scenes?	The entrances and exits of the characters Oedipus summons define the scenes, which are further delineated by choral odes between scenes.
How does the environment raise the stakes of the action?	The domineering pillars upstage increase the awareness of how much power is a stake. Over the course of the play, the pillars reveal, through their scale and possibly through symmetry, how small Oedipus becomes in light of powers higher than his – Creon and the gods.

CHAPTER TWO

Structure and Action

In Chapter One, we worked on acquiring the tools to establish the larger context for the action of a play: the big picture. Now we will begin to learn how to break down a script into playable units of action by first examining the text for the most obvious indications of structure, to which a playwright draws attention through dialogue, stage directions, and formatting – the division of the play into acts and scenes; characters' entrances and exits; changes in location from scene to scene; and changes in subject matter in each scene. These signs provide a readily accessible starting point for breaking down the play into a series of units, each one with a clear sense of purpose and a common thread of action.

For a full-length play running 80–120 pages, I usually expect to find twenty-five to thirty-five units. You should aim for the shortest unit to be at least one page and the longest up to five pages (There will be some obvious exceptions to this recommendation: brief scenes in Shakespearean or other Elizabethan plays, for example; monologues that stand on their own; and short, stand-alone scenes.). In reading a play, the rule of thumb is that one page will take one minute to perform on stage; by this measure, a ten-minute play would usually be about ten pages. In practice, most plays take a bit longer than this to perform. Most of my units are one to four pages – about two to six minutes of stage time, depending on the tempo of the scene and the time required for physical action.

Before we look at our case study plays for signs of structure, we should discuss the most basic types: climactic and episodic dramatic structure. Keep in mind that most plays do not clearly meet all the criteria for either type of dramatic structure; it is best to think of dramatic structure on a continuum from climactic to episodic, with most plays somewhere along that continuum. Rather than categorize a play as episodic or climactic, describe a play as 'predominantly climactic or episodic', or consider its 'climactic or episodic features'.

Most theatre scholars delineate seven elements that help us place a play on the continuum from climactic to episodic:

1. **Point of Attack.** Where does the plot start in relation to the overall story?

2. **Number of Scenes.** Into how many scenes is the play divided?

3. **Number of Locations.** In how many locations does the play take place?

4. **Number of Characters.** How many characters are in the play?

5. **Number of Plots.** Is there one dominant plot or more than one?

6. **Type of Causality.** Does one event lead to the next or do events accrue?

7. **Duration of Action.** Does the action of the play take a long period of time to unfold, or is it compressed?

As I define each of these elements of dramatic structure, I focus on how that element helps us understand the relationship of each unit to the others.

POINT OF ATTACK

Let us start by looking at **point of attack,** which depends upon an understanding of the difference between plot and story. The distinction between plot and story is significant, yet these two words are so common in our daily speech that we might find the definitions elusive. For our purposes, assume that the plays we are analysing all have a plot and a story.[1] The story of a play is a chronological account of everything we learn about the characters. This includes everything that occurs on stage, as well as any and all events that the characters tell us about that occur offstage – before the action of the play, between scenes or acts, or offstage during a scene.

For example, the story of *Oedipus the King*, most of which was well known to its audiences even before they came to see the premiere of Sophocles's version, includes a lot of action that takes place offstage, before the play, and some significant offstage action during the play. Before the play, much has happened

---

[1]Some experimental and avant-garde plays have little or no plot or story, such as Peter Handke's *Offending the Audience*, Mac Wellman's *Terminal Hip*, or Robert Whitman's *The Night Time Sky*, but these are rare. In fact, our desire for a story and plot to help us make sense of what we see on stage is so strong that even the most experienced spectators tend to find them even in their absence. Our method of analysing scripts will work even with plays that lack a plot, but it will require some modification.

that is integral to the events that will transpire. An oracle has told Oedipus's father, Laius, that his son will murder him; to avoid this fate, Laius ordered a shepherd to kill Oedipus, but another shepherd rescued the child; while being raised by Polybus and Merope, king and queen of Corinth, Oedipus heard a rumour that he is not their biological son, then saw an oracle who told him that he is destined to murder his father and sleep with his mother; attempting to avoid this fate, Oedipus fled Corinth, only to chance upon his biological father on the road and murder him, and so on. There is no time 'between scenes' in the plot of *Oedipus* because the action takes place in real time (that is, the time covered by the play's action is the same as the time it takes to tell the story in the theatre). But some of the most violent and atrocious action takes place offstage, at the climax of the play. When Jocasta, Oedipus's mother, realizes that he is her son, she goes into the palace, offstage, to kill herself; upon discovering her body, Oedipus blinds himself with the pin of her brooch, again offstage. Sophocles decided to place these actions offstage – a choice that de-emphasizes the violent spectacle of suicide and blinding, instead focusing the audience's attention on the characters' emotional reactions to these violent actions.

Most plays reveal a number of events that have taken place before the action of the play. Likewise, many playwrights construct their plots so that some time passes between acts and scenes, and fill that time with offstage events that fuel the action. Between Acts 2 and 3 of *Hedda Gabler*, Løvborg gets drunk at Judge Brack's party and loses the only copy of the manuscript of his new book. These offstage events lead him to break up with Thea towards the end of Act 3 and accept Hedda's offer of one of her pistols, all of which leads to Løvborg's deadly offstage confrontation with Mademoiselle Diana between Acts 3 and 4.

For either *Oedipus* or *Hedda*, if we relate all the events in chronological order – starting with the earliest parts of the story, which take place before the play, then proceeding to recount the events of the play, adding in the offstage events – we will have recounted the entire **story**. The plot, however, is more selective; it reveals one of the playwright's most significant artistic contributions. The **plot** is the playwright's patterned arrangement of events: his or her selection of certain events to dramatize on stage, set in a certain order for dramatic effect. Based on the story of *Oedipus*, a different playwright might create a different plot, and indeed several playwrights (including Seneca, Voltaire, and Frank McGuinness) have done so. The plot could dramatize all the major events of the story, starting with the original prophecy for Laius, or earlier, with the crime or sin that lead to his fate: the rape of the son of King Pelops of Elis, whom Laius had been teaching to race chariots.

If a playwright starts the plot near the beginning of the story, we call this an early **point of attack**. Sophocles's plot begins just before Oedipus discovers that by attempting to avoid his fate, he has stepped right into it. This is a late point of attack, because in a story that spans from before Oedipus's birth up to his self-blinding, the plot begins in the hours just before that major event. To visualize this, we can create a timeline of the story and mark the point at which the plot begins: the point of attack or, more literally, the point at which the playwright 'attacks' the story and initiates the plot:

1. Oedipus is born. Oracle tells Laius the prophecy. Laius orders shepherd to kill Oedipus. Another shepherd saves Oedipus, who is raised by King Polybus and Queen Merope.

2. Oracle tells Oedipus the same prophecy. He flees to avoid his fate.

3. On his way to Thebes, Oedipus fights with an older man (his biological father, Laius) and murders him.

4. Oedipus solves the Riddle of the Sphinx, saving Thebes from her, and is rewarded with the throne of Thebes and the hand of the widowed Queen Jocasta in marriage. This fulfils the prophecy.

5. The plot starts here: Oedipus uncovers the truth about his birth, the murder of Laius, and his marriage. Jocasta kills herself; Oedipus discovers her body and blinds himself. Creon banishes Oedipus, according to Oedipus's own decree for the murderer of Laius.

The late attack of the plot of Sophocles's *Oedipus the King* (point 5 above) is one indication of its predominantly climactic dramatic structure. It reveals that the playwright has chosen to use a short time to unfold the plot and action of a story that covers a much larger period of time. Thus, the plot compresses the action of the play. Plots with a late point of attack tend to have a stronger relationship between units, scenes, and acts – each one driving to the next, each building momentum from the previous one.

Plots with an earlier point of attack, as in the epic theatre of Bertolt Brecht – think of *Mother Courage and Her Children*, which takes place in twelve scenes over twelve years – tend to have looser relationships between scenes, so point of attack is a strong sign of the types of action we should find or create from scene to scene. Keep in mind that there might well be more than one unit in each scene, and the relationships between units within a scene might be far more causal than the relationships between scenes or acts. What we are looking for, overall, is the flow or pulse of the play. For a play with a late point of attack, the pulse is likely to be very driven, with a marked acceleration over the course of the play. With an early attack, the pulse might be more start and stop, as the action moves forward within one scene, only to restart during the next one.

NUMBER OF SCENES

The number of scenes in a play can also reveal the tendencies of the dramatic structure. In plays with very few scenes, the action is more likely to be climactic; in plays with a lot of scenes, the action tends to be episodic. The pattern created by a lot of different scenes allows the playwright a certain amount of freedom, whereas in a play with few scenes, or one sustained scene, the absence of a pattern created by scenes leaves a structural gap that many playwrights come to grips with by giving the internal actions of the play a stronger sense of driving, linear action. It might be most useful to think of each of the seven elements of dramatic structure as interrelated, as one element of climactic structure, for example, tends to be associated with the others. For a theatre artist analysing a play for production, the ways in which a particular play diverges from its dominant structural tendencies might be the most significant information. An avant-garde play such as Mac Wellman's *Terminal Hip*, for example, meets four of the seven criteria for climactic action: one scene, one location, one character, in real time. Yet arguably the play still has an early point of attack because the character has no past; there is no real plot; and the causality of the action lacks any easily discernible logic other than that created by Wellman's linguistic gymnastics. This strange concoction of climactic and episodic dramatic structure tendencies is a valuable first glimpse into the qualities that make this play unique.

The number of scenes in a play, however, does not always line up with the other six elements of a particular dramatic structure. A play with a few scenes – each act a single uninterrupted stretch of time, divided only by entrances, exits, and changes in subject matter – might have any number of characters. A play with many scenes might have many characters, as in *Twelfth Night*, or relatively few significant ones, as in *How I Learned to Drive*. The important thing to note about a play with few scenes is that it is an element of climactic structure, but it is the combination of all seven elements that creates the qualities of dramatic structure for any particular play.

NUMBER OF LOCATIONS

A play that sets its scenes in a large number of locations almost always, by definition, also involves a large number of scenes, but not all plays with a large number of scenes use a large number of locations. Ultimately, the presence of a large number of scenes is the stronger indication of episodic structure, but the addition of many locations makes it more likely that the connections among scenes will be more associative than directly causal. A play such as *Woyzeck* has both a large number of scenes and locations, both indicative of episodic structure. *Hedda Gabler* and *The Importance of Being Earnest*, conversely, have limited locations and scenes. *Hedda* has four acts in one location, each act made up of continuous, uninterrupted action in a single location, whereas *Earnest* has three acts in three locations. Both indicate a tendency towards climactic structure.

A *Streetcar Named Desire*, however, reveals a combination of climactic and episodic tendencies through these measures. *Streetcar* has a large number of scenes, but it calls for only one location. Although the play unfolds through eleven scenes stretching from early May to mid-October of the same year, Williams contains the action in Stanley's and Stella's apartment – a hothouse for the battle between Stanley and Blanche, surrounded by the carnival-esque sounds of New Orleans's French Quarter, epitomized by Williams's opening stage directions evoking the sounds of the 'blue piano':

> In this part of New Orleans you are practically always at a barroom just around the corner, or a few doors down the street, from a tinny piano being played with the infatuated fluency of brown fingers. This 'Blue Piano' expresses the spirit of the life which goes on here.

From this we should recognize that *Streetcar* is a bit less definitively climactic than *Earnest* or *Hedda*, given the larger number of scenes and earlier point of attack.

NUMBER OF CHARACTERS

The number of characters is another clue to the structural tendencies of a play: A large number of characters tends to indicate a more sprawling, episodic structure, whereas a small number suggests a more climactic structure, because smaller casts tend to encourage a more compressed story, focused on a limited circle of acquaintances. But again, these tendencies might blend with the other elements to create a hybrid structure, as in *How I Learned to Drive*, which has an early point of attack, with many scenes and locations (episodic), but a limited number of characters. Among our case study plays, the ones that thus far exhibit the most elements of climactic structure, *Hedda* and *Earnest*, also have relatively few characters, whereas *Streetcar*, already a blend of elements, has a few more characters, though they serve primarily to build up the atmosphere of the French Quarter: the upstairs neighbours, Steve and Eunice, whose abusive relationship echoes Stanley's and traumatizes Blanche; the men in Stanley's poker game; the boy collecting for the newspaper; the Mexican woman selling 'flowers for the dead'; and the doctor and nurse whom Stanley summons to take Blanche away to an asylum several weeks after he rapes her.

Many scholars consider *Oedipus the King* a strongly climactic dramatic structure, and certainly the limited number of characters and single location indicate that tendency. The point of attack is very late, as noted: the story goes back to before Oedipus was born, but the plot begins just an hour or so before he learns what he has done, discovers that his mother/wife, Jocasta, has hanged herself, and blinds himself. Despite these strong indications of climactic dramatic structure, *Oedipus* exhibits some episodic attributes. Although all the action takes place in real time, in a single location (in front of the Theban palace), the play's structure drives forward with dramatic scenes for two or three characters alternating with choral passages sung and danced by the chorus members. There are five scenes and six choral odes in *Oedipus*, for a total of eleven scenes. Taken by themselves, the five dramatic scenes exhibit a single line of action (see 'Causality' below), but the odes, though they capture the chorus's reactions to the events that occur in the dramatic scenes and offstage, tend to break up the line of action somewhat, if only because of the introduction of music and spectacle.[2]

NUMBER OF PLOTS

Despite the texture added to the play through the use of the chorus, *Oedipus the King* focuses on a single plot: Oedipus must discover who killed Laius, the king of Thebes, to rid the land of the plague. His investigation of the murder leads him to ask further questions about his own identity, in the end discovering that he is the murderer he seeks. Yet *Oedipus* remains a clear-cut example of a single-plot play, which is one of the hallmarks of climactic dramatic structure. *Hedda Gabler* has two or three subplots that converge: Hedda's desire to see Løvborg kill himself 'beautifully' converges with Brack's behind-the-scene manipulations of the Tesmans's financial affairs, which lead him to have substantial control over Hedda's life. We might add Thea's plot line, which involves her attempts to maintain her relationship with Løvborg, and then, after his death, pursue a relationship with her old flame, George Tesman. Similarly, *Earnest* has two central plot lines that converge into one – while Jack pursues Gwendolen, Algernon pursues Cecily – as well as the somewhat absurd romantic subplot involving Chasuble and Miss Prism.

For a clearer example of multiple plots that move forward independently of each other, some of the best examples come from the plays of William Shakespeare, one of the great craftsmen and artists of episodic structure. In *Twelfth Night*, for example, there are at least two major plots, each with a related subplot or two:

1. **The Viola-Orsino-Olivia-Sebastian love rectangle.** Viola dresses like her twin brother, Sebastian, becomes 'Cesario', and pursues her love

---

[2]I might also observe that Greek tragedy reveals a shape similar to many modern musical theatre pieces: plot, followed by spectacle, followed by plot again, and so on.

for Orsino, all while mourning the loss of her brother in the storm that starts the action. Orsino pursues his love for Olivia, meanwhile (much to his own bewilderment) falling in love with Cesario, not realizing that 'he' is actually a woman (Viola). Meanwhile, Olivia also falls in love with Cesario, convinced that she is a man. When Sebastian appears, Olivia falls for him, mistaking him for Cesario, and Sebastian in turn falls in love with Olivia.

2. **The Toby-Feste-Malvolio-Olivia prank.** Sir Toby and his gang, looking to have some fun with his nemesis, Olivia's stuck-up servant, Malvolio, trick Malvolio into thinking Olivia is in love with him, and set him up to make a fool of himself by courting her in cross-gartered yellow stockings while smiling incessantly. Thinking Malvolio has lost his mind, Olivia asks Toby to look after him, and Toby blindfolds and imprisons him and sends Feste to mock him. Meanwhile, Sir Toby encourages his foolish friend, Sir Andrew, to continue to pursue his crush on Olivia, setting up Sir Andrew to challenge Cesario to a duel.

Clearly, there is a different feeling or shape to the multiple plots of *Twelfth Night*, as compared with the more linear plots of *Hedda* and *Earnest*. Reading the latter two plays, one senses that the plot lines are so closely related that they appear to move forward in lockstep. In *Twelfth Night*, however, the plot lines diverge for much of the play, interweaving at times, then separating again. When Malvolio storms on to the stage at the very end of Act 5, his plot line requires a separate resolution, as compared with the plot lines of *Earnest*, which are resolved at the same time. Of course, *Oedipus*, with its singular plotline, is even more narrowly focused, with a clear resolution of a single plot.

TYPE OF CAUSALITY

Of the seven elements that help determine where a play stands on the continuum from climactic to episodic dramatic structure, the sixth, the type of causality, is arguably the most significant one to examine before we break down a play into units of action. When we look at causality, we scrutinize the relationship between units of action: how one unit builds upon the previous one, contrasts with it, or simply layers on top of it. In plays with more climactic tendencies, the causality is usually very direct and linear, with each unit flowing from the action of the previous one. In plays with more episodic tendencies, particularly in ones that have multiple plot lines, the transitions from unit to unit, particularly between scenes and acts, may appear more abrupt, contrasting with each other or accruing. It might help to think of plays with linear causality as building horizontally, with one scene following logically from the next, and plays with episodic structure as building vertically, with one scene stacking on top of the other, or with two or more plots building horizontally, but alternating, as in *Twelfth Night*. These types of dramatic structure exhibit a very different shape; they require us to analyse the movement from unit to unit, particularly from scene to scene, quite differently.

To best understand the feel of a play with linear causality, I usually refer to the long-running television series *Law & Order* (For this example, any of the three *Law & Order* franchises will do, although the original tends to be the most linear.). There is a sound effect that the directors use repeatedly, a sort of deep 'bah-bump' that we hear between many of the scenes. That sound almost always telegraphs the progression of linear causality in the show. For example, during the first half of an episode – the part that is focused on the police investigation of a crime – the detectives will go to the scene and find a clue, for example, a fingerprint on a murder weapon. The investigator will show the detectives the print; we will hear the 'bah-bump', and the screen will go black; then there will be a black screen with a few printed words (an 'intertitle' stating 'Crime Lab', along with the date and time); and then, lo and behold, the detectives will be at the lab, talking to an expert about the print – a clear, linear progression from crime scene discovery to crime lab analysis.

Oedipus the King moves from unit to unit in much the same way. In fact, one of the things that makes *Law & Order* such an excellent example of linear causality when studying *Oedipus* is that *Oedipus* is also a murder investigation: Oedipus is trying to figure out who killed King Laius. We can even imagine adding the *Law & Order* sound effect between scenes. When, in the first dramatic scene, Oedipus discovers that his brother-in-law, Creon, gave up on his search for the murderer when the screams of the Sphinx became overwhelming for the citizens of Thebes, he calls for Creon to question him – 'bah-bump' – and in the next dramatic scene, Creon appears at precisely the right moment for the meeting. The only significant difference between the structure of scenes in *Law & Order* and *Oedipus* is that in the latter, instead of the 'bah-bump', there is a choral scene, in which the chorus reacts to the latest revelation. When we examine the progression of scenes more closely, I would also point out that the choral scenes in *Oedipus* allow the play to continue in uninterrupted real time by allowing for enough time for a servant to get Creon and bring him to Oedipus. In a way, the intertitle that states the time and location of the next scene in *Law & Order* fulfils the same purpose: it helps shape the transition from one time to another by focusing our attention on the linear causality, using the tight progression of events to move forward in time without losing the logical thread of the action. And the 'bah-bump' of the chorus – the spectacle of seeing a dozen chorus members chant and dance the choral interlude – functions in a similar way, standing in contrast to the rhythm, pitch, and sight of a dramatic scene and moving the action forward in a linear way to the next piece in the puzzle.

Duration of action

Finally, the duration of the action – how much time is covered by the events of the play, the distribution and concentration of the action across that time – reveals how compressed or sprawling the action will appear. The more compressed the action, the more climactic the structure is likely to be. In *Oedipus*, for example, the action appears to unfold in real time: The duration of the action on stage is the same as that action would take in reality, with no time cut out or skipped over. If it were not for the choral interludes that interrupt and comment on the action, the line of action would be as tightly compressed as possible. In contrast to this, *How I Learned to Drive* is told in flashback from L'il Bit's point of view years after the central events in the story; the plot covers events that span from when she was 12 (1962) to her present day, giving the action a more episodic feeling.

If we take several of our case study plays and evaluate them according to each of these criteria, we could create a chart for these qualities that would look something like this:

Climactic	Play	Episodic
Late point of attack, one location, 1 plot, linear, compressed time (real time)	*Oedipus the King*	5 scenes + 6 choral interludes, 8 characters + chorus
Late point of attack, 4 scenes, 1 location, 7 characters, one dominant plot, linear, compressed (24–48 hours)	*Hedda Gabler*	
Relatively late point of attack, 1 location, 1 dominant plot, linear	*A Streetcar Named Desire*	11 scenes, many characters, less compressed (4–5 months)
Few characters, 1 dominant plot	*How I Learned to Drive*	Early point of attack, many scenes, many locations, non-linear/non-chronological, sprawling (many years)
	Twelfth Night	Early point of attack, many scenes, several locations, many characters, more than one plot, non-linear, action takes months
Late point of attack, compressed time/action (real time)	*Information for Foreigners*	20 scenes, many rooms in one house, many characters, many plots, non-linear

The point of such a chart is not to simply count the number of episodic and climactic elements present in each play but to look at the pattern of elements. The outliers – the elements that prevent a play from being purely episodic or climactic, as well as those that fall into the grey area for any particular element – tell us as much about a play's structure as the elements that are easily categorized. For example, *Hedda Gabler* meets all seven criteria for climactic dramatic structure, but the action of the play covers roughly 24 hours, a bit less compressed than the real-time action in *Oedipus*. By observing that, we can see that more happens in the gaps between the four acts in *Hedda* than in between the five scenes and six choral odes in *Oedipus*. Yet despite the more compressed action in *Oedipus*, Sophocles used the convention of choral interludes to disrupt the otherwise-uninterrupted action and create room for some off-stage action between the play's dramatic scenes.

In *Information for Foreigners*, we can observe extremely loose associations between scenes. All the scenes involve torture, but they do not revolve around the same characters or a single plot: each is a separate event, brought together thematically to create an atmosphere of terrorism, which each group of audience members views in a different order. Notwithstanding this experimental technique, part of a style of theatre that we would now call 'immersive', the play exhibits some significant elements of climactic dramatic structure: a late point of attack and compressed time. To effectively break down a play like this into units of action, we need to begin by observing that the scenes, though non-linear, still take place in real time with a late point of attack. This lends the action a sense of urgency and leads me to believe that though the scenes are non-linear, the effect of each scene will be strongly climactic.

Units

Having analysed a play's overall dramatic structure and noted its distinguishing characteristics, we next need to break down the action into a series of units that we can analyse in more detail. The first step in breaking down any play into units of action is to look for the most obvious divisions of action provided by the playwright: acts, scenes, and 'French scenes'. Not all plays are divided into acts, but of the three types of divisions, acts are the largest major units of a play. Most plays have one to five acts. Although Shakespeare's plays are among the most famous examples of the five-act play structure, the first quarto editions of his plays were not divided into acts and scenes; there is no evidence that he wrote the plays with this structure in mind. In subsequent Folio editions, editors imposed on his plays a five-act structure, one that we readily accept to this day.

For the purposes of analysing structure in terms of units of action, I am going to use Wilde's *The Importance of Being Earnest* and Shakespeare's *Twelfth Night* as the primary case study plays – one with a primarily climactic dramatic structure, one with a predominantly episodic structure. *Earnest* has three acts, whereas *Twelfth Night* has five, so we immediately can divide the action into some big chunks. We can also see that the act structure of a play is not always associated with a particular type of dramatic structure. Within each act of *Twelfth Night*, we see different quantities of scenes and progressions of locations:

> Act 1, Scene 1: Duke Orsino's palace.
>   Scene 2: The sea coast.
>   Scene 3: Olivia's house.
>   Scene 4: Duke Orsino's palace.
>   Scene 5: Olivia's house.
> Act 2, Scene 1: The sea coast.
>   Scene 2: A street.
>   Scene 3: Olivia's house.
>   Scene 4: Duke Orsino's palace.
>   Scene 5: Olivia's garden.
> Act 3, Scene 1: Olivia's garden.
>   Scene 2: Olivia's house.
>   Scene 3: A street.
>   Scene 4: Olivia's garden.
> Act 4, Scene 1: Before Olivia's house.
>   Scene 2: Olivia's house.
>   Scene 3: Olivia's garden.
> Act 5, Scene 1: Before Olivia's house.

The first thing to note is that Shakespeare has already given us eighteen units of action, a very good start towards breaking down the action for analysis. Many scholars have noted that Shakespeare, through his use of verse, prose, and iambic pentameter, directs his own plays. Yet the structure of scenes in his plays is equally significant for the purposes of script analysis.

We might also note a significant pattern of locations. Though Acts 1 and 2 alternate fairly regularly between Duke Orsino's palace and Olivia's house and garden, Act 3 takes place almost entirely in Olivia's house and garden, and Acts 4 and 5 do so solely. We can also see a second pattern of decreasing numbers of scenes as the acts progress: 5 in Acts 1 and 2; 4 in Act 3; 3 in Act 4; and 1 in Act 5. All these structural clues would lead me to see whether each act, as a self-contained chunk or larger unit of action, is progressively more climactic, eventually bringing together the various strands of the plot in the single, extended scene that takes up the entirety of Act 5. And I can already see that we are going to want to break up Act 5 into a few units to provide us with a structure from which we can find a progression to the actions in this longer, single-scene act.

To further break down the units of action of a play, we next look for entrances and exits of characters. So called because the French neoclassical plays depended upon entrances and exits for structure, a 'French scene' often works as a unit of action because the entrance or exit of a character frequently causes a change in the subject matter of the dialogue, along with a change in what the characters want and what they do to get it. Not all French scenes in all plays will be useful units of action. If a play has a lot of entrances and exits, as in a bedroom farce, for example, there might be too many to be useful (Remember, we are aiming for twenty to forty units in a full-length play, with most units two to five pages. So if a character comes in and out of the room several times in a few pages, it will not be useful for us to create a new unit for every entrance and exit.).

Finally, moving beyond the playwright's given indications of structure, we would then look for changes in the subject matter of the dialogue for further unit divisions. Of course, if a play is a single act, with no acts, scenes, or French scenes, we will have to depend more upon subject matter to determine our breakdown. I would also point out that although there are unit breakdowns for any play that can be more useful than others, there is no single 'right' way to break down a play. Breaking down a play into units is part craft, part art, and, ultimately, an act of interpretation by each theatre artist. In most rehearsal and production processes, the director's breakdown will be the decisive one and will determine the rehearsal units for the production. But all theatre artists benefit from doing this for themselves and understanding the logic behind whatever unit breakdown the creative team agrees upon.

Let us begin by examining *Twelfth Night* in a bit more detail. Just from examining the act and scene structure, we have found eighteen units. Because this is an almost pure example of episodic structure, the playwright has given us almost enough units to work with. By writing his plays in this way, Shakespeare had already given his company units of action that could be rehearsed as such – an efficient and effective way of writing plays in a time when there was no 'director', in a contemporary sense, to divide the play into units for the cast. We can see the same quality in the alternation of dramatic scenes and choral interludes in Greek tragedy. Both the Elizabethans and the ancient Greeks preferred dramatic structures that encouraged their ensembles to discover the texture in the shape of the action, whether through the alternation of dramatic scenes among two or three characters and choral sections, filled with music and spectacle (in the case of Greek tragedy), or through a continual variety of locations, character combinations, and even style in Elizabethan plays (for example, Shakespeare's use of fool in a tragedy such as *King Lear* adds comic texture to the shape of the action).

Within the eighteen scenes in *Twelfth Night*, we now would look for longer scenes that need further division to be manageable in rehearsal. I would start by observing the length of each of the eighteen scenes. In most plays, I would look at the number of pages for each scene, but that approach can be misleading, as different editors and publishers will lay out the text in different ways (In most of the major anthologies of drama, for example, a play takes up fewer pages than in its acting edition.). Whatever text you are analysing, you need to take into account the layout and size of the typeface. For Shakespeare, though, there is another, more readily accessible measure of the length of a scene: the number of lines of text. The rule of thumb when working on Shakespeare's plays in production is that sixteen to eighteen lines of text will equal about one minute of stage time, so if we count the lines in each scene, we should get a pretty good idea of which scenes would be most easily divided into more than one unit. Uncut – keep in mind that most directors make cuts to Shakespeare's plays, for clarity or to simply reduce the running time for contemporary audiences – *Twelfth Night* has 2,711 lines. Here is a breakdown by act, with the scenes with running times over eight minutes long in bold:

Total lines in Act 1: 629
    Act 1, Scene 1: 41
    Act 1, Scene 2: 62
    Act 1, Scene 3: 152
    Act 1, Scene 4: 42
    Act 1, Scene 5: 332
Total lines in Act 2: 658
    Act 2, Scene 1: 51
    Act 2, Scene 2: 42
    Act 2, Scene 3: 210
    Act 2, Scene 4: 126
    Act 2, Scene 5: 229
Total lines in Act 3: 755
    Act 3 Scene 1–178
    Act 3 Scene 2–93
    Act 3 Scene 3–50
    Act 3 Scene 4–434
Total lines in Act 4: 249
    Act 4 Scene 1–69
    Act 4 Scene 2–144
    Act 4 Scene 3–36
Total lines in Act 5–420
    Act 5 Scene 1: 420

If we break down those scenes with more than 128 lines (16 lines/minute ×
8 minutes of running time = 128 lines) into two or more units, then we would
end up with a minimum of twenty-nine scenes. If we then look for French
scenes to further divide some of these units, we will end up with thirty to thirty-
five units, a workable number for rehearsal and production. We would then put
these units into a chart that also captures the characters who appear in each
scene, as well as the locations and a summary title for each unit (I mark each
character's appearance in a unit with a 'X', noting brief appearances in a unit
with a lower-case 'x' or one in parentheses, '(X)'):

Twelfth Night unit breakdown, Act 1

| Unit number | 1 | 2 | 3 | 4 | 5 | 6 | 7 | 8 | 9 |
Act-scene	1.1		1.2	1.3		1.4[a]	1.5		
Duke Orsino	X	X				X			
Curio	X	X				X			
Valentine	X	X				X			
Duke's attendants	X	X				X			
Viola/Cesario			X			X			
Captain			X						
Sir Toby Belch				X	X				x
Maria				X	X		X		x
Sir Andrew					X				
Feste							X	X	x
Olivia								X	X
Olivia's attendants								X	X
Malvolio								X	x

[a] Act 1, scene 4 is a bit more complicated structurally than this breakdown reveals, as Valentine
and Viola/ Cesario enter for six lines of dialogue before being joined by Duke Orsino, Curio,
and other attendants.

I have started by examining a Shakespeare play because the episodic structure
and quantity of scenes provides us with so many obvious breakpoints between
units. As a rule, most plays with episodic dramatic structures will be easier for
us to break down into units. When looking at a play with a predominantly
climactic dramatic structure, such as *The Importance of Being Earnest*, we will
need to depend more on French scenes and changes in subject matter to find the
break points between units. I am going to focus on the first act of *Earnest*, so
that we can get a closer look at each breakpoint. I will give each unit a title – a
quote from the unit, seven words or fewer, selected to capture the essence of
the action. The chart for Act 1 might look something like this:

Unit	Title	Algernon	Lane	Jack	Lady B	Gwen
I, 1	The Science of Life	X	X			
I, 2	The Truth is Rarely Pure & Never Simple	X	x	X		
I, 3	Poor Bunbury	X	x	X	X	X
I, 4	I Must Get Christened at Once			X		X
I, 5	To Lose Two Parents Seems Like Carelessness			X	X	X
I, 6	All Women Become Like Their Mothers …	X		X		
I, 7	It May Be Necessary To Do Something Desperate	X	X	X		X

Each unit title should capture its essential action, so that seeing or speaking the title is sufficient to conjure up the action of the scene or, at the very least, its subject matter or conflict. If we do this well, the chart can reveal the structure of the scene and progression of the action, which will allow us to visualize its shape. In the chart above, I would observe that the action of the act intensifies as characters invade Algernon's space. Unit I, 1 establishes Algernon's apartment in its normal state, with just he and his servant, Lane, talking about the norms of Algernon's society: how servants drink the champagne, how dreary the life of a married man can be ('The Science of Life'). The status quo is interrupted, first by the entrance of John ('Jack') Worthing, who interrogates Algernon about his cigarette case and the lies it betrays ('The Truth is Rarely Pure and Never Simple') before confessing his intention to ask Algernon's cousin, Gwendolen, to marry him, and then by the arrival of Gwendolen and her mother, Lady Bracknell, the latter of whom forces Algernon to again lie about his poor friend, the profligate Bunbury ('Poor Bunbury'). Upon realizing that Gwendolen will marry him only if his name is Earnest (Jack uses the name 'Earnest' in the city), Jack realizes that he must change his name through christening ('I Must Get Christened at Once').

Once we have perceived the basic structure of Act 1 of *Earnest*, we must then look at the precise placement of each unit break. Breaking down a play into units is an art, not a science; otherwise like-minded artists can disagree on the placement of unit breaks, as well as the number of units in any act or play. These are true artistic differences, in the best sense of that phrase, ones that reveal each artist's unique view of a play's action. It is fair to say that there is no single right way to break down any particular script into units, but there are certainly wrong ways. As our working definition of a unit is for it to have a consistent action or subject matter, unit breaks that interrupt a single action or disrupt the flow of the action are counterproductive.

When we look at the unit breakdown chart for *Earnest* (above), we can see that the units are French scenes: for each new unit, there is an entrance or exit by one of the characters. Thus, the subject matter and action of each unit change in large part because the combination of characters has changed. Yet we still need to find the best placement for the break points between units. In searching for the idea break point, I follow three criteria: subject matter, action, and rehearsal pragmatics.

Let us look at the transition from the first French scene to the second in Act 1 of *Earnest*:

ALGERNON [Languidly]   I don't know that I am much interested in your family life, Lane.

LANE   No, sir; it is not a very interesting subject. I never think of it myself.

ALGERNON   Very natural, I am sure. That will do, Lane, thank you.

LANE   Thank you, sir [LANE goes out].

ALGERNON   Lane's views on marriage seem somewhat lax. Really, if the lower orders don't set us a good example, what on earth is the use of them? They seem, as a class, to have absolutely no sense of moral responsibility.

Enter LANE

LANE   Mr. Ernest Worthing.

Enter JACK

LANE goes out

ALGERNON   How are you, my dear Ernest? What brings you up to town?

In just a few lines, we see Lane exit and re-enter, followed quickly by Jack's entrance and a final exit by Lane. For this reason, there are several points at which we might observe a French scene and mark a new unit. Looking first at subject matter, we note that after Lane's first exit, Algernon continues to talk about the same subject matter (seemingly as direct address to the audience), family life/marriage. For this reason, I would not mark a new unit after Lane's first exit, as it would interrupt the flow of the scene. Moreover, starting a new unit by having Algernon address the audience and talk about the same subject matter as the previous unit will be more difficult for the actors in rehearsal, as it disconnects the discussion about family life between Algernon and Lane from Algernon's comments to the audience about that very discussion.

When Lane re-enters to announce Jack Worthing's arrival, there is a clear change of subject matter, so there is a reasonable case to be made that this is the start of a new unit. And the action has changed as well: by announcing Jack's entrance, Lane has changed the dynamics of the scene. It is no longer a master-servant scene between Lane and Algernon; the actions will now be predominantly between Algernon and Jack. Yet we might consider a later start to unit 1, 2, from the perspective of pragmatism. Aside from one brief moment later in the unit, when Lane brings in Jack's silver cigarette case at Algernon's request, Lane is not present in unit 1, 2; in fact, despite that brief appearance, Lane does not have any lines until he announces the arrival of Lady Bracknell and Gwendolen around the break point between units 1, 2 and 1, 3. So if we mark the break point between units 1, 1 and 1, 2 after Lane exits, we might be able to excuse the actor playing Lane from the rehearsal of unit 1, 2 and add him later, when we start to put the units together into a more sweeping arc. I would also note that the subject matter does not change clearly until Algernon addresses Jack directly, asking him why he has come to town.

But I am also always on the lookout for patterns in the entrances and exits of any play. In Act 1 of *Earnest*, Lane (and, in subsequent acts, his servant-doppelganger, Merriman) enters several times to announce the arrival of Algernon's guests. In a play with such a clear, at times formal structure, I would look to reinforce that by trying, as much as is practical, to have Lane's entrances support the structure of the act by having them follow a consistent pattern. It is ultimately an artistic choice on my part, but I would put each of Lane's announcements in the subsequent unit, so that the announcement of guests serves as a reminder of the subject matter, or at least the players, in that unit. In this way, Lane's announcement of 'Mr. Ernest Worthing' proclaims the start of the Ernest-Algernon unit, whereas Lady Bracknell and Miss Lady Bracknell and Miss Fairfax's heralds the start of their unit with Jack and Algernon. This might seem to result in calling Lane for more unit rehearsals, but this can be managed by having the actor rehearse the announcement at the start of the unit rehearsal, then releasing him and having an assistant stage manager stand in for Lane. For this reason, I would mark the break point like this:

ALGERNON   Lane's views on marriage seem somewhat lax. Really, if the lower orders don't set us a good example, what on earth is the use of them? They seem, as a class, to have absolutely no sense of moral responsibility.

1, 2. The Science of Life

Enter LANE

LANE   Mr. Ernest Worthing.

Enter JACK

LANE goes out

ALGERNON   How are you, my dear Ernest? What brings you up to town?

The placement of each unit break is essential to our understanding of the structure of a play. Each unit covertly tells everyone working on a production that the actions of the characters within belong together and therefore are part of the rhythm and texture of that unit. In the case of the break point between units 1 and 2 in *Earnest*, the placement of Lane's announcement of a guest sets a pattern. If we placed the unit break later, after Lane's announcement of Ernest's arrival, we would see it as connected to Algernon's direct address speech in unit 1, which might lead the ensemble to see the announcement as an interruption; with the break marked before the announcement, I would be more inclined to see Algernon's direct address as a clean conclusion to unit 1, with Lane's introduction of Ernest as a flourish at the start of unit 2. Each of these possible unit breaks would then have different ramifications for designers as well, affecting the placement and rhythm of the light cues, for example.

Once we divide the entire act into units that both capture unified actions and divide up the action in ways that will facilitate rehearsal calls, the next step is to give each unit a title. I recommend keeping each title relatively short – seven words or fewer – and using a direct quote from the unit. I favour this approach for a number of reasons. Using the dialogue as a title limits the possibilities, which usually makes the task less time-consuming. It forces us to pay attention to the playwright's words, and the title selected is more likely to connect with and echo the action of the unit. We are looking for a title that captures the essence of the action, so that it immediately conjures up the right unit for us when we hear it. If well selected, it will serve as shorthand for the scene, so that the mere mention of the title immediately causes anyone in the ensemble to recall the entire unit. Finally, if all the units meet this standard, then listing all the titles in order should help reveal the overall arc or shape of the play's action. Adding unit titles, dates, and places to a unit breakdown chart will help us trace a virtual map of the action from unit to unit, with the pattern of character appearances and conflicts registering in the far-right columns. Once we have established these units, we can analyse the action in each unit from moment to moment.

ACTIONS AND OBJECTIVES

To define the action of each unit, we need to examine more closely the actions and objectives of each character. An **objective** is what a character wants from another character during a particular unit. It must be something that is achievable during the time the two characters will be together on stage, in that moment. Different acting teachers and directors might use any of the following words to signify the character's objectives: needs, wants, desires, or goals. The most effective objective should be stated as a desired response from the other character – something the other character could do during the unit. By thinking of the objective as a desired response from the other character, we remind the actors to look for their partners' responses. This encourages actors to establish a better connection with each other on stage and often prompts them to make stronger tactical changes to their actions from moment to moment, in reaction to the responses they receive.

The second element is the **action**: what one character does to another character to achieve his or her objective. I have introduced them in this order – objective first, action second – so that you will always think of action in the service of a character's objective, but in practice you can analyse either action or objective first. Sometimes the objective will be obvious but the action will be unclear; sometimes, the action will be evident but the objective will be obscure. Both approaches have their place in your toolbox of script analysis skills.

An action is always a verb; the best actions are 'playable verbs', meaning that they will 'play' or work on stage and in rehearsal. The best playable verbs will be concrete actions – 'down and dirty' verbs that we use in everyday conversation – which one actor or character could do to another for several minutes. In rehearsal, a director might ask any one of the following questions to elicit a playable verb:

What are you doing?
What are you playing?
How are you trying to achieve your objective?

There are several types of verbs to avoid because most actors will find them difficult, if not impossible, to commit to for five or ten minutes. In *A Sense of Direction*, William Ball describes five categories of unplayable verbs: intellectual verbs, behaviour or condition verbs, existential verbs, adjectival verbs, and trigger verbs (85–86). Intellectual verbs are overly complicated verbs that can easily be replaced or upgraded with more everyday forms. For example, *mystify*, *befuddle*, and *confuse* are the more ordinary forms of the intellectual verb *obfuscate*. Behaviour and condition verbs usually describe reflexive activities, such as *fear*, *like*, or *recover*, and are frequently physical actions that do not require commitment, such as *walk*, *laugh*, and *belch*. Although these verbs can describe things that an actor does in a scene, they do not require sufficient conscious commitment by the actor. Existential verbs usually prove to be too vague for actors: *think*, *create*, *intend*, *hope*, and *die*. Of course a character can die in a scene, but an actor playing that role will need to commit to some other action until the moment the character dies.

Adjectival verbs are the most subjective category. The key is to avoid verbs that will cause actors to indicate how they are feeling rather than play an action. Ball asks, 'Does the choice of the verb sound dangerously close to indicating – or playing the adjective?' (86). For example, *aggravate* risks becoming *aggravating*; *forgive* might turn into *forgiving*; and *adore* leads to *adoring*. The final test comes in rehearsal and performance: Can the actor play the verb so that it results in powerful action on stage? But it is best to be wary of adjectival verbs. Trigger verbs include actions that an actor can and usually does complete quite quickly, such as *slice*, *notice*, *kick*, and *snap*.

After years of teaching action-objective to theatre students, I have come to believe that the best way to learn how to select strong playable verbs is to work regularly with a list of them, divided into a few different categories for easy reference. In *An Actor's Craft: The Art and Technique of Acting*, David Krasner discusses the actor's six basic actions, based on his years of study with actress Kim Stanley: to *beg* (or *plead*), *destroy*, *seduce*, *dominate*, *celebrate*, and *accuse*. These are meant to be a distillation of the maximum range that an actor can play or a director can encourage. Krasner's six actions are meant to be the most aggressive or bold forms of action, but they also serve as a starting point for creating categories or types of playable action-verbs. To these six, I have added four action categories – to *defend*, to *soothe*, to *discourage*, and to *provoke* – as these types of action fill in some of the less aggressive actions that fall between the six basic actions. I include an extensive list of playable actions in Appendix A, grouped in these ten broad categories for ease of reference when scoring a script. By using it regularly, you will expand your vocabulary of playable verbs.

In each category, I try to offer a range of actions from the most aggressive to the most deferential – different notes, tones, and tactics. For example, a character can celebrate another in various ways, from the more aggressive (*glorify*) to the less so (*accept*). Many of the actions listed fit in more than one category, depending upon the objective with which they are paired. The purpose of this list is not to consign each action to a single category but to give theatre artists easy access to a large range of actions for script analysis.

The final element in a complete action-objective sentence is the receiver: the one on whom the first character focuses action and hopes will respond as desired, fulfilling his or her objective. If we put all three elements together, we should arrive at a sentence that captures the overall action succinctly:

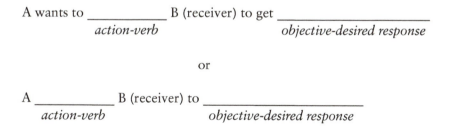

The latter version of this formula is the most succinct, but the former acknowledges that the action and objective is a want or desire. I prefer the shorter version, as I think of script analysis as geared towards creating a visual document, and I am looking for something that will communicate the maximum amount of information in the fewest words and least space. Whether I am in a design meeting, rehearsal, or tech rehearsal, I want to be able to glance down at my script analysis and quickly recall how I see a particular scene or unit. Some of my students have condensed the formula even more, so that it resembles a fraction, with the action above a vertical line and the objective below it:

$$\frac{A \; (action\text{-}verb) \; B}{(objective\text{-}desired \; response)}$$

Here are some examples of effective actions-objectives in proper forms:

> Hedda wants to *persuade* Løvborg to *take the pistol.*
> Cecily wants to *humiliate* Gwendolen so she will *break off her engagement.*
> Blanche wants to *soothe* Mitch so he will *relax and fall for her.*
> Troy wants to *taunt* Cory so he will *back off.*

Each of these has a strong playable action-verb: persuade, humiliate, soothe, taunt. Each has a clear objective, stated as a desired response from the other character; each objective could be achieved during that scene or unit.

As I have mentioned, sometimes it will be easier to start with a character's action, and other times it will be easier to start with the objective. If you encounter trouble selecting a strong action for a character, start by looking for the most literal action you can think of, and then search for an action other than the literal. I say this because the literal, by definition, captures the action in the words, but as an overall rule, the most compelling actions on stage do something different than the literal. When we talk about subtext – what exists beneath the surface of the dialogue – we are really talking about actions and objectives that differ from the literal meaning of the words:

> The difference between the action you choose and the character's literal action creates a dynamic between the lines of the script and what you are doing on stage. This dynamic is part of what creates the illusion of character in the eyes of the audience…what brings the scene to life. (*Practical Handbook* 27)

I would go one step further and assert that the most intriguing and creative formulations of action-objective frequently involve a combination of action and objective that seems contradictory at first blush:

> Hedda wants to *seduce* Løvborg so he will *want to kill himself.*
> Cecily wants to *praise* Gwendolen so she will *break off her engagement.*

Blanche wants to *accuse* Mitch so he will *fall in love with her*.
Troy wants to *dominate* Cory so he will *lose his temper and attack him*.

Please note that these reformulations of our initial sentences are meant to illustrate the technique of choosing actions and objectives in opposition to each other; they are not necessarily the only or optimal choices for these characters and scenes, which would depend upon the script analysis of the rest of the scene and play. Nevertheless, by searching for actions and objectives that expose the needs that lurk beneath the dialogue, or expose the irrational and contradictory ways in which characters pursue their wants and needs, we are developing our eye for what is unique in an ensemble's approach to the production of a play.

It is important to write the action and objective for each character at the top of each unit, right beneath the unit number and title, not in the margins towards the middle of the unit. We call this **scoring** a scene. For your scoring to be most useful, you need to position your analysis visually so it is available and evident where you will need it. The scoring of a scene should be designed to create a compelling visual document. The visual form and format of your notations are as significant as the content. Some students use different colours of ink for different elements, or different fonts or font sizes. I do not advocate one particular way of presenting this information, but I strongly recommend that the finished product places important information where it will do the most good, where you have easy and quick access to it.

Once we have determined the initial action and objective for each character in each unit, there are two questions we can ask to help refine our choices:

1. Can I raise the stakes for the characters?
2. Can the characters pursue their objectives differently: either more aggressively or more indirectly?

When we consider whether it is possible to raise the stakes for a character, we focus on revising the objective. By selecting an objective that is more difficult to achieve or more important to the character, you might be able to create greater conflict or emotional commitment to the action. But higher stakes are not always better. Over the course of an entire play, we are looking to shape the action, and persistently high stakes may become 'top heavy' – even the highest-stakes drama needs some down time. The great benefit of asking whether we can raise the stakes, though, is that it will challenge us to look beyond our initial analysis and consider alternatives.

When we ask whether a character can pursue his or her objective in a different way, we are re-examining the character's action-verb. Perhaps the character can be more aggressive, simply 'upgrading' the action to a more powerful verb. Or perhaps the character can use an indirect or even counterintuitive action towards achieving the objective: one that creates texture and surprise by avoiding the most obvious and direct route or action to the goal. As with raising or lowering the stakes, it is not always the most aggressive action that creates the strongest scene. Remember, in a scene with two characters, the conflict is created by the clash between two sets of actions and objectives.

Many times, the values of the story might be better served by modulating the strength of a character's pursuit of an objective. For example, in *Oedipus the King*, we might decide that Oedipus uses aggressive actions towards Creon and Tiresias, such as bully, dominate, and lambast. But if both Creon and Tiresias answer these attacks with the most aggressive counter-actions, then these two scenes might come off as too similar, sacrificing texture in the pursuit of maximum conflict. Instead, we might consider how the differing class and status of each character (one a co-ruler, brother-in-law, and uncle; the other a blind prophet) and personal qualities might lead them to pursue their objectives in distinctive ways.

Their characters are different, so their actions will differ, too. Creon is a member of the royal family and a co-ruler of the kingdom. Tiresias knows who Oedipus is and what he has done (killed his father, married his mother). All these differences should encourage us to search for different actions for each character, in response to similar attacks by Oedipus. By pushing to consider actions that are less obvious, we might discover intriguing surprises. Perhaps we expect that Creon, as a co-ruler of the kingdom, would be more willing to confront Oedipus aggressively, whereas Tiresias, as a class below the king, would be more respectful. Yet the opposite could be true and might be more captivating on stage. After all, Tiresias is a blind old man who knows the truth. He may be blatantly disrespectful of Oedipus, or he might mock or belittle him. Creon, in contrast, might believe he is the odd man out in the triumvirate of rulers; the other two rulers, Oedipus and Jocasta, are married and can easily outvote him or decide to exclude him on important matters of state. So Creon might choose a more conciliatory action, such as honour or glorify. The contrast and texture created by seeing a co-ruler glorify the king, only to be followed by a blind old man mocking him, could be quite compelling on stage.

To further our understanding, let us analyse sample units from two of our case study plays for possible actions and objectives: *The Importance of Being Earnest*, at the start of Act 1, and *Hedda Gabler*, at the end of Act 3. In the first unit of *Earnest* (lines 1–30), the scene opens on Algernon's flat in the West End of London; Lane sets the table for afternoon tea with Lady Bracknell, as Algernon is heard playing the piano offstage. Algernon questions Lane, his servant, about the number of bottles of champagne written down as consumed on Thursday night and asks him why bachelors' servants always drink the champagne. The two banter about marriage; Lane admits that he has had little experience with marriage, having only been married once, 'in consequence of a misunderstanding between myself and a young person'. Algernon tells Lane he is not interested in his personal life and dismisses him, ending the unit with an aside to the audience, in which he glibly dismisses the lower classes for not setting a good example for the upper class.

At first glance, there is very little at stake in this unit – just some playful banter to establish who and where they are, their basic relationship (master-servant), and Algernon's flippant attitude towards life. But whatever the shape of the action in Act 1, this is its starting point; the characters must need something from each other and pursue these objectives. What does Algernon want from Lane? He asks four questions:

'Did you hear what I was playing, Lane?' (line 1)
'[H]ave you got the cucumber sandwiches cut for Lady Bracknell?' (7–8)
'Why is it that at a bachelor's establishment the servants invariably drink the champagne?' (15–16)
'Is marriage so demoralizing as that?' (19)

Of these four questions, the one with the clearest and most significant objective is the third. Although he asks about servants drinking champagne in what I would suggest is a light comic manner, Algernon seems to want to an answer, and he is clearly implying that Lane has been drinking his champagne. So what does Algernon want from Lane? A confession? An explanation? An excuse? Or simply for Lane to amuse him, so that he will not mind Lane's drinking his expensive champagne?

For his part, Lane repeatedly refers to Algernon as 'sir', which could be seen as a formality but is certainly an indicator of their master-servant relationship (see 'Status' below). His responses to Algernon are brief, until Algernon mentions the consumption of champagne, at which point Lane makes a witty observation about the quality of champagne in married households, followed by a lengthier admission and description of his limited experience with marriage. It seems, therefore, that the unit builds towards the banter about champagne, which takes up about one-third of the unit. Yet because Lane does not ask any questions, and all his lines are in response to Algernon, it is a little more difficult to uncover and interpret Lane's objective.

When I encounter difficulty analysing a character's objective, I turn to the character's action next. Sometimes a character's action is more overt than the objective. If I can figure out Lane's action, it might help me discover his possible objectives. To me, Lane seems self-deprecating, pointing out his lack of experience with marriage and disparaging his personal life: '[I]t is not a very interesting subject. I never think of it myself' (25). In terms of broad action categories, I tend to think he 'celebrates', 'seduces', or 'encourages' Algernon.

When I search these categories for fitting actions, I come up with pampers, coddles, charms, flatters, respects, glorifies, or entertains. At this point, we are looking for an action and objective that encompass the entire unit. Algernon's questioning about the champagne, though central to the minor conflict in this unit, takes Lane by surprise; it is not a part of Lane's goals for the scene, but an obstacle to achieving them, more central to Algernon's agenda than Lane's. So I believe that Lane is pampering or glorifying Algernon, perhaps to gain his trust or approval.

By putting this altogether, we might arrive at the following actions-objectives for this unit:

Lane wants to *glorify* Algernon for *his approval*.
Algernon wants to *tease* Lane so he will *confess to drinking the champagne*.

Once we have found the starting point for the characters' actions and objectives, we need to see whether there is sufficient conflict between the two characters to sustain the tension in the unit. In most cases, this means that the objectives need to be in conflict, though occasionally the objectives might be the same or complimentary, but the actions prevent the two characters from giving each other what they want. In this case, Lane's need for Algernon's approval is in direct conflict with Algernon's goal of getting Lane to confess to drinking his champagne.

For a higher-stakes example, consider the final unit in Act 3 of *Hedda Gabler*, just after Thea has stormed off in the wake of Løvborg's lie to her about destroying the only copy of the manuscript he wrote with her help (lines 415–477). Løvborg confesses the truth to Hedda: he lost the manuscript, an act he believes Thea will see as even worse than destroying it, because of his extreme neglect of their mutual creation. When he tells Hedda that he intends to 'put an end to it all', she offers him one of her pistols, reminding him that she had once pointed it at him, and urges him to use the pistol 'beautifully', a reincorporation of her idealized vision of his suicide: a single shot to the head.

Hedda's objective seems evident: to get Løvborg to accept the pistol and go off to shoot himself in the head. Løvborg, having already decided to commit suicide, has chased off Thea so he can be alone with Hedda before killing himself. Løvborg's objective is more open to interpretation: he might want her approval for having chased away Thea, her encouragement for his plans to kill himself, or for her to stop him from doing so. This unit comes at the end of the third act of a four-act play, and it is the last unit between Hedda and Løvborg, so we should be looking to keep the stakes high, fuelled by aggressive actions.

For the purposes of this example, I want the maximum conflict, by having Løvborg seek to have Hedda stop him from committing suicide. Or, better, as he knows that she is drawn to his destructive side, let us say that he wants her to become excited by his suicide threats in the hopes of finally getting her to respond to him sexually, or that he wants her to divulge her true feelings for him. To complete their actions and objectives for the unit, we would need to fill in their actions:

Hedda _____ Løvborg to accept her pistol and kill himself.
Løvborg _____ Hedda so that she will reveal her love for him.

Løvborg is distraught, at the end of his tether, but still wants one final reaction from Hedda before he leaves. The more interesting actions might be ones that are quite at odds with his objective: an unexpected tactic could do much to conceal his true goal from her and create an element of surprise for the audience. I could imagine Løvborg committing to any of the following action-verbs – threatens, baits, ensnares, tests, bluffs, shocks, unnerves – all coupled, perversely, with his desire to have her reveal she loves him.

In a literal sense, Hedda is offering her pistol to Løvborg, but the most revealing choice of action will veer from this, giving us a window into Hedda's innermost desires. If she wants him to take the pistol and shoot himself in the head, how might she pursue this objective? If she sees Løvborg's feelings for her, Hedda might take advantage at this point, using his own goal against him. For this reason, I might consider actions that appeal to his interest in her, again hoping for an element of surprise: entrance, inflame, seduce, tantalize. So we might score the actions for this unit as follows:

Hedda *inflames* Løvborg to accept her pistol and kill himself.
Løvborg *unnerves* Hedda so that she will reveal her love for him.

Their objectives are in conflict. Their actions stand in stark contrast to the literal action of the scene: inflaming someone into killing himself and unnerving someone to reveal her love are slyly perverse formulations of action and objective, and yet, at times, true to human nature.

Keep in mind that these are only starting points for analysis. To fine-tune these choices, we would next examine how the action in this unit contrasts with the action in other units. Most important, I would examine the contrast between Løvborg's action towards Hedda in this unit and his action towards Thea in the previous unit. Such contrast helps shape the action so there is significant variety from unit to unit. We always need to be alert to these contrasts. In terms of story, I am interested in the differences between how Løvborg lies to a woman who loves him (Thea) so she will leave him, compared with how he tells the truth to a woman who is fascinated by him, in the hopes that she will reveal her deeper feelings. Last, for actors and directors, always remember that these choices will be explored and negotiated in rehearsal. Actors still need to explore and help shape these decisions, and rehearsal might expose more effective choices for the combination of performers in a particular cast. Scoring actions and objectives before rehearsal allows directors and designers to find the overall arc of the action for a production, but these choices should always be tested and further refined in rehearsal with the actors, each of whom should come to know his or her character better than anyone else working on the production.

Shifts

No matter how single minded a character might be in pursuit of an objective, his or her actions change in response to a variety of stimuli. I refer to these tactical changes as 'shifts' because of the term's association with the gears in a car – the sense of shifting from one gear to another, which brings with it a change in speed (tempo) and retains a sense of momentum. Several types of stimuli can bring about a change in a character's action. Shifts are an interpretative tool, not limited to the playwright's intentions. There might be some weak choices for the placement of shifts in a unit, but there is no single correct choice.

By analysing the dialogue for several types of information, we can detect likely points for shifts:

- **Change in subject matter**. When characters start talking about a new subject, they frequently change to a different action.
- **Change in tactic**. Sometimes the dialogue suggests an overt change in tactic.
- **New information**. When one character reveals new information to another, it creates an opportunity for a shift – in the revelation or in the other character's response to it.
- **Realization**. During a unit, a character might realize something new, giving him or her an opportunity to shift.
- **Physical action**. Any time a character takes physical action, there is the opportunity to change his or her action-verb.

Any time I see a shift – a significant change in a character's action – I mark its exact placement with an 'S' in a circle [Ⓢ], followed by a new action-verb. These are short-term changes in action in pursuit of the same objective. In truth, there are many small shifts in action in any given unit. In analysing a play, we want to be selective, marking only the most significant shifts. I usually aim to have one to three shifts in a unit, although occasionally I might mark more than that, if it is a particularly long unit or a volatile interaction. Even under these circumstances, though, I find that it is most useful for me to keep to one to three shifts; any more than that simply gets too detailed. As a collaborative director, I prefer to find the rest of the shifts in rehearsal, in collaboration with the cast. In analysing a script before rehearsal, we must always remember that our focus is on the big picture; too much detail might weigh us down, making it more likely that we will lose sight of the larger shape of the action.

Shifts and unit actions are both action-verbs, though, so what is the difference? A unit action always comes with an objective, but a shift is a change in action without a change in objective. In his book *How Life Imitates Chess: Making the Right Moves from the Board to the Boardroom*, political activist and former world chess champion Garry Kasparov distinguishes between strategy and tactics:

> Whereas strategy is abstract and based on long-term goals, tactics are concrete and based on finding the best move right now. Tactics are conditional and opportunistic, all about threat and defense. . . . As Sun Tzu wrote centuries ago, 'Strategy without tactics is the slowest route to victory. Tactics without strategy is the noise before defeat.' (16)

To translate this into script analysis terminology, unit actions are strategic; taken together, a list of a character's unit actions makes up his overall strategy for reaching his objectives. A character's shift actions, however, are tactical: the actions (threats) and reactions (defences) that a character makes in the heat of the moment, without changing his objective. These shifts, although less important to the big picture of a play's action, are very important to the texture of a play, and they help us find the changes in tone, rhythm, and tempo that are essential to creating a compelling production.

Let us return to the final unit of Act 3 in *Hedda Gabler* and search for the most significant shifts for each character. This is a fairly short unit, so I would aim for only one or two shifts for each character. Because I have already suggested what I might select as actions and objectives for Hedda and Løvborg in this unit, we will start from there, looking for the moments when the characters veer strongly from their overall action for the unit. It is also possible, though, to find the significant shifts first and then deduce from that the unit actions. In fact, I recommend you try both ways of working – moving from big picture, strategic actions to finer, tactical shifts, and vice versa – to develop both ways of discovering the action. In practice, I usually begin with the strategic choices, but I use the shifts that I discover to test the validity of my initial decisions about unit actions.

Here is what this unit would look like with the unit break, title, number, and actions-objectives marked, ready for the analysis of shifts, using Michael Meyer's translation[3]:

---

[3]Due to the length of the excerpts from *Hedda Gabler*, I have used Michael Meyer's translation with the permission of the copyright holder, Bloomsbury Methuen Drama. For all other extended units of dialogue, I have selected excerpts from plays in the public domain. All excerpts from plays protected by copyright constitute fair use, as they are of limited length, used only for the purposes of commentary, criticism, and analysis.

3, 7. Beautifully, promise me that.

Hedda inflames Løvborg to accept her pistol and kill himself.
Løvborg unnerves Hedda so she will reveal her love for him.

HEDDA [Waits a moment]   Aren't you going to escort her home, Mr. Løvborg?

LØVBORG   I? Through the streets? Do you want me to let people see her with me?

HEDDA   Of course, I don't know what else may have happened last night. But is it so utterly beyond redress?

LØVBORG   It isn't just last night. It'll go on happening. I know it. But the curse of it is, I don't want to live that kind of life. I don't want to start all that again. She's broken my courage. I can't spit in the eyes of the world any longer.

HEDDA [As though to herself]   That pretty little fool's been trying to shape a man's destiny [Looks at him]. But how could you be so heartless towards her?

LØVBORG   Don't call me heartless!

HEDDA   To go and destroy the one thing that's made her life worth living? You don't call that heartless?

LØVBORG   Do you want to know the truth, Hedda?

HEDDA   The truth?

LØVBORG   Promise me first – give me your word – that you'll never let Thea know about this.

HEDDA   I give you my word.

LØVBORG   Good. Well; what I told her just now was a lie.

HEDDA   About the manuscript?

LØVBORG   Yes. I didn't tear it up. Or throw it in the fjord.

HEDDA   You didn't? But where is it, then?

LØVBORG   I destroyed it, all the same. I destroyed it, Hedda!

HEDDA   I don't understand.

LØVBORG   Thea said that what I had done was like killing a child.

HEDDA   Yes. That's what she said.

LØVBORG   But to kill a child isn't the worst thing a father can do to it.

HEDDA   What could be worse than that?

LØVBORG   Hedda – suppose a man came home one morning, after a night of debauchery, and said to the mother of his child: 'Look here. I've been wandering round all night. I've been to – such-and-such a place and such-and-such a place. And I had our child with me. I took him to – these places. And I've lost him. Just – lost him. God knows where he is or whose hands he's fallen into.'

HEDDA   I see. But when all's said and done, this was only a book –

LØVBORG   Thea's heart and soul was in that book. It was her whole life.

HEDDA   Yes, I understand.

LØVBORG   Well, then you must also understand that she and I cannot possibly ever see each other again.

HEDDA   Where will you go?

LØVBORG   Nowhere. I just want to put an end to it all. As soon as possible.

HEDDA [Takes a step towards him]   Eilert Løvborg, listen to me. Do it – beautifully!

LØVBORG   Beautifully? [Smiles] With a crown of vine leaves in my hair? The way you used to dream of me – in the old days?

HEDDA   No. I don't believe in that crown any longer. But – do it beautifully, all the same. Just this once. Good-bye. You must go now. And don't come back.

LØVBORG   Adieu, madame. Give my love to George Tesman [Turns to go].

HEDDA   Wait. I want to give you a souvenir to take with you.

She goes over to the writing-table, opens the drawer and the pistol case, and comes back to LØVBORG with one of the pistols.

LØVBORG [Looks at her]   This? Is this the souvenir?

HEDDA [Nods slowly]   You recognize it? You looked down its barrel once.

LØVBORG   You should have used it then.

HEDDA   Here! Use it now!

LØVBORG [Puts the pistol in his breast pocket]   Thank you.

HEDDA   Do it beautifully, Eilert Løvborg. Only promise me that!

LØVBORG   Goodbye, Hedda Gabler.

He goes out through the hall. HEDDA stands by the door for a moment, listening. Then she goes over to the writing-table, takes out the package containing the manuscript, glances inside, pulls some of the pages half out and looks at them. Then she takes it to the armchair by the stove and sits down with the package in her lap. After a moment, she opens the door of the stove; then she opens the packet.

HEDDA [Throws one of the pages into the stove and whispers to herself]   I'm burning your child, Thea! You with your beautiful, wavy hair! [She throws a few more pages into the stove] The child Eilert Løvborg gave you [Throws the rest of the manuscript in]. I'm burning it! I'm burning your child!

As you examine this unit for shifts, first do so instinctively. Look for moments when you see (or perhaps a better word is 'feel') a change in tactics: when one character seems to shift what he or she is doing to the other character. Wherever you see a shift in action, mark it in the script with an Ⓢ.

In units such as this one, with such high stakes at the end of the third act of a four-act play, it should come as no surprise that we could mark many such moments. But we need to be selective so that we do not over-analyse the unit before the director has gotten the opportunity to shape the action in rehearsal with the actors. We are looking for the major shifts so that we can find the overall arc of the action in the play – the landmarks in the characters' journey. Frequently, I find that a shift in action by one character triggers a shift in the other character. When this happens, I tend to favour marking the first character's shift; I assume that if the actor playing that role hits that shift, then the other actor will respond and naturally find his or her shift. For example, the first prominent shift I see occurs somewhere in the vicinity of Løvborg's confession to Hedda that he lied to Thea:

> HEDDA   Of course, I don't know what else may have happened last night. But is it so utterly beyond redress?
> LØVBORG   It isn't just last night. It'll go on happening. I know it. But the curse of it is, I don't want to live that kind of life. I don't want to start all that again. She's broken my courage. I can't spit in the eyes of the world any longer.
> HEDDA [As though to herself]   That pretty little fool's been trying to shape a man's destiny [Looks at him]. But how could you be so heartless towards her?
> LØVBORG   Don't call me heartless!
> HEDDA   To go and destroy the one thing that's made her life worth living? You don't call that heartless?
> LØVBORG   Do you want to know the truth, Hedda?
> HEDDA   The truth?
> LØVBORG   Promise me first – give me your word – that you'll never let Thea know about this.
> HEDDA   I give you my word.
> LØVBORG   Good. Well; what I told her just now was a lie.

You should be able to sense that the characters' actions have changed here. But at what moment does the change begin? Who initiates it? What is the most effective placement for this shift?

I am drawn to the exchange between Hedda and Løvborg in which they debate whether his treatment of Thea was heartless. There is conflict: Hedda accuses Løvborg of treating Thea heartlessly, by destroying the manuscript that the two of them had created, whereas Løvborg sees it differently. Because he knows the truth – that he did not destroy the manuscript but lost it – he believes he has been compassionate by saving Thea from the truth about his recklessness and neglect. I see two possible placements for a shift here: when Hedda asks

Løvborg how he could be so heartless to Thea, or when Løvborg decides to tell Hedda the truth about his actions that night.

Either shift could work; both capture the change that occurs at this moment in the unit. I favour the earlier moment, particularly as it follows what appears to be a realization by Hedda and is followed by such a clear response by Løvborg, who echoes her words:

> HEDDA [As though to herself]   That pretty little fool's been trying to shape a man's destiny [Looks at him]. But how could you be so heartless towards her?
> LØVBORG   Don't call me heartless!

We mark the shift with an 'S' in a circle [Ⓢ] at the exact point where we see the change in action. I would mark it right after the stage direction 'Looks at him', at the start of her line 'But how could you ... .'

Having marked the shift, we next need to define it, by selecting a playable verb to capture the new action. What is Hedda doing to Løvborg by asking him how he could treat Thea this way? If we look at the broad categories of verbs, is it a positive action, such as encouraging or approving, or a negative action, such as provoking or harming? It might seem to be a negative action, such as 'accuses', 'blames', 'aggravate', or 'shame'. But given Hedda's fascination with Løvborg's irresponsible actions in the past, she could just as easily be expressing her admiration with an action such as 'revere' or 'stoke'. Much as I am usually drawn to the more surprising choice of action (which might be the more positive actions for Hedda in this case), we need to stay focused on the big picture of the unit, even while analysing this smaller moment.

Two bits of information help guide my choice here. First, Løvborg's reaction – 'Don't call me heartless!' – seems defensive, which makes me think that Hedda's action was more attack than support. Second, Hedda's objective is to make Løvborg 'accept her pistol and kill himself'. If she will, in the end, attempt to seduce or inflame Løvborg so that he will take the pistol, what tactic might she be using at this point in the unit, and what tactic will make for the most intriguing and absorbing journey towards the end of Act 3? In a dramatic and climactic scene between two major characters – the last scene in the play for one of them – I am usually looking for maximum conflict, as well as maximum contrast between actions. If Hedda will end up seducing Løvborg with her pistol, then I am drawn to choices such as 'shames' or 'accuses' as contrasting points in the journey towards seduction.

I would also pay attention to Løvborg's unit action-objective, 'to threaten Hedda so she will reveal her love for him'. If we choose a positive action for Hedda at this moment, such as 'revere', Løvborg will have achieved his objective, and that will lower the stakes of the scene for him. That is not to say that 'revere' is out of the question for a shift at this moment; it is possible that Hedda teases Løvborg by almost giving him what he wants, only to withdraw her love at the last moment. It is always a good idea to consider the opposite of your initial action, as this type of choice could be revelatory. In the end, your choice is a starting point for discussions between the director and designers, to be articulated in rehearsal in collaboration with the cast.

Further in the unit, there is a point at which Hedda turns more directly towards her objective, eventually offering Løvborg one of her pistols and asking that he use it to end his life 'beautifully'. We are looking for the most significant shift in action (tactics) that leads to the climactic moment when Hedda actually offers the pistol. This will usually occur before the climax of the unit or scene, not at the moment of the climax. We are looking for the change in action that triggers the climax, not the change, if any, at that key moment (we will talk about key moments and how to score them later). Again, I must caution that the placement of this shift is an act of interpretation, first undertaken by the director and designers in preparation for design and production meetings, but ultimately articulated in rehearsal through the collaboration of the director and actors. Let us look at the chunk of dialogue wherein this shift falls:

HEDDA   Where will you go?

LØVBORG   Nowhere. I just want to put an end of it all. As soon as possible.

HEDDA [Takes a step towards him]   Eilert Løvborg, listen to me. Do it – beautifully!

LØVBORG   Beautifully? [Smiles] With a crown of vine leaves in my hair? The way you used to dream of me – in the old days?

HEDDA   No. I don't believe in that crown any longer. But – do it beautifully, all the same. Just this once. Good-bye. You must go now. And don't come back.

LØVBORG   Adieu, madame. Give my love to George Tesman [Turns to go].

HEDDA   Wait. I want to give you a souvenir to take with you.

She goes over to the writing-table, opens the drawer and the pistol case, and comes back to LØVBORG with one of the pistols.

LØVBORG [Looks at her]   This? Is this the souvenir?

HEDDA [Nods slowly]   You recognize it? You looked down its barrel once.

LØVBORG   You should have used it then.

HEDDA   Here! Use it now!

LØVBORG [Puts the pistol in his breast pocket]   Thank you.

HEDDA   Do it beautifully, Eilert Løvborg. Only promise me that!

LØVBORG   Goodbye, Hedda Gabler.

He goes out through the hall

I would gravitate towards the moment when Løvborg tells Hedda he intends to end it all, and Hedda asks him to do it beautifully. But which moment is the trigger here? Ultimately, we could safely mark Hedda or Løvborg's line as the shift, and we would be observing the same basic shape to the action. So what is the difference between these two scores? I believe this choice indicates who is driving the action. Does Løvborg threaten to kill himself as a last-ditch effort to provoke an admission of love from Hedda? Or does Hedda see the opportunity created when Løvborg confesses his plans to commit suicide, seize it, and urge him to do it in a particular way, one that satisfies her idealized, destructive-romantic desires? I believe that either might work; ultimately the ensemble will discover the best choice in rehearsal. We can also think of this in terms of the overall shape of the unit or scene, looking for where this shift fits into the pattern of shifts. At this point, I am taken with the idea of Hedda being the aggressor, but I am on the lookout for a moment when Løvborg might assert himself again.

There seems to be one last shift worth noting, when Løvborg turns to leave and Hedda offers him a souvenir:

> HEDDA   No. I don't believe in that crown any longer. But – do it beautifully, all the same. Just this once. Good-bye. You must go now. And don't come back.
> LØVBORG   Adieu, madame. Give my love to George Tesman [Turns to go].
> HEDDA   Wait. I want to give you a souvenir to take with you.
> *She goes over to the writing-table, opens the drawer and the pistol case, and comes back to LØVBORG with one of the pistols.*
> LØVBORG [Looks at her]   This? Is this the souvenir?

To me, 'Give my love to George Tesman' contains Løvborg's most powerful action: He taunts Hedda by reminding her that after he leaves, Hedda will be left with only George Tesman to amuse her. So although Hedda's offer of the 'souvenir', the pistol, appears to be an extremely aggressive action, I might score the shift on Løvborg's final line before he turns to leave. What is his action when he says 'Give my love to George Tesman'? Throughout the play, Løvborg makes quite a show of calling Hedda by her maiden name; in his very last words in the play, he calls her Hedda Gabler one last time. By purposefully invoking George Tesman's name one last time, Løvborg mocks Hedda with visions of her future after his death. In fact, there is a wonderful echo here: first, Løvborg says goodbye using the name Tesman, then he says goodbye with the name Gabler. I would look first at the negative action categories, 'provoke', 'harm', and 'destroy'. I might choose one of the following actions from those categories: abandon, antagonize, horrify, infuriate, ridicule, belittle, cheapen, demean, disown, taunt, banish, or nullify.

Finally, after Løvborg leaves, Hedda must make a final shift when she turns to burn the manuscript:

HEDDA [Throws one of the pages into the stove and whispers to herself] I'm burning your child, Thea! You with your beautiful, wavy hair! [She throws a few more pages into the stove] The child Eilert Løvborg gave you [Throws the rest of the manuscript in]. I'm burning it! I'm burning your child!

This is a clear shift in tactics, but also, technically, a change in objective, if only because Løvborg has left the house: If the receiver has changed, then the objective has changed as well. As there is no other character on stage, upon whom is Hedda acting? When a character appears onstage alone, there are several ways to analyse action and objective. If the character addresses the audience directly, then the audience is the receiver (though often the audience is a stand in for another character). In this case, we might see the action as Hedda talking to the audience as if it is Thea; Hedda talking to the manuscript as if it is Thea; Hedda talking to Thea as if she is there; or Hedda talking to herself. For her objective to be achievable on stage in this moment, the receiver must be on stage, so we might see this as Hedda doing something to herself. Why is she destroying the manuscript, Thea and Løvborg's 'child'? To celebrate her victory, perhaps, but in an almost maniacal way. This is the final image of Act 3: Hedda, kneeling by a wood burning stove – whispering to herself, according to the stage direction – bathed in the glow of the swelling fire. And yet she is also pretending to talk to Thea, so we might want to capture a sense of her hostility towards her rival. The combination of celebration and antagonism leads me first to the list of 'manipulative' verbs – beguile, bewitch, blackmail, entrap, mesmerize – or stronger actions from the 'loving' verb list, such as admire, enthral, inflame, spellbind.

Subunits

Once Løvborg takes the pistol from Hedda and leaves her house, she has achieved her objective (or so she believes). As noted above, she is acting upon herself for these last few lines, or acting upon the manuscript as a stand-in for Thea. Because Hedda can only achieve an objective that involves herself, I might score this as a reflective moment, with Hedda as actor and receiver. Usually, when the objective and receiver change, we mark this as a new unit. Yet it would be a very short unit – too short to rehearse by itself, to my mind. For situations such as this, I would mark the final lines as a subunit (3-7b), still connected to the preceding action between Hedda and Løvborg (3-7a). By breaking down the unit into subunits, I can see each as distinct parts of the same unit of action. In rehearsal, I might rehearse each subunit separately once or twice, but I would always make sure to combine the subunits at the end of each rehearsal, so the actors understand how Hedda's and Løvborg's actions in unit 3-7a lead Hedda to burn the manuscript in unit 3-7b.

Using one of the actions I suggested above, at the end of the section on units, our analysis for the two subunits might look something like this:

3-7a. Beautifully, promise me that.

Hedda inflames Løvborg to accept her pistol and kill himself.
Løvborg unnerves Hedda so she will reveal her love for him.

HEDDA [Waits a moment] Aren't you going to escort her home, Mr. Løvborg?

LØVBORG I? Through the streets? Do you want me to let people see her with me?

HEDDA Of course, I don't know what else may have happened last night. But is it so utterly beyond redress?

LØVBORG It isn't just last night. It'll go on happening. I know it. But the curse of it is, I don't want to live that kind of life. I don't want to start all that again. She's broken my courage. I can't spit in the eyes of the world any longer.

HEDDA [As though to herself] That pretty little fool's been trying to shape a man's destiny [Looks at him]. But how could you be so heartless towards her?   ⑤ **shames**

LØVBORG Don't call me heartless!

HEDDA To go and destroy the one thing that's made her life worth living? You don't call that heartless?

LØVBORG Do you want to know the truth, Hedda?   ⑤ **teases**

HEDDA The truth?

LØVBORG Promise me first – give me your word – that you'll never let Thea know about this.

HEDDA I give you my word.

LØVBORG Good. Well; what I told her just now was a lie.

HEDDA About the manuscript?

LØVBORG Yes. I didn't tear it up. Or throw it in the fjord.

HEDDA You didn't? But where is it, then?

LØVBORG I destroyed it, all the same. I destroyed it, Hedda!

HEDDA I don't understand.

LØVBORG Thea said that what I had done was like killing a child.

HEDDA Yes. That's what she said.

LØVBORG But to kill a child isn't the worst thing a father can do to it.

HEDDA What could be worse than that?

LØVBORG   Hedda – suppose a man came home one morning, after a night
   of debauchery, and said to the mother of his child: 'Look here. I've been
   wandering round all night. I've been to – such-and-such a place and such-
   and-such a place. And I had our child with me. I took him to – these
   places. And I've lost him. Just – lost him. God knows where he is or
   whose hands he's fallen into.'
HEDDA   I see. But when all's said and done, this was only a book.
LØVBORG   Thea's heart and soul was in that book. It was her whole life.
HEDDA   Yes, I understand.
LØVBORG   Well, then you must also understand that she and I cannot
   possibly ever see each other again.
HEDDA   Where will you go?
LØVBORG   Nowhere. I just want to put an end to it all. As soon as
   possible.   ⓢ threatens
HEDDA [Takes a step towards him]   Eilert Løvborg, listen
   to me. Do it – beautifully!
LØVBORG   Beautifully? [Smiles] With a crown of vine leaves in my
   hair? The way you used to dream of me – in the old days?
HEDDA   No. I don't believe in that crown any longer. But – do it
   beautifully, all the same. Just this once. Good-bye. You must go now.
   And don't come back.
LØVBORG   Adieu, madame. Give my love to George Tesman.   ⓢ taunts
   [Turns to go]
HEDDA   Wait. I want to give you a souvenir to take with you.
   *She goes over to the writing-table, opens the drawer and the pistol
   case, and comes back to LØVBORG with one of the pistols.*
LØVBORG [Looks at her]   This? Is this the souvenir?
HEDDA [Nods slowly]   You recognize it? You looked down its barrel once.
LØVBORG   You should have used it then.
HEDDA   Here! Use it now!
LØVBORG [Puts the pistol in his breast pocket]   Thank you.
HEDDA   Do it beautifully, Eilert Løvborg. Only
   promise me that!   ⓢ seduces
LØVBORG   Goodbye, Hedda Gabler.
   *He goes out through the hall. HEDDA stands by the door for a moment,
   listening.*

3, 7b. I'm burning your child.

Hedda inflames herself/Thea to ecstasy/misery.

*Then she goes over to the writing-table, takes out the package containing
the manuscript, glances inside, pulls some of the pages half out and looks*

at them. Then she takes it to the armchair by the stove and sits down with the package in her lap. After a moment, she opens the door of the stove; then she opens the packet.

HEDDA [Throws one of the pages into the stove and whispers to herself] I'm burning your child, Thea! You with your beautiful, wavy hair! [She throws a few more pages into the stove]. The child Eilert Løvborg gave you [Throws the rest of the manuscript in] I'm burning it! I'm burning your child!

The next step is to decide at what moment in the overall unit the climax or key moment occurs. With that decision in mind, the ensemble can further interpret the major changes to tempos and rhythms in each unit – for example, when Hedda offers Løvborg the gun in the first subunit, or as she burns the manuscript in the second subunit.

Obstacles

One significant but often underused tool in scoring a unit, scene, or play is to identify the **obstacles** to the characters' objectives. What stands in each character's way? 'Remember the old adage that something difficult to obtain is always more strongly desired than something readily available', Uta Hagen observed. 'The obstacle itself will strongly influence what you must do to overcome it in the pursuit of the objective.'[4] The greater the obstacle, the more powerful the need to overcome it. In the absence of obstacles, actors will find it more difficult to commit strongly to their actions over longer periods; relationships might lack the deep-seated conflict and sustained tension that lead to striking **shifts** in tactics (actions), a fully articulated dramatic arc, peaks (**key moments**), and, therefore, maximum audience engagement.

Actors tend to think of obstacles as significant because they help create conflict and raise the stakes. An obstacle does serve as one important test of whether a character's objective will be sufficiently difficult to attain, but I also find that obstacles help stimulate actors to experiment with tactics, and those tactics (shifts) open up a wider dynamic range of potential actions for each character. Consequently, obstacles help the ensemble better articulate the shape of the action in greater detail.

Hagen delineates six types of elements established or suggested in the script that might lead us to identify formidable obstacles:

1. **Character.** A character's obstacle might be the nature of his or her character; in other words, an internal obstacle. For example, Hedda

---

[4]*Respect for Acting* 180.

Gabler's fear of scandal might prevent her from taking certain actions or achieving her goals because she is risk-averse.

2. **Past and present circumstances**. The character's background and personal or professional circumstances might make it more difficult to achieve particular goals. In *A Streetcar Named Desire*, Mitch's relationship with his mother might prevent him from forgiving and accepting Blanche once he learns of her hometown reputation and sexual history.

3. **Relationships and other characters' objectives**. Quite frequently, a character is directly opposed to another character's objective, or a relationship stands in the way of it. In *Fences*, Troy's failure to make it as a major league ballplayer due to his race prevents him from seeing the value in his son Cory's desire to earn a scholarship to play college football. Blanche's relationship with Stella holds Stanley's violence towards Blanche in check until the penultimate scene of the play; only after Stella leaves for the hospital does Stanley feel at liberty to assault Blanche.

4. **Events**. Løvborg's death between Acts 3 and 4 robs Hedda of the life she most desperately desires to control. Once Brack realizes that Løvborg was shot with one of Hedda's matching pistols, he has the power to blackmail her. In the wake of these events, Hedda shoots herself at the end of the play, unable to overcome her obstacles, or perhaps in a last-ditch effort to achieve her objective, to control life.

5. **Surroundings**. The small living quarters, together with the noise and bright lights surrounding Stanley and Stella's apartment in the New Orleans French Quarter, stand in the way of Blanche's creating the romantic atmosphere that she believes she needs to lure Mitch into love and marriage. In Act 2 of *Hedda Gabler*, the presence of Hedda's husband, Tesman, in the next room stands in the way of Løvborg's attempts to seduce Hedda.

6. **Objects**. The presence of one of Hedda's pistols at the scene of Løvborg's death reveals her complicity to Brack, exposing her to blackmail. At the end of scene 10 in *Streetcar*, a broken bottle is Blanche's last defence and Stanley's last obstacle to rape.

Let us examine two examples from our case study plays, the 'tea scene' from Act 2 of *The Importance of Being Earnest* and scene 10 from *A Streetcar Named Desire*. The tea scene is a marvellous example of comedy of manners, as Cecily and Gwendolen do battle over their misconception that each is engaged to the same 'Ernest' – and attempt to preserve what their society sees as the proper manners for serving and sharing tea. I would divide this scene into two units or subunits: the first (lines 498–599), in which they discover that they are both engaged to a man named Ernest Worthing, and the second (lines 600–640), in which Cecily serves tea to Gwendolen as they attempt to make polite small talk. We will focus primarily on the second unit, as it offers two additional circumstances that complicate the characters' pursuit of their objectives: Cecily's butler, Merriman, and a footman are present, assisting her with tea service; and the action of the tea service itself, which allows Cecily to bring express her actions physically.

> *Enter MERRIMAN, followed by the footman. He carries a salver, tablecloth, and plate stand. CECILY is about to retort. The presence of the servants exercises a restraining influence, under which both girls chafe.*

MERRIMAN   Shall I lay tea here as usual, Miss?

CECILY [Sternly, in a calm voice]   Yes, as usual [MERRIMAN begins to clear table and lay cloth. A long pause. CECILY and GWENDOLEN glare at each other]

GWENDOLEN   Are there many interesting walks in the vicinity, Miss Cardew?

CECILY   Oh! yes! a great many. From the top of one of the hills quite close one can see five counties.

GWENDOLEN   Five counties! I don't think I should like that; I hate crowds.

CECILY [Sweetly]   I suppose that is why you live in town?

> *GWENDOLEN bites her lip, and beats her foot nervously with her parasol.*

GWENDOLEN [Looking round]   Quite a well-kept garden this is, Miss Cardew.

CECILY   So glad you like it, Miss Fairfax.

GWENDOLEN   I had no idea there were any flowers in the country.

CECILY   Oh, flowers are as common here, Miss Fairfax, as people are in London.

GWENDOLEN   Personally I cannot understand how anybody manages to exist in the country, if anybody who is anybody does. The country always bores me to death.

CECILY   Ah! This is what the newspapers call agricultural depression, is it not? I believe the aristocracy are suffering very much from it just at present. It is almost an epidemic amongst them, I have been told. May I offer you some tea, Miss Fairfax?

GWENDOLEN [With elaborate politeness]   Thank you. [Aside] Detestable girl! But I require tea!

CECILY [Sweetly]   Sugar?

GWENDOLEN [Superciliously]   No, thank you. Sugar is not fashionable any more.

> *CECILY looks angrily at her, takes up the tongs and puts four lumps of sugar into the cup.*

CECILY [Severely]   Cake or bread and butter?

GWENDOLEN [In a bored manner]   Bread and butter, please. Cake is rarely seen at the best houses nowadays.

CECILY [Cuts a very large slice of cake, and puts it on the tray]   Hand that to Miss Fairfax.

MERRIMAN does so, and goes out with footman. GWENDOLEN drinks the tea and makes a grimace. Puts down cup at once, reaches out her hand to the bread and butter, looks at it, and finds it is cake. Rises in indignation.

GWENDOLEN   You have filled my tea with lumps of sugar, and though I asked most distinctly for bread and butter, you have given me cake. I am known for the gentleness of my disposition, and the extraordinary sweetness of my nature, but I warn you, Miss Cardew, you may go too far.

CECILY [Rising]   To save my poor, innocent, trusting boy from the machinations of any other girl there are no lengths to which I would not go.

GWENDOLEN   From the moment I saw you I distrusted you. I felt that you were false and deceitful. I am never deceived in such matters. My first impressions of people are invariably right.

CECILY   It seems to me, Miss Fairfax, that I am trespassing on your valuable time. No doubt you have many other calls of a similar character to make in the neighbourhood.

Before we analyse the obstacles in this unit, we will score the actions and objectives of each character. The two young women, operating under the erroneous belief that they are engaged to the same man, each want to take down the other in some way. I would note that Gwendolen opens the unit with questions and observations, whereas Cecily appears to focus on the superficial manners of the encounter. I might score the scene like this:

Gwendolen belittles Cecily so she will feel disgraced.

Cecily teases Gwendolen so that she will explode from frustration.

So what are the obstacles to the characters' achieving their objectives? What will help the unit build tension and momentum, rather than become a shapeless brawl?

In terms of Hagen's first two elements, the women's characters and circumstances hold them back, at least initially, from pursuing their objectives as aggressively as possible. Each comes from a wealthy or prominent family. Gwendolen's family name is well respected, but her parents have squandered much of their wealth. After the decline of their fortunes, manners and presentation have become even more important to her. Cecily's family has money but not an aristocratic name, because her ward, John Worthing, does not know the identity of his birth parents. It could be argued that each woman sees herself as polite and gentile and has had little opportunity to engage in this kind of fight, though perhaps this kind of sparring is a part of their lives and the stakes are simply higher in this scene, because they are fighting over their futures.

Their objectives put them in direct conflict: each wants to embarrass the other without embarrassing herself. And there is the element of their relationship – they share a connection to John/Jack Worthing (though Gwendolen knows him as Ernest) and Algernon Moncrief (though Cecily knows him as Ernest), yet the two women have never met before. Their connection greatly raises the stakes and conflict, whereas their having just met pushes them towards greater formality and decorum. As for events, each woman's recent engagement – both in the past twenty-four hours – adds to the heightened pressure.

Yet for me, the surroundings and objects create the most interesting and distinctive obstacles in the scene. For forty lines of this unit, the women's battle takes place under the watchful eyes of the butler, Merriman, and a footman, the two servants acting as silent witnesses and accomplices to the battle. They function as a Greek chorus often does – as a stand-in for the audience, to show how less-privileged, 'average' citizens might react to this behaviour – and hold the women's most severe responses in check for a while, as the upper-class women do not wish to display their basest instincts in front of the servants. The tea set, sugar, cakes, and butter eventually supply the weapons with which Cecily taunts Gwendolen and she, in turn, ridicules Cecily. But before the tea service becomes a weapon, it serves as the foundation for the proper manners of the scene and setting, hence an obstacle to the humiliation that each woman wishes to inflict upon the other.

In scene 10 of *A Streetcar Named Desire*, Stella's doctors have sent Stanley home from the hospital to get some sleep, as they do not expect her to give birth until the next morning. While he was gone, Mitch, having learned of the rumours about Blanche's past from Stanley, has insulted Blanche and broken off their courtship. Blanche has been drinking and fantasizing about a moonlight swim with some friends and lovers. Stanley makes a big show of putting on the silk pajamas he wore on his wedding night, as Blanche invents a story about a millionaire from Dallas who has invited her to cruise the Caribbean with him on a yacht. By the end of the scene, Stanley will rape Blanche.

Whether Stanley intends early in the scene to rape Blanche – his final threatening line 'We've had this date with each other from the beginning!' implies he might have been thinking about her as a likely sexual conquest since the day she arrived – is open to debate. But I would suggest that there is more conflict in the scene if Stanley actually wants something else – to celebrate the imminent birth of his child and what it portends for Blanche: with a baby in the house, there will be no room for her to stay in the Kowalskis' tiny apartment. For her part, until Stanley enters, Blanche appears to be trying to drown her sorrows over the loss of Mitch's affections, fantasize about a past that no longer exists, and pretend that she has a future grander than poor Mitch could have provided. In a sense, then, each of them must adapt to the other's unexpected disruption of his or her plans. I might score their actions and objectives along these lines:

> Stanley wants to belittle Blanche until she breaks down.
> Blanche wants to mesmerize Stanley so that he will be in awe of her.

Because Blanche is drunk, alone, and desperate, and Stanley is sceptical of anything she claims, she has little to no chance of achieving her objective. Stanley's objective is more attainable, but in his unbridled desire to force Blanche to break down and admit that she is a liar, he will never be completely satisfied, and thus he will escalate the action until he decides to attack her.

In terms of character, I see no internal obstacles to Stanley's pursuing and achieving his objective; perhaps that is why he appears to win this scene. Blanche, however, has an internal obstacle that might prevent her from winning over Stanley: She is so desperate for his approval, and the approval of men in general, that she constantly overreaches and exaggerates and eventually gets caught in her own lies. Recognizing this obstacle might help the actress and director find a wider range of actions. As each of her actions is met by Stanley's ridicule, Blanche feels compelled to attempt ever more reckless and overblown actions to support her transparently fictitious stories. Her circumstances provide little in the way of obstacles to her pursuing Stanley's admiration, particularly as she is not attempting to seduce him in this scene. Stanley, though, is quite mindful that Blanche is his sister-in-law, and much as he wants her out of his house, he knows from experience that his wife, Stella, remains very protective of her older sister.

Perhaps the most powerful obstacles to Stanley and Blanche are each other. When two characters' objectives stand in direct opposition, a hard-fought battle is almost guaranteed. For a scene such as this, with a key moment that could be seen as the climax of the play, the greater the number and intensity of the obstacles that we discover, the more the actors will be able to build the tension and momentum of the scene. Clearly, the already contentious relationship between Stanley and Blanche will fuel their conflict in this scene. Similarly, a key event occurring offstage simultaneously – Stella is in the hospital in labour, about to give birth to the Kowalskis' first child – gives a major boost to both characters' pursuit of their objectives. Stanley might feel emboldened by the absence of his wife, as well as by his heightened awareness of his own virility. Once Stella becomes a mother, Blanche might fear that Stella will not allow her to stay in the apartment.

Finally, the surroundings and objects in the Kowalskis' apartment seem to conspire to thwart Blanche's attempts to salvage her dignity and earn Stanley's respect. Blanche's rhinestone tiara, her 'crumpled white satin evening gown and a pair of scuffed silver slippers with brilliants set in their heels', initially help her prop up her fantasy life, but now that Stanley has uncovered her past, he easily shatters her illusions:

> What've you got on those fine feathers for? (12)
> And you come up with that – gorgeous – diamond – tiara? (32)
> Gosh. I thought it was Tiffany diamonds. (34)

At the same time, Williams's stage directions heighten the sense that the environment is set against Blanche or reflects her inner turmoil: the 'lurid reflections' on the walls around her (118), 'inhuman voices like cries in a jungle' (123); the blue piano (127, 134); and the sordid action revealed through the transparent back wall:

> Through the back wall of the rooms, which have become transparent, can be seen the sidewalk. A prostitute has rolled a drunkard. He pursues her along the walk, overtakes her and there is a struggle. A policeman's whistle breaks it up. Some moments later the NEGRO WOMAN appears around the corner with a sequined bag which the prostitute has dropped on the walk. She is rooting excitedly through it. (123)

Whether these are real events taking place around the action or expressions of Blanche's inner state of mind, they serve as powerful atmospheric obstacles to her achieving her objective, because they stand in stark opposition to her fantasies.

All in all, it seems that Blanche has much greater obstacles to achieving her objectives than Stanley has to his. This might indicate just how far she has fallen. She has lost her last hope of a romantic salvation in the form of Mitch, because of Stanley's meddling. With the baby on the way, Stella will have other responsibilities, other places to focus her love and caring, than her unstable older sister – yet seemingly little stands in Stanley's way. So what pushes Stanley to his final, dreadful assault on Blanche? I can think of two things. First, he will not be satisfied until Blanche completely breaks down, which will set the stage for her institutionalization in scene 11. Second, Blanche resists with the threat of violence, just as Stanley seems to have thought of his most aggressive action:

STANLEY   Come to think of it – maybe you wouldn't be bad to – interfere
   with . . .
   BLANCHE moves backward through the door into the bedroom.
BLANCHE   Stay back! Don't you come toward me another step of I'll –
STANLEY   What?

BLANCHE   Some awful thing will happen! It will!
STANLEY   What are you putting on now?
   They are now both inside the bedroom.
BLANCHE   I warn you, don't, I'm in danger!
   He takes another step. She smashes a bottle on the table and faces him,
   clutching the broken top.
STANLEY   What did you do that for?
BLANCHE   So I could twist the broken end in your face! (134–142)

One observation of this scene is that the many things standing in the way of Blanche's objective – the most dangerous being Stanley himself – push her to threaten him with a broken bottle in self-defence. Armed with that knowledge, we would then look to articulate the shape of the unit actions and tactical shifts that trace her descent from dress-up fantasy at the start of the scene to physical confrontation with Stanley at the end.

Key moments

Key moments are brief passages of time during which a play reaches its peaks of tension and conflict. In contemporary script analysis, the most intense, highest-stakes key moment in the play, after which the action resolves, is referred to as the climax. Yet if we think of a play as a dramatic landscape, with plateaus, peaks, and valleys, the most significant key moments are noteworthy landmarks: the events or incidents that stand out amid their surroundings and therefore help us find our bearings. By marking these, we can map the emotional, intellectual, and psychological journey of the characters and action.

By the same measure, in each scene or unit we can usually detect a mini-key moment – the emotional 'top' of the scene, which the action builds towards before resolving in some way or leading, causally or by accrual, to the next scene. All good plays and productions maintain interest and build momentum through such moments. Even in the most understated scene – a quiet, low-conflict discussion between family members, for instance – it is almost always possible to detect or define a small key moment. Keep in mind that a key moment is always perceived in relation to the surrounding action; not every key moment comes at the end of a volatile, knockdown, drag-out fight.

The playwright might have many waves of different sizes leading to the climax. In contrast to the others, the climax might appear as a tidal wave caused by an asteroid falling into the ocean. If, however, we imagine a much quieter set of events in a unit, the key moment might be merely the largest of several small ripples, each caused by a pebble thrown into the water. Similarly, we could return to the image of a landscape painting. In an entire work, we might see only two or three landmarks that grab our eye immediately – whereas if we zoom in and focus on a small part of the canvas, we will see smaller landmarks that escaped our notice earlier. In a play, when we zoom in on a scene, we will observe moments that pop out within their context but escape notice in a larger context with more dramatic, high-stakes events. In most realistic plays, the largest key moments tend to fall at the end of acts, but the smaller key moments are equally significant, as they enable a play or production to build momentum leading to the larger key moments and, eventually, the climax.

In *Hedda Gabler*, each of the four acts builds to a major key moment in the final minute or so of action. Act 1 builds to Brack's revelation that Eilert Løvborg has published a major new book, returned to town, and will be competing for the position as a professor that Tesman had been promised and upon which he and Hedda have mortgaged their future. As this is Act 1, the stakes are just beginning to rise; next to the key moments at the ends of Acts 3 and 4, this seems far less significant, but it starts the overall progression of the four acts. Brack's revelation disrupts the uneasy but relatively peaceful status quo at the start of the play. In the context of the entire play's landscape, we can see this key moment as one of four major key moments that build tension and momentum from act to act. Yet if we zoom in on Act 1 after we conclude that this is the most significant key moment in the act, we can then see a series of smaller key moments building to this one – Miss Tesman's news about putting up the security for the Tesmans's house; Tesman's implication to Miss Tesman that Hedda might be pregnant; and Hedda's winning Thea's confidence. The first of these, the revelation that Miss Tesman has mortgaged her future for the newlyweds, pales next to Brack's revelation that Løvborg might use the publication of his new book to compete for Tesman's coveted job and livelihood. But in this earlier unit, we might observe an interesting dynamic between the tension created by Miss Tesman's revelation of the mortgage and the understated disclosure of Løvborg's new book:

> MISS TESMAN But, George dear, the expense! It's going to make a
>   dreadful hole in your pocket, all this.
> TESMAN [a little down cast] Yes, I – I suppose it will, won't it?
> MISS TESMAN Oh, George, really!
> TESMAN How much do you think it will cost? Roughly, I mean? What?
> MISS TESMAN I can't possible say till I see the bills.
> TESMAN Well, luckily Judge Brack's managed to get it on very favourable
>   terms. He wrote and told Hedda so.
> MISS TESMAN Don't worry, George dear. Anyway, I've stood security for
>   all the furniture and carpets.
> TESMAN Security? But dear, sweet Auntie Juju, how could you possibly
>   stand security?
> MISS TESMAN I've arranged a mortgage on our annuity.

TESMAN [Jumps up]   What! On your annuity – and Auntie Rina's?

MISS TESMAN   Yes. Well, I could think of no other way.

TESMAN [Stands in front of her]   Auntie Juju, have you gone completely out of your mind? That annuity's all you and Auntie Rina have.

MISS TESMAN   Alright, there's no need to get so excited about it. It's a pure formality, you know. Judge Brack told me so. He was so kind to arrange it all for me. A pure formality; those were his very words.

TESMAN   I dare say. All the same –

MISS TESMAN   Anyway, you'll have a salary of your own now. And, good heavens, even if we did have to fork out a little – tighten our belts for a week or two – why, we'd be happy to do so for your sake.

TESMAN   Oh Auntie Juju! Will you never stop sacrificing yourself for me?

MISS TESMAN [Gets up and puts her hands on his shoulders]   What else do I have to live for but to smooth your road a little, my dear boy? You've never had any mother or father to turn to. And now at last we've achieved our goal. I won't deny we've had our little difficulties now and then. But now, thank the good Lord, George dear, all your worries are past.

TESMAN   Yes, it's wonderful really how everything's gone just right for me.

MISS TESMAN   Yes! And the enemies who tried to bar your way have been struck down. They have been made to bite the dust. The man who was your most dangerous rival has had the mightiest fall. And now he's lying there in the pit he dug for himself, poor misguided creature.

TESMAN   Have you heard any news of Eilert? Since I went away.

MISS TESMAN   Only that he's said to have published a new book.

TESMAN   What! Eilert Løvborg? You mean – just recently? What?

MISS TESMAN   So they say. I don't imagine it can be of any value, do you? When your new book comes out, that'll be another story. What's it going to be about?

In a more understated unit such as this, we might mark the line in which Tesman reacts to his aunt's sacrifice as the key moment ('Auntie Juju, have you gone completely out of your mind?'), which allows us to sneak in another significant bit of exposition in its wake, the publication of Løvborg's book.

I mark these key moments with a capital 'K' in a triangle. As with all the symbols that we will use, the shape of the symbol is indicative of its function. A triangle with a point at the top captures the sense of a peak in the action, so that the director, actor, or designer can simply glance at the page and recognize the significance of the moment. I recommend restraint in marking key moments; if there are too many notations such as this in a full-length play, they might lose their usefulness. Select smaller key moments carefully but feature the major key moments prominently, using a larger triangle for the major climaxes.

Occasionally, it might be useful to extend a bracket to the preceding dialogue to indicate where the key moment begins to escalate.

Let us analyse the scene in Act 1 of *The Importance of Being Earnest*, in which Jack proposes to Gwendolen, so that we can see how the key moment relates to actions, objectives, shifts, and obstacles. Several moments appear to be significant in this unit. From the standpoint of humour, the line in which Jack inadvertently admits that he will need to be christened as Ernest to satisfy Gwendolen's obsession with that name is likely to be the biggest laugh in the scene. If the laughs overwhelm the emotional stakes of the scene, however, we might lose the thread of the narrative. Therefore, I would suggest that the most effective choice of key moment might be Jack's actual proposal and Gwendolen's acceptance. In a more traditional and realistic proposal, the *acceptance* might be the key moment, but as Gwendolen has already told Jack she intends to accept, I think the key moment is *when* he proposes.

If this is the key moment, then the actions and objectives should propel the characters in that direction. Jack's objective, framed as a desired response from Gwendolen, is for her to agree to marry him; Gwendolen's objective is for Jack to propose to her. There seems to be little conflict and no obstacles, and one might expect that the action will be easy, restrained only by the characters' nerves. But there are clearly other obstacles. Gwendolen's mother, who is obsessed with social status and has not yet fully approved of Jack, is in the next room (surroundings). Algernon, who has taken his aunt, Lady Bracknell, into the next room to distract her, is impulsive and unpredictable, fully capable of encouraging her to interrupt the couple at the most inopportune time, just to amuse himself. Finally, Gwendolen appears to be obsessed with appearances. Jack, whom she knows as Ernest, must have the right name and must propose in the proper fashion (character).

In response to these obstacles, each character might alter his or her original strategy (overall unit action) in favour of a different tactic – a shift. Remember, strategies (overall actions) are for the long term, persisting for at least one unit, whereas tactics (shifts) are short term and more immediate, responsive to the obstacles that a character discovers in a unit. With rare exception, and regardless of a character's strength, almost all dramatic situations require and benefit from varied tactics – shifts in action in response to obstacles.[5]

Once again, we will mark shifts with an 'S' in a circle [Ⓢ], in the margin to the right side of the dialogue or above the precise line, dialogue, or word at

---

[5]The most common exceptions are characters that are emotionally stunted or intellectually limited, and characters whose single-minded pursuit of the same action might be used for comedy, such as Sir Andrew in *Twelfth Night*.

which point the shift occurs. After the shift mark, write the new action verb. For example, in the last scene we analysed, from *Hedda Gabler*, if Tesman had been playing the action 'brags' while marvelling at how well things have been going for him, we might mark a shift after he discovers that Løvborg has released a new book:

TESMAN What! Eilert Løvborg? You mean – just recently?
    What?   Ⓢ **challenges**

In this way, although Tesman might still be pursuing the same objective from his aunt – perhaps to celebrate with her – the obstacle from newly discovered present circumstances (Eilert's book) forces him to change his tactics.

Returning to the unit in *Earnest* in which Jack proposes to Gwendolen, our unit analysis might look something like this:

Unit 1.7: May I propose to you now?

> Jack wants to impress Gwendolen so that she will accept his proposal. Gwendolen wants to train Jack so that he will propose perfectly.

JACK   Charming day it has been, Miss Fairfax.
GWENDOLEN   Pray don't talk to me about the weather, Mr. Worthing. Whenever people talk to me about the weather, I always feel quite certain that they mean something else. And that makes me so nervous.
JACK   I do mean something else.
GWENDOLEN   I thought so. In fact, I am never wrong.
JACK   And I would like to be allowed to take advantage of Lady Bracknell's temporary absence . . .
GWENDOLEN   I would certainly advise you to do so. Mamma has a way of coming back suddenly into a room that I have often had to speak to her about.
JACK [Nervously]   Miss Fairfax, ever since I met you I have admired you more than any girl . . . I have ever met since . . . I met you.
GWENDOLEN   Yes, I am quite well aware of the fact. And I often wish that in public, at any rate, you had been more demonstrative. For me you have always had an irresistible fascination. Even before I met you I was far from indifferent to you [Jack looks at her in amazement]. We live, as I hope you know, Mr. Worthing, in an age of ideals. The fact is constantly mentioned in the more expensive monthly magazines, and has reached the provincial pulpits, I am told; and my ideal has always been to love some one of the name of Ernest. There is something in that name that inspires absolute confidence. The moment Algernon first mentioned to me that he had a friend called Ernest, I knew I was destined to love you.
JACK   You really love me, Gwendolen?   Ⓢ **idolizes**
GWENDOLEN   Passionately!

JACK   Darling! You don't know how happy you've made me.

GWENDOLEN   My own Ernest!

JACK   But you don't really mean to say that you couldn't love me if my name wasn't Ernest?

GWENDOLEN   But your name is Ernest.

JACK   Yes, I know it is. But supposing it was something else? Do you mean to say you couldn't love me then?

GWENDOLEN [Glibly]   Ah! that is clearly a metaphysical speculation, and like most metaphysical speculations has very little reference at all to the actual facts of real life, as we know them.   Ⓢ **proclaims**

JACK   Personally, darling, to speak quite candidly, I don't much care about the name of Ernest . . . I don't think the name suits me at all.

GWENDOLEN   It suits you perfectly. It is a divine name. It has a music of its own. It produces vibrations.   Ⓢ **inflames**

JACK   Well, really, Gwendolen, I must say that I think there are lots of other much nicer names. I think Jack, for instance, a charming name.

GWENDOLEN   Jack? . . . No, there is very little music in the name Jack, if any at all, indeed. It does not thrill. It produces absolutely no vibrations . . . I have known several Jacks, and they all, without exception, were more than usually plain. Besides, Jack is a notorious domesticity for John! And I pity any woman who is married to a man called John. She would probably never be allowed to know the entrancing pleasure of a single moment's solitude. The only really safe name is Ernest.

JACK   Gwendolen, I must get christened at once – I mean we must get married at once. There is no time to be lost.   Ⓢ **rushes**

GWENDOLEN   Married, Mr. Worthing?

JACK [Astounded]   Well . . . surely. You know that I love you, and you led me to believe, Miss Fairfax, that you were not absolutely indifferent to me.

GWENDOLEN   I adore you. But you haven't proposed to me yet. Nothing has been said at all about marriage. The subject has not even been touched on.

JACK   Well . . . may I propose to you now?   Ⓢ **tests**

GWENDOLEN   I think it would be an admirable opportunity.
   And to spare you any possible disappointment, Mr. Worthing,
   I think it only fair to tell you quite frankly beforehand that
   I am fully determined to accept you.

JACK   Gwendolen!

GWENDOLEN   Yes, Mr. Worthing, what have you got
   to say to me?   K

JACK   You know what I have got to say to you.

GWENDOLEN   Yes, but you don't say it.   Ⓢ **intimidates**

JACK   Gwendolen, will you marry me? [Goes on   KEY MOMENT
   his knees]

GWENDOLEN   Of course I will, darling. How long you have been about it! I am afraid you have had very little experience in how to propose.

JACK   My own one, I have never loved anyone in the world but you.

GWENDOLEN   Yes, but men often propose for practice. I know my brother Gerald does. All my girlfriends tell me so. What wonderfully blue eyes you have, Ernest! They are quite, quite, blue. I hope you will always look at me just like that, especially when there are other people present.

I note several things about the way in which I have scored this unit. First, almost every line could be marked as a shift in action, either subtle or blatant. The key in most scenes is to avoid over-scoring the action. Aim to capture the broad shape or arc of the action, without marking so many actions as to stifle the actors' choices in rehearsal or the synthesis that occurs when two or more actors' choices combine, conflict, and create reactions and chain reactions. When you see an action and reaction, always try to mark the first action, as the reaction should come about in rehearsal naturally. By marking the earlier action, you will also note the instigator of the action: the character or actor who first shifts his or her tactics and stimulates a reaction from the other character or actor.

Yet frequently, such moments can be scored in more than way. For example, about half a page into the dialogue, Gwendolen declares, 'The moment Algernon first mentioned to me that he had a friend called Ernest, I knew I was destined to love you'. In response, Jack replies, 'You really love me, Gwendolen?' I mark Jack's response as a shift in action from his overall action in the unit, 'impress', to a new action, 'idolize', because I can still imagine Gwendolen playing her original action, 'to train Jack', on her declaration of love. In truth, her line is not as clear of a declaration of love as Jack takes it to be. Gwendolen says she knew she was destined to love Jack (Ernest) before she had met him – simply upon hearing that Algernon had a friend with the name Ernest. Only after Jack asks her whether she loves him does Gwendolen say, 'Passionately'. For this reason, I see her 'declaration of love' as part of her overall unit action, 'to train Jack so that he'll propose perfectly'. Then I see Jack shift his action to 'idolize', which is a step in the right direction, from Gwendolen's point of view. In this reading of the scene, Gwendolen wins the first point, by successfully training Jack and forcing him to shift his action accordingly.

Scoring the key moment in the unit – the literal 'peak' – helps us find the escalation of action leading to it. In this unit, Gwendolen expresses her frustration at Jack's inability to propose properly in her shift to the action 'intimidates' on her line, 'Yes, but you don't say it', and then playfully teases him after he finally proposes with her line, 'Of course I will, darling. How long you have been about it! I am afraid you have had very little experience in how to propose.' Her two shifts, in my analysis, help define the key moment in which Jack proposes, between Gwendolen's intimidation and her teasing of him.

Relationships

We begin to analyse a **relationship** between two characters from facts that the playwright provides through stage directions and dialogue. The text provides a wealth of information, which offers a starting point, or baseline, for each basic relationship in the play. We can then get more precise by examining the changes in a relationship in a particular unit by looking at the characters' social positions, where a scene takes place, and the subject matter of their conversation. Finally, we can examine a relationship in even greater detail by analysing how the characters treat each other from moment to moment. To describe these moment-by-moment changes in a relationship, we will use a concept, **status**, developed by British improvisation and playwriting teacher Keith Johnstone to analyse the ways in which characters raise or lower themselves relative to others.

When we examine how two characters relate, we start by describing the **generic** and **specific relationship**. The generic relationship characterizes the first level of analysis: the type of relationship and its general circumstances. Ask yourself, 'What type of relationship is this?' Think generically – a class, type, or group. In *Hedda Gabler*, we would note that Tesman and Hedda are husband and wife. In *Oedipus the King*, Oedipus and Jocasta are husband and wife, yet they are also mother and son, although they do not realize it until the end of the play. In *A Streetcar Named Desire*, Stanley and Blanche are brother-and sister-in-law. In each case, the characters' social positions further detail the relationship.

Hedda's more affluent upbringing shapes her relationship with Tesman, who comes from more humble roots – she is the daughter of a respected general; he was raised by his poor aunt, Miss Tesman. Their class difference still weighs on Miss Tesman, who divulges her reverence of Hedda, bordering on fear, in her exchange at the top of Act 1 with her former maid, Bertha,[6] whom Miss Tesman has provided to the young couple:

> BERTHA   But, Miss Juju, there's another thing. I'm frightened madam may not find me suitable.
>
> MISS TESMAN   Oh, nonsense, Bertha. There may be one or two little things to begin with –
>
> BERTHA   She's a real lady. Wants everything just so.

---

[6]Meyer anglicizes the Norwegian 'Berta' to 'Bertha'. For a quick look at the dramaturgy of translations, compare the excerpts from Meyer's British translation to any other translation of *Hedda Gabler*.

MISS TESMAN   But of course she does! General Gabler's daughter! Think of what she was accustomed to when the general was alive. You remember how we used to see her out riding with her father? In that long black skirt? With the feather in her hat?

BERTHA   Oh, yes, miss. As if I could forget! But, Lord! I never dreamed I'd live to see a match between her and Master George.

MISS TESMAN   Neither did I. By the way, Bertha, from now on you must stop calling him Master George. You must say Dr. Tesman.

Note the way that Miss Tesman counters their awe of Hedda's social position with her nephew's newly earned title, doctor (for his Ph.D.). This early exposition sets up the relative status of several characters and exposes the class differences that define the starting points for several characters' relationships with Hedda: Bertha, Miss Tesman, and George Tesman.

Later in Act 1, the following exchange reveals that Tesman and his aunt find Hedda's stature and beauty intimidating, but attractive, as these qualities raise their status in the eyes of George's friends and, presumably, within their social circle:

MISS TESMAN [With a sudden change of mood]   Oh, but, George, fancy you being a married man! And to think it's you who've won Hedda Gabler! The beautiful Hedda Gabler! Fancy! She was always surrounded by admirers.

TESMAN [Hums a little and smiles contentedly]   Yes, I suppose there are quite a few people in this town who wouldn't mind being in my shoes. What?

We might say that Tesman is insecure about not being good enough for her, or that he thinks of her as a great 'catch'. Similarly, Oedipus does not believe he is a natural-born Theban, but he is king of Thebes, so we might say that he overcompensates, at times, by pressing Creon, Tiresias, and the shepherds for information more obstinately than a native king might feel appropriate to his rank.

Blanche was born to a higher class than Stanley, and throughout the first act of *Streetcar*, she clings desperately to the trappings of her past life. But in scene 7, after Stanley has investigated Blanche's past in her hometown, he can see that their social positions have reversed, once he realizes that she has lost her social status and ruined her own reputation:

STANLEY   The trouble with Dame Blanche was that she couldn't put on her act any more in Laurel! They got wised up after two or three dates with her and then they quit, and she goes on to another, the same old act,

same old hooey! But the town was too small for this to go on forever! And as time went by she became a town character. Regarded as not just different but downright loco – nuts.
STELLA *draws back*
And for the last year or two she has been washed up like poison. That's why she's here this summer, visiting royalty, putting on all this act – because she's practically told by the mayor to get out of town! (lines 68–76)

Stanley now sees Blanche's behaviour differently. It is not that of a woman born into money and enjoying a relaxed, high status; it is that of a fallen woman trying her best to keep up the pretence that she is still a woman of means, above Stanley and his rowdy, uncouth crowd. Now Stanley's relationship with Blanche changes – from trying to catch an aristocratic woman in a lie designed to hide her wealth and property from her sister, to trying to tear down a crazy woman with a bad reputation before she can get her hooks into his best friend, Mitch.

When we analyse a **specific relationship**, we can zoom in even further on the relationship at the start of a particular scene. Let us look at how the location of a scene can affect specific relationships. Hedda and Tesman live in a house they cannot afford, in a part of town where Hedda feels more comfortable than Tesman, though Hedda confesses to Judge Brack that she secretly hates the house. Moreover, Brack made the arrangements to purchase the house, and Miss Tesman put up her pension for collateral to purchase the furnishings. For these reasons, it is not a house that Hedda can fully enjoy, and for most of the play she is stuck there, unable to afford to invite over anyone from her larger circle of friends, once Brack informs George and Hedda that George might have to compete for his once-promised professorship. The financial pressure caused by the cost of the house and its furnishings creates a great deal of tension between Hedda and the other characters, changing her relationships with Brack and Miss Tesman in particular to ones in which she owes them something – a debt that will come back to haunt her in Act 4.

Oedipus speaks to Creon in front of the palace, a public seat of power, with citizens hearing and witnessing every public word and deed. As king, he feels superior to everyone whom he interacts with at the start of the play – even his brother-in-law, Creon, with whom he technically shares power. Yet by the end of the play, his relationship with Creon has changed, as Creon becomes king and Oedipus is about to be banished from Thebes; the public nature of their power transition only amplifies the shift in their relationship from near-equals to king and banished subject.

In *Streetcar*, the Kowalskis live in a vibrant, loud, freewheeling part of New Orleans, multicultural and raucous – a very uncomfortable place for Blanche to attempt to cling to her last shred of dignity. The tight quarters of the first floor one-bedroom apartment render Blanche more vulnerable to Stanley, particularly as he learns more about her past. The lack of a bedroom door combined with the folding cot that the Kowalskis provide for Blanche to sleep on accentuate the temporary quality of her residence and her lack of privacy, as displayed in the first scene:

BLANCHE   What kind of bed's this – one of those collapsible things?
   She sits on it
STELLA   Does it feel alright?
BLANCHE [Dubiously]   Wonderful, honey. I don't like a bed that gives much. But there's no door between the two rooms, and Stanley – will it be decent? (lines 161–164)

To further analyse a specific relationship in a scene, we next look at the subject matter. Each of the relationships above changes depending upon what has been happening just before a scene, and then the subject matter of the scene further changes the relationship. Hedda and Tesman are husband and wife, but more specifically, they are newlyweds arriving in their new home for the first time, after a long European honeymoon. In Act 1, Hedda likely knows that she is pregnant, and Tesman appears to suspect as much, as shown in the following exchange, in which he implies that Hedda is pregnant to distract his aunt after Hedda has insulted her new hat and parasol:

TESMAN   But, Auntie Juju, take a good look at Hedda before you go. Isn't she pretty and charming?
MISS TESMAN   Dear boy, there's nothing new in that. Hedda's been a beauty since the day she was born [Nods and goes right].
TESMAN [Follows her]   Yes, but have you noticed how strong and healthy she's looking? And how she's filled out since we went away?
MISS TESMAN [Stops and turns]   Filled out?
HEDDA [Walks across the room]   Oh, can't we forget it?
TESMAN   Yes, Auntie Juju – you can't see it so clearly with that dress on. But I've good reason to know –
HEDDA [By the French windows, impatiently]   You haven't good reason to know anything!
TESMAN   It must have been the mountain air up there in the Tyrol –
HEDDA [Curtly, interrupts him]   I'm exactly the same as when I went away.
TESMAN   You keep saying so. But you're not. I'm right, aren't I, Auntie Juju?

The subject matter, Hedda's body and health, and its implication that the couple might already be expecting a child change Hedda and Tesman's relationship from the general description 'newlywed husband and wife' and the more specific 'in a new home that they owe to Brack and Miss Tesman'. Merely the suggestion of her pregnancy affects her relationship with her husband and his aunt. Hedda snaps at Tesman immediately, perhaps because she does not want to be a mother (which she will later tell Brack), or because she dreads the changes to her body and her lifestyle that a baby would bring. In any case, in this moment in Act 1 we can see how the subject matter of Hedda's body and possible pregnancy exposes Hedda's vulnerability, and how this changes her relationships with the characters in this scene, particularly Miss Tesman, who goes from being fearful of Hedda to becoming protective and motherly. A baby will give Miss Tesman something new to live for – someone to take care of – now that her nephew/adopted son, George, has moved out of her home.

We can trace how the specific relationship between Hedda and Tesman changes throughout the play, whenever the subject matter of their conversations shifts. At the end of Act 1, when Brack reveals that Hedda's old flame Løvborg has released a new book and might be competing for the job as professor that had been all but promised to Tesman, Tesman panics – suddenly worried because he married Hedda and borrowed money to buy the house based on his belief that the job was his. Yet Hedda, perversely, seems to get a thrill at the prospect of her husband's competition against her old flame.

> TESMAN   No, but – Judge Brack, they couldn't be so inconsiderate towards me! [Waves his arms] I mean, by Jove, I – I'm a married man! It was on the strength of this that Hedda and I *got* married! We've run up some pretty hefty debts. And borrowed money from Auntie Juju! I mean, good heavens, they practically promised me the appointment. What?
> BRACK   Well, well, I'm sure you'll get it. But you'll have to go through a competition.
> HEDDA [Motionless in her armchair]   How exciting, Tesman. It'll be a kind of duel, by Jove.
> TESMAN   My dear Hedda, how can you take it so lightly!
> HEDDA [As before]   I'm not. I can't wait to see who's going to win.

Suddenly the details of Hedda and Tesman's relationship have changed again in reaction to the news that Løvborg might compete for the job that Tesman believed was his. Excited by the news of the competition, Hedda appears to be empowered again. Tesman, apparently shocked by Hedda's reaction to the news, is stripped of the swagger that her pregnancy afforded him at the start of the scene. Instead of bragging about expecting a baby, he now worries about the cost of raising a child if he is not gainfully employed. Rather than disregard his wife's concerns, he shifts to a term of endearment, 'my dear Hedda', in a desperate attempt to secure her as an ally.

In *Streetcar*, the specifics of place do not change, as all the action occurs in the Kowalskis' apartment. But the particulars of subject matter change the specific relationships greatly from scene to scene. Consider two scenes involving Stanley and Blanche. We have described their general relationship as brother- and sister-in-law. We have observed that the setting – a cramped, one-bedroom apartment with very little to protect Blanche from the sounds of New Orleans nightlife and nothing between the bedroom and living room to shield Blanche from the sounds of Stanley and Stella's intimacies – makes Blanche more vulnerable in her relationships, particularly her relationship with Stanley. New Orleans is Stanley's turf; his poker buddies occupy the apartment with their colourful shirts and off-colour language in scene 3. Only when Stanley is out can Blanche use her paper lantern to dim the lights for her slow seduction of Mitch. Yet the subject matter of each scene hones the specific relationship.

Towards the end of scene 2, Stanley and Stella have a unit alone (lines 175–239), in which Stanley rifles through Blanche's trunk in search of the papers for Belle Reve, the DuBois family estate. Stanley finds the papers but also comes across intimate poems written by Blanche's late husband. The subject matter of the unit – touching upon the 'epic fornications' of Blanche's and Stella's grandfathers and father, the loss of Belle Reve by foreclosure, and the poems – increases Blanche's vulnerability, which she tries to ward off at the start of the next unit with a flirtatious mist of perfume. For this reason, though their general relationship is sister- and brother-in-law, in this unit their relationship is more specifically vulnerable and flirtatious, a feeling that will come to a head in scene 10, when Stanley, drunk and exuberant about the imminent birth of his first child, crosses the line and rapes Blanche.

For *Hedda Gabler* and *Streetcar*, I would note the general relationship for the play and the specific relationship for each scene on a character blueprint, so that I can see the changes in the relationship. Our blueprints for the case study relationships might look something like this:

Hedda-Tesman

Generic relationship	
Type	Husband and wife. Newlyweds.
Social positions	Hedda's father was a general, highly respected. Tesman's poor aunts raised him. Most people consider Hedda out of his league.
Specific relationship	
Place	Their home, heavily mortgaged, set up by Judge Brack and Tesman's aunt, Miss Tesman.
Subject matter	Act 1, lines 272–285: Tesman implies that Hedda is pregnant, which irritates Hedda but empowers Tesman. Act 1, lines 749–760: Brack tells them that Løvborg might compete for the professorship Tesman thought was his. This weakens Tesman and empowers Hedda, who loves the idea of her old flame and husband in a competition.

Stanley-Blanche

Generic relationship	
Type	Brother-in-law/sister-in-law
Social positions	Stanley is a working-class Polish immigrant. Blanche was raised as Southern aristocracy and considers Stanley beneath her.
Specific relationship	
Place	New Orleans. A loud and raucous district in the city with a multicultural, working-class population. A basement apartment with no door to the single bedroom.
Subject matter	Lines 175–239: Stanley goes through Blanche's possessions, trying to put her on the defensive, but she still holds to some semblance of her superiority because he does not know her secret yet. Scene 10: Emboldened by liquor, Mitch's rejection of Blanche, and the impending birth of his first son, Stanley feels invincible.

Status

Now let us consider **status,** a concept that Johnstone originally used to describe the relative standing of two characters within a scene. Focusing on status helps give shape and definition to improvisations, enhances a scene and benefits all theatre artists, as it can be applied to playwriting and design as well as acting and directing.[7] It is essential to realize that status is always in flux, so we can examine the action for the continual moment-to-moment raising and lowering of character status: one character raises or lowers the other, the other responds in kind. Most characters have a baseline status that they play most of the time, but that status changes depending upon whom they are paired with and where the action takes place. Think of the self-confident politician who plays high status to his or her colleagues at the statehouse – and low status to his or her partner in the kitchen. Or the young doctor who plays high-status expert with patients at a hospital – but extremely low status to the attending doctor or to the other senior doctors when he or she is presenting a case.

When analysing status in a scene or unit, note the overall status between two characters and then look for the most significant moments when status changes. Mark these moments succinctly and sparingly in the margins of the script: Hedda lowers Tesman, Hedda raises Tesman, Hedda lowers herself to Tesman, or Hedda raises herself above Tesman (In his classic book *Impro*, Johnstone describes the many physical and vocal indications for changes in status, from

---

[7] A high-status character will often dress differently than a low-status one. Think of the status implications of what we wear to work: a doctor's white lab coat, a lawyer's pinstripe suit, the police officer's uniform, the fitness instructor's tights. All are symbols of status; many bring attention to certain physical features and help create a façade or project a quality or quantity of power.

posture to vocal patterns. For the purposes of analysis, I am less concerned with these, though I highly recommend his book for actors and directors alike.). We can employ simple marking when looking at the status shifts in one of our case study plays, Shakespeare's *Twelfth Night*.

Let us examine the relationship between Olivia's steward Malvolio and her clown, Feste. Neither is a high-status character; each owes his status to his relationship to Olivia, a countess. Malvolio appears to be her chief steward and secretly has a crush on her – one that is only intensified by his discovery of a prank letter left behind by Sir Toby and his gang of mischief-makers to imply that Olivia might hold romantic feelings for Malvolio. As for Feste, in Shakespeare's plays, clowns hold a special status. Although they serve as entertainment for royalty, their status as entertainers is a double-edged sword: they are lower status by virtue of their profession, but because no one takes them seriously, they can say things to royalty that other characters cannot. Shakespeare's clowns often break through status barriers because the nature of a clown is to slip back and forth across the borders of propriety.[8]

Now we will examine a scene that involves Olivia, Feste, and Malvolio, Act 1, scene 5 (lines 29–104). After Maria warns Feste that Olivia is upset with him, Feste greets Olivia (with Malvolio in waiting) and tries to amuse her so as to put himself back into her good graces after a prolonged absence. After some successful banter with Olivia, she turns to Malvolio and asks him his opinion of Feste's foolery, and Feste and Malvolio match wits briefly:

OLIVIA   What think you of this fool, Malvolio? doth he not mend?

MALVOLIO   Yes, and shall do till the pangs of death shake him: infirmity, that decays the wise, doth ever make the better fool.

FESTE   God send you, sir, a speedy infirmity, for the better increasing your folly! Sir Toby will be sworn that I am no fox; but he will not pass his word for two pence that you are no fool.

OLIVIA   How say you to that, Malvolio?

MALVOLIO   I marvel your ladyship takes delight in such a barren rascal: I saw him put down the other day with an ordinary fool that has no more brain than a stone. Look you now, he's out of his guard already; unless you laugh and minister occasion to him, he is gagged. I protest, I take these wise men, that crow so at these set kind of fools, no better than the fools' zanies.

OLIVIA   Oh, you are sick of self-love, Malvolio, and taste with a distempered appetite. To be generous, guiltless and of free disposition, is to take those things for bird-bolts that you deem cannon-bullets: there is no slander in

---

[8]In contemporary television, this has allowed American comedians such as Bill Maher, Jon Stewart, and Stephen Colbert, and British comedians such as Eddie Izzard and Russell Howard, to be more aggressive in their political critiques than the most acerbic political journalists.

an allowed fool, though he do nothing but rail; nor no railing in a known
discreet man, though he do nothing but reprove.

FESTE   Now Mercury endue thee with leasing, for thou speakest well of
fools! (lines 67–92)

In this brief interchange, Malvolio enters the scene with higher status than
Feste: He holds an inherently more serious position in Olivia's court, and Feste
is in trouble for having been absent for so long. But when Feste succeeds in
amusing her just before the lines quoted above, Olivia's approval raises Feste's
status, and Malvolio feels threatened and lowered in relationship to Feste.
Malvolio tries to raise his status above that of Feste, but he tries too hard, and
when Olivia chastises him, she lowers him and raises Feste once again.

I might note that Malvolio and Feste are each of lower status than their
employer, Olivia, and that they are dependent upon her approval for their status
in any scene. That should add dynamics to any scene that the three of them
share. If, however, they are surrounded by Sir Toby and his gang (as in Act 2,
scene 3), all of whom despise and ridicule Malvolio and support Feste, then Feste
enjoys higher status and Malvolio must try very hard to assert his higher status.

Gathering the status information above, I would write down overall status as
part of my notes on the relationship between Malvolio and Feste:

Status	Overall, Malvolio enjoys higher status within Olivia's court than Feste. But when Feste's jokes please Olivia, or when a sympathetic audience surrounds him, he raises himself above Malvolio. Further, when Malvolio takes himself too seriously, he risks lowering his status to Feste.

I would then note the major status changes in the margins of the script, as we
see in Act 1, scene 5, lines 84–90. A simple note in the margin, 'Olivia lowers
Malvolio', is enough to remind a director, actor, or designer of this important
shift in status and the glee in Feste's response that follows.

Language

A playwright's choice of words and phrasing for characters provides a wealth
of information for theatre artists, but it often remains unexplored, awaiting
analysis. It frequently acts upon actors subconsciously, the word choices
and rhythms of a play exerting their influence just by being spoken. Some
playwrights make characters' voices so clearly stylized that the use of language
is impossible to miss (among classic playwrights, think of Shakespeare and
Molière). But as theatre artists, we should be sensitive to language in all
modern plays, though it might be more evident in the colloquial language

of August Wilson, the stylized language of Suzan-Lori Parks, and the poetic
language of Tennessee Williams, to mention just a few. In this section, we will
focus on Shakespeare's *Twelfth Night* and Wilson's *Fences* to analyse.

Shakespeare and his contemporaries used verse in their plays for several
reasons, some artistic and some pragmatic. Because verse has such a clear
rhythm, it is, by and large, easier to memorize than prose. Given that
Elizabethan theatre companies performed plays in true repertory fashion – a
different play each night of the week – and with very little rehearsal, verse
served a pragmatic aim, making it easier for the actors to recall their lines.
But Elizabethan playwrights used verse to achieve their artistic aims as well.
Shakespeare tended to use verse for upper-class characters and more formal
situations; prose was the province of lower-class characters, fools, and clowns.
In *Twelfth Night*, the upper-class characters, Duke Orsino, Olivia, Viola, and
Sebastian, speak mostly in verse; it lends them an air of sophistication, wealth,
and prestige. But the servants Malvolio, Maria, and Fabian speak almost
entirely in prose (with one notable exception); Feste the clown speaks entirely
in prose, although his language displays the extraordinary word play of his
trade; and Sir Toby and Sir Andrew, although upper class, speak in prose, an
indication of their drunkenness, comic nature, and ultimate status as fools. The
contrast between Sir Toby's and Sir Andrew's class and use of language reveals
their lower status in the world of the play.

Because Shakespeare wrote in a particular type of verse (iambic pentameter),
his manipulation of language and decisions about who speaks in verse or prose
and when provide us with a wealth of opportunity to explore language. Let us
start by looking at three passages from *Twelfth Night*, beginning with Olivia,
Act 3, scene 1, lines 144–155:

> OLIVIA   O, what a deal of scorn looks beautiful
>   In the contempt and anger of his lip!
>   A murderous guilt shows not itself more soon
>   Than love that would seem hid: love's night is noon.
>   Cesario, by the roses of the spring,
>   By maidhood, honour, truth and every thing,
>   I love thee so, that, maugre all thy pride,
>   Nor wit nor reason can my passion hide.
>   Do not extort thy reasons from this clause,
>   For that I woo, thou therefore hast no cause,
>   But rather reason thus with reason fetter,
>   Love sought is good, but given unsought better.

The first thing we notice is the way Shakespeare arranges Olivia's speech on
the page. Even the most casual reader of Shakespeare can see that her speech is
written in verse, as evidenced by the jagged edge formed by the ends of each line

and the capitalization of each line, even if it does not begin a sentence. In every Shakespearean play, he alternates prose and verse, creating a linguistic pattern.

In the first four lines of Olivia's speech, she addresses the audience directly. The rest of her speech to Cesario is in rhyming couplets, giving the passage a singsong quality that functions much as a song in a musical: Olivia is so impassioned that she speaks in rhymes. We might also see Olivia's use of rhyming couplets as an indication that she is deliberately wooing Cesario with poetry.

To fully understand the passage, we need to know the precise meanings of the words Shakespeare chose during this time. If an actor understands the meaning, he or she will be able to communicate it even if a modern audience does not easily grasp the meaning of all the words. Numerous annotated editions of Shakespeare are available to help us understand the meaning of his more antiquated and colloquial words, but most professional Shakespearean actors prefer to look up confusing words in several reference sources. David and Ben Crystal's *Shakespeare's Words* defines more than 14,000 words for contemporary theatre artists and readers, with precise notations of the different meanings of each word in particular plays. Alexander Schmidt's bulkier two-volume *Shakespeare Lexicon and Quotation Dictionary,* which covers three times as many words and quotations, remains the gold standard for the most exacting theatre artist.[9] Eric Partridge's *Shakespeare's Bawdy* covers most of Shakespeare's sexual and scatological references, making it an indispensable source, particularly as most editors tend purposefully or inadvertently to conceal the dirtier sides of his plays.

Olivia's speech contains a number of words that had more specific meanings in the Elizabethan era than in ours:

Maidhood:	virginity (*Bawdy* 143)
Honour:	reputation (*Words* 226) or female chastity (*Bawdy* 122)
Maugre:	in spite of (*Words* 277)
Wit:	cunning plan, intelligence (*Words* 500)
Reason:	(*v.*) debate the pros and cons; (*n.*) common sense, as opposed to passion (*Words* 364)
Passion:	sexual love, physical desire (*Bawdy* 158)
Nor … nor:	neither, nor (*Words* 298)
Fetter:	suppress (*Words* 174)

When we discover the original meanings of these words, we see that Olivia's speech is more impassioned than we might suspect: she appears to be trying to

---

[9]C.T. Onions's *A Shakespeare Glossary* covers a good deal of the same territory but is much shorter and lighter, making it a valuable book to bring to rehearsal.

seduce Cesario in a more suggestive or explicitly sexual way than the formality of the rhyming couplets might suggest, offering her virginity, sacrificing her pride, and declaring her love in the absence of any indication that Cesario is interested in her ('Love sought is good, but given unsought better.').

Beyond the meaning of the words, Shakespeare's language reveals several patterns that shape the rhythm and flow of Olivia's speech. First, Shakespeare has written Olivia's speech in iambic pentameter, his dominant verse form, in which a standard line has ten or eleven syllables broken down into five ('penta') feet ('meters'). Each foot has two or three syllables, the most common being an 'iamb', a foot with two syllables, the first unstressed and the second stressed. Actors call the analysis of verse for stress patterns 'scansion'. With rare exception, scansion reveals that the stressed syllables fall where they would in an actor's natural pronunciation of the words; if well delivered, the lines frequently sound less poetic than they appear to be on the page because the iambic stress pattern is close to the natural patterns created by the English language. The most common three-syllable foot is a feminine ending to a line of verse in which, in place of a standard iamb, Shakespeare adds a third unstressed syllable, as in the last two lines of this speech:

But rather reason thus with reason fetter,
Love sought is good, but given unsought better.

Both lines have eleven syllables, ending in words that rhyme and naturally finish on the unstressed '-er'.

Olivia's language displays another pattern: the pauses and full stops created by its sentence structure, including all punctuation. If we break down the speech into sentences, we can see this pattern to Shakespeare's use of language:

O, what a deal of scorn looks beautiful in the contempt and anger of his lip!
    A murderous guilt shows not itself more soon than love that would seem hid: love's night is noon.
    Cesario, by the roses of the spring, by maidhood, honour, truth and every thing, I love thee so, that, maugre all thy pride, nor wit nor reason can my passion hide.
    Do not extort thy reasons from this clause, for that I woo, thou therefore hast no cause, but rather reason thus with reason fetter, love sought is good, but given unsought better.

The first two sentences are relatively short, punctuated by only four marks: a comma after the first word ('O'), an exclamation point at the end of the first sentence, a colon before the final clause ('love's night is noon'), and a period at the end of the second sentence. These lines, which appear to be addressed to the audience, then give way to much longer sentences to Cesario with multiple commas – to my eyes and ears, an indication that Olivia is forgoing any restraint she had been exercising in her pursuit of him. In the last sentence, we might also note Shakespeare's use of alliteration ('rather reason') and antithesis ('sought...unsought'), which further shapes the sound of Olivia's speech in performance.

Towards the end of Act 5, Malvolio confronts Olivia, believing that a love letter she left for him led to his humiliation:

> MALVOLIO   Madam, you have done me wrong,
>   Notorious wrong.
> OLIVIA   Have I, Malvolio? no.
> MALVOLIO   Lady, you have. Pray you peruse that letter:
>   You must not now deny it is your hand:
>   Write from it, if you can, in hand or phrase;
>   Or say 'tis not your seal, not your invention:
>   You can say none of this. Well, grant it then,
>   And tell me, in the modesty of honour,
>   Why you have given me such clear lights of favour;
>   Bade me come smiling and cross-garter'd to you;
>   To put on yellow stockings, and to frown
>   Upon Sir Toby and the lighter people;
>   And, acting this in an obedient hope,
>   Why have you suffer'd me to be imprison'd,
>   Kept in a dark house, visited by the priest,
>   And made the most notorious geck and gull
>   That e'er invention played on? tell me why. (lines 294–310)

This is the only time in the play that Shakespeare has Malvolio speak in verse. Why? We might conclude that the setting for this scene, in front of Olivia's and Orsino's entire courts, demands that Malvolio speak more formally to her, despite his extreme embarrassment and anger. The use of verse might indicate that Malvolio is clinging to his last shred of self-control to confront Olivia. Finally, in the sentence structure within the verse, there are two relatively short sentences, followed by an extremely long one, which suggests that halfway through this confrontation, Malvolio unleashes the full fury of his frustration:

> Well, grant it then, and tell me, in the modesty of honour, why you have given me such clear lights of favour; bade me come smiling and cross-garter'd to you; to put on yellow stockings, and to frown upon Sir Toby and the lighter people; and, acting this in an obedient hope, why have you suffer'd me to be imprison'd, kept in a dark house, visited by the priest, and made the most notorious geck and gull that e'er invention played on? tell me why.

In this rant, the verse structure and punctuation – specifically, the commas and semicolons – help the actor playing Malvolio break this speech into chunks that will be easier to handle, in both meaning and breathing. I would also note Shakespeare's deliberate use of a lower case 't' in Malvolio's final sentence, 'tell me why', which might suggest that he has run out of steam and can no longer muster the courage to confront her as powerfully as when he started. In any case, it is an extremely long sentence, with Shakespeare's verse lines and punctuation helping define the shape and flow of the speech in performance.

Most contemporary playwrights write in prose, yet their dialogue frequently plays with many of the same elements we have seen in Shakespeare's verse: emphasis, suggestive or symbolic meaning, rhythm, punctuation, and sentence length. In Act 1, scene 1 of Wilson's *Fences*, for example, when Rose Maxson worries that her husband, Troy, will drink himself to death, Troy compares death to a fastball, using baseball to argue that his fearlessness at the plate proves his courage in the face of death:

> Death ain't nothing. I done seen him. Done wrassled with him. You can't tell me nothing about death. Death ain't nothing but a fastball on the outside corner. And you know what I'll do to that! Lookee here, Bono . . . am I lying? You get one of them fastballs, about waist high, over the outside corner of the plate where you can get the meat of the bat on it . . . and good god! You can kiss it goodbye. (lines 185–190)

I would first note Wilson's repeated use of the word 'death', which echoes through the first half of the speech but disappears in the second half. Next, I would observe that the speech starts with seven short lines, followed by the long line, 'You get one of those fastballs. . . .' The length and location of this sentence indicate its prominence, whereas Troy's comparison of death to a fastball calls upon the actor's vocal and emotional power, undermining Troy's bravado with the shallowness of the analogy: he describes a pitch he believes he can hit out of the park, not the most difficult one. By the time Troy finishes describing how he hit the pitch, he no longer mentions death; by fantasizing about his glory days as a ballplayer, he has completely lost track of the original subject, death.

Tempo and rhythm

A playwright's use of language not only offers us a great deal of information about a play's characters, their status, and their education, it also suggests ways in which an ensemble may further shape the action of the play through tempo and rhythm. We have already seen how Shakespeare's decisions about when to use verse or prose alter the flow of a scene. Before we go any further, though, I would like to get more specific about the meaning of tempo and rhythm, as these words are often conflated. I will add into the mix two additional terms that we frequently hear in the theatre: pacing and momentum.

Let us start with tempo and rhythm. Simply put, **tempo** refers to speed, whereas **rhythm** reflects pattern. To describe the tempo of a unit of a play, we use words on a continuum from slow to fast: very slow, slow, medium, fast, very fast. We might also think of a metaphor for speed, such as 'at a snail's pace' for a unit that is extremely slow, or 'lightning fast' for a unit that is as fast as one can imagine playing it.

When we seek to describe rhythm, we're looking for words that describe the pattern created by moments of emphasis or by the alternation of faster and slower moments within a unit. If you have been trained in ballet or orchestral dance music, you might use terminology such as waltz, mazurka, or tarantella; for example, in a waltz, the music is in triple meter, emphasizing the first chord in each measure. Classical music offers terms such as accelerando (increasing tempo) and time signatures that specify the number of beats per measure. As we touched upon in the previous section on language, iambic pentameter is based on variations of a standard five meter line: five (penta-) meters, each containing an **iamb** (a meter in which the first beat is unstressed and the second beat is stressed, lending the standard iambic line its distinctive, regular pulse: ba-bump, ba-bump, ba-bump, ba-bump, ba-bump. When Shakespeare wanted an actor to sound controlled or formal, he wrote lines that were remained very close to a standard line of iambic pentameter; when he varied the verse rhythm by starting a line with an inverted foot (a **trochee** – stressed, unstressed), he was signalling to the actors in his company that the rhythm and emphasis had changed, frequently meaning that the character was taking charge by starting with a stressed syllable.

For most of you, the easiest way to capture a rhythm is to find a piece of music that fits your vision of the unit. When I am directing, I almost always listen to music as I analyse a script in preparation for rehearsals and design meetings, and I will gravitate towards music that matches up well with the mood or rhythm of the play, scene, or unit on which I am working. Sometimes this music makes its way into the production as underscoring for a scene or as transitional music between scenes or acts. Other times, if I have a sound designer, I will give them one or two pieces of music as a starting point for our design collaboration. But in any case, I will write the tempo and the name of a piece of music that captures the rhythm I detect in the dialogue in the margin of my promptbook, just beneath the unit title, actions, and objectives.

The way I look at it, most if not all plays have what I would call 'short' and 'long' rhythms. A short rhythm reflects the rhythm of a small section of the play, frequently a unit or a subunit. But plays also have long rhythms – patterns created by the alternation in speed from unit to unit and scene to scene. For example, we might divide up a ten-minute play into five units, alternating among three different tempos: slow, fast, slow, fast, medium. Each of these units has a different pattern or beat (short rhythm), but the alternation of tempos from unit to unit creates a pattern over the entirety of the scene (long rhythm), reflected by the change in rhythm and tempo.

Furthermore, not every unit hews closely to a single rhythm or tempo. Without cluttering your script analysis with too many notations, if you see a point in a unit at which the tempo or rhythm changes significantly, mark it in the margin of the script at the exact point the change occurs. In rehearsal, actors may end up playing the tempo or rhythm change in a different place, but noting the most prominent changes will help capture the shifts in tempo and rhythm in greater detail. If a performance is uniformly the same speed and tempo, it has no pulse (literally and figuratively), and this reflects one of my central beliefs about what makes good theatre compelling: in performance, the ensemble should articulate a play's tempos and rhythms like a piece of music.

I would like to define two more terms that many people use in theatre: **momentum** and **pacing**. For me, a play, scene, or unit is well paced if there is no unnecessary air between the lines. In other words, all silences and pauses appear to be justified by the action and filled by the tension among characters; otherwise, actors must learn to 'pick up their cues' more quickly. Momentum sounds very similar to this, but more accurately reflects an increase in the tempo or pace: a sense of acceleration. Most traditional, realistic plays build momentum as they near the climax or key moment of each act.

Keep in mind that realism is a style of theatre; it does not actually capture the real, everyday tempos and rhythms of life. Life frequently has a lot more air between lines and words than most audiences will tolerate on stage. Very few plays come close to capturing these real, everyday rhythms. Among recent plays, Annie Baker's 2014 Pulitzer Prize-winning play, *The Flick*, comes very close to everyday rhythms and tempos. Baker calls for long segments in which characters clean a movie theatre without saying a word to each other. Yet despite the Pulitzer Prize and acclaim of several positive reviews, many audience members who attended the premiere in New York City were not prepared for such an unusually slow and silent production. During this short first run in New York, large numbers of audience members did not return from intermission to see the second half of the production.[10]

I would also note that as with action and objective, there is no single right tempo and rhythm for a unit. The director and actors will have the greatest influence in creating this rhythm, but the designers should be on the same page in order to support or contrast the tempos and rhythms of a production, particularly during entrances, exits, and transitions between scenes. For

---

[10]Nonetheless, after winning the Pulitzer, *The Flick* re-opened and played to packed houses for a much longer run, a testament to audiences' abilities to adapt, or to the power of good publicity created by winning a major award.

example, if scene 1 of a performance ends with a fast unit and scene 2 picks up at the same tempo, a glacially slow transition between the two scenes may create an unintended long rhythm that might not facilitate the best overall pacing of the performance. Furthermore, tempo and rhythm choices are closely connected to the characters' actions and objectives, and the combinations created by these choices are limitless and inherently interesting. For example, a character might dominate the other character slowly or quickly, and they may do so in a variety of rhythms that the actors and director discover in rehearsal, suggested by the playwright's use of language.

When I teach script analysis, I use an app called 'Tempo SloMo', which allows the user to take any piece of music and slow it down or speed it up without a change in pitch. With this tool, I can alter the tempo to fit the scene, and note it in the margins of my promptbook, for example, Beethoven's 'Moonlight Sonata', slowed down to 85 per cent of its regular tempo. In analysing any play, tempo and rhythm are ultimately used to interpret the action, though this can work in either direction: your feel for tempo and rhythm might help you define the fundamental action, or your vision of the action might help define the tempo and rhythm.

In Act 1, scene 1 of *Twelfth Night*, for example, Orsino's first line calls for music from one of his entourage in the hopes that it will 'feed' his love:

If music be the food of love, play on;
Give me excess of it, that, surfeiting,
The appetite may sicken, and so die.
That strain again! it had a dying fall:
O, it came o'er my ear like the sweet sound,
That breathes upon a bank of violets,
Stealing and giving odour! Enough; no more:
'Tis not so sweet now as it was before. (lines 1–8)

To my director's ear, this fairly regular verse speech sounds like it would be best done slowly, with a clear change in tempo and rhythm when Orsino stops the music, 'Enough; no more: 'Tis not so sweet now as it was before.' The rhythm, in keeping with Orsino's character and his willingness to wait for years for Olivia to return his love, seems to me to be rolling, sentimental, languishing, and almost lazy. I might describe it that way in my promptbook and coach my cast accordingly, but I might just as easily find a song that captures the tempo and mood, which I might further refine by making it slower or faster on Tempo Slow. Try reading Orsino's eight lines out loud while playing the classic folk music group The Weavers' version of the song 'Kisses Sweeter Than Wine', and then see what happens to the reading by increasing or decreasing the tempo.

For a scene with the play's clown, Feste, I might look for something much faster and more playful. Let us examine a few lines of Act 1, scene 5, between Olivia, who has been mourning the death of her father and brother for years, and Feste, who tries to amuse her and rouse her from her melancholy with his word play in this prose scene:

FESTE Good madonna, why mournest thou?
OLIVIA Good fool, for my brother's death.
FESTE I think his soul is in hell, madonna.
OLIVIA I know his soul is in heaven, fool.
FESTE The more fool, madonna, to mourn for your brother's soul being in heaven. Take away the fool, gentlemen. (I, 5, lines 66–72)

In analysing this unit, I might describe the tempo as fast and the rhythm as playful, jumpy, and driving. Alternately, I might capture the rhythm and tempo by selecting a piece of upbeat swing music with a driving drum beat, such as Gene Krupa's 'Drum Boogie'. To further capture the dynamic of this unit, I might also observe that Feste's bouncy clown rhythms dominate the unit, forcing Olivia into Feste's rhythm. If possible, Feste's rhythm will match his actions: to amuse, dazzle, or outwit.

In the same way, the tempo and rhythm changes over the course of several units of a play will create a long rhythm that is a vital part of the shape and texture of the action. We might most easily discover or create long rhythm in an episodic play like *Twelfth Night*, because the frequent changes in characters and location from scene to scene renders the rhythm and tempo changes more evident. We might match up the rhythms and tempos with the places, characters, and actions:

Twelfth Night, Act 1

Scene	Location	Characters/actions	Tempo/Rhythm
1	Orsino's palace	Duke Orsino laments + Curio, Valentine, lords	Slow Melancholy 'Kisses Sweeter Than Wine'
2	Sea coast	Viola inquires + Captain, sailors	Medium After the storm Pensive, jittery
3	Olivia's house	Sir Toby agitates + Sir Andrew, Maria	Medium-fast Boisterous, mischievous
4	Orsino's palace	Duke Orsino confesses & implores + Cesario, Valentine, Curio, attendants	Medium-slow Accelerating
5	Olivia's house	Feste manipulates & dazzles + Maria, then Olivia, Malvolio, attendants	Very fast Playful 'Drum Boogie'

CHAPTER THREE

Process

CORE ACTION

Having broken a play into units and analysed each part and element, you are
ready for the next crucial step: to synthesize your findings into a persuasive and
inspirational statement about the play. This statement must capture the essence
of your approach to interpreting the action of the play. It should be written
primarily for your collaborators: the actors, designers, and director who make
up your ensemble.

Throughout this book, we have worked from the assumption that good
theatre must convey a strong point of view about how the action of a play
unfolds in time and space. Action differs from theme. As a director, I deliberately
avoid thematic statements, because my experience as a director and audience
member has convinced me that the static nature of theme risks flattening the
shape of the action in rehearsal and performance. In other words, you cannot
act a theme. For this reason, we shall focus on defining the action and leave
the ultimate meaning of the play to those who attend the production. Each
audience member will view the action of a play through the lens of his or her
personality, beliefs, experience, and culture. An Argentine audience will view
Information for Foreigners differently than an American one; Argentines know
the history of their country's 'dirty war', whereas most Americans have little or
no experience similar to the action of the play. I believe there is no way for a
production to send a single thematic message that all will receive and interpret
in the same way; even if this was possible, in my opinion, it would not make for
very interesting theatre. The best theatre thrives on ambiguity, not certainty; it
succeeds by prompting or provoking audience members to ask questions, rather
than by convincing them to accept the artists' predetermined answers.

I call the theatre artist's statement of intent about a production the **core action statement**: core, because it must be central to what unfolds on stage; action, because 99 per cent of plays rely on action to create interest, conflict, and momentum. Some plays may seem, on first reading, to have very little action: the full-length plays of Samuel Beckett, some of the early Symbolist plays of Maurice Maeterlinck, and some more recent avant-garde plays, such as the plays of Mac Wellman, Suzan-Lori Parks, and Annie Baker. Yet if we examine these plays more closely, we can still find action, though the action may be non-traditional – action that never resolves, for example – or place greater emphasis on other elements of theatre, such as rhythm in the plays of Mac Wellman and Suzan-Lori Parks, or spectacle in the immersive theatre of Punchdrunk (UK) and Third Rail Projects (NY).

A core action statement should be approximately 500–1,000 words: long enough to explore the action in detail, but not so long as to seem like a lecture or manifesto that loses your readers. Inspire your collaborators without treading too heavily on their territory. In my opinion, each person in a production ensemble will come to know more about his or her portion of the production than the other ensemble members. When writing a core action statement as a director, aim to inspire the rest of the ensemble, not to tell them exactly what to do. If you are writing a core action statement to prepare to design, look to contribute to the collaboration from your point of view as set, costume, lighting, or sound designer. As an actor, the director will usually begin the rehearsal process with his or her statement about the production and a presentation by the designers, but the actor will shape their character's journey through strong, committed choices about action. Understanding how a core action statement functions will help the actor use it as a guide.

I work primarily as a theatre director. The more I direct, the shorter my core action statements become. Instead of fleshing out my ideas more fully, I try to condense them, and then I follow up with specific questions about the production for each member of the design team. In the best of all worlds, I will pitch the core action statement at the start of the first design meeting. But when it proves impossible to assemble the creative team in one place and time, I send a core action statement to the designers by e-mail. Whether you direct, design, or act, you need to develop your ability to pitch your core action persuasively both verbally and in writing and adapt your statement to several audiences: your collaborators, producers, media outlets, and potential audience members. I use the word **pitch** to capture the need to win over your audience – to sell them on your interpretation.

Before I offer some examples of core action statements, I would like to describe the goals and uses of these statements, the process I use to generate a core action, and the criteria I use for evaluating one. The goals of a core action are three-fold:

- To explain your interpretation of the central action and through-line of a play clearly.
- To inspire your ensemble to believe in your core action so that the entire ensemble will flesh out and give shape to a singular production.
- To create a guide or benchmark for artistic choices throughout the process.

Of the three, theatre artists overlook the last goal, to create a guide for artistic choices, at their greatest peril, for it helps facilitate productive collaboration. Process is as important as product. When the ensemble creates a constructive working environment and process and all members of the ensemble feel good about their contributions, the product almost always improves. Under these circumstances, the ensemble becomes like a family, with a common language, a core set of beliefs, and a shared vision of the world of the play.

By using the core action statement as a guide, any member of the ensemble can evaluate and critique a choice without making it personal. You may have been involved in a production in which one of the collaborators rejected another's idea. Sometimes this creates a great deal of tension during design meetings or rehearsals; occasionally, this becomes an obstacle to productive collaboration. As a general rule, as long as there is sufficient time in the process, I think it is better to try out every reasonable idea. If time is short, or if the idea does not appear to work, relying on the core action statement for guidance helps make a rejection seem less personal. Rather than say, 'I don't like that idea. It doesn't work', we might say that the idea might work in a different production but does not work given the core action that the ensemble has agreed upon.

A shrewd theatre artist will realize when and how to adapt the core action statement for a particular purpose or a different audience. Start by writing a full version, usually about 500–1,000 words for a full-length play. The full version might be used to propose a play to a producer or theatre, to start the design process, and to start the rehearsal process. Because it is geared towards an audience of theatre makers, it can and should describe the ending of the play. Don't worry about 'spoiler alerts'. You will be working with these people on this production; they know or will soon know how the play ends. You might pitch the core action slightly differently to a theatre or producer than to your designers and actors, but the underlying interpretation should remain essentially the same. For producers and theatres, you may simply have to make a stronger argument for why you think this production is relevant, or why it will attract an audience.

I also find it useful to have a short version of my core action statement. I use this condensed version primarily to attract audience members. You can adapt it for use as a press release, and you can use it for applications to fringe festivals, such as the Edinburgh and New York International Fringe Festivals.

Some people call it an 'elevator pitch'. If you have a minute to talk to some people in an elevator, what would you tell them about your production to get them to buy a ticket? You may find it useful to condense your statement even further, into what filmmakers call a 'logline': a single sentence designed to grab attention, which could be used in a festival programme, for example.

For my 2009 production of Neil LaBute's *bash* at the Paradise Factory in New York City, I worked with one designer and two actors on a limited budget. One of LaBute's earliest plays, *bash* is made up of three one-acts: two monologues and a duologue, in which two characters address the audience but do not directly acknowledge each other. LaBute loosely based the first two plays, *medea redux* and *iphigenia at orem*, on Greek tragedies; the final duologue, *a gaggle of saints*, although not drawn from a specific myth or tragedy, involves the same level of brutality as the first two.[1]

Our production deliberately aimed to make the audience uncomfortable by bringing them as close as possible to the performers, both physically and emotionally. The audience sat at tables identical to the one on stage; the stage area was at the same level as the audience; the closest audience member was a mere three feet from the actors; and the actors addressed the audience directly, making eye contact as widely and frequently as possible. The producers, actors, and I had agreed upon this approach before we brought a designer on board or started rehearsal. But I still needed a core action statement for each of the three plays and a unifying action for the three one-acts as a production.

bash core action

The plays work by misdirection: audience members believe they are seeing and hearing one story, and it turns out to be something else entirely. We need to be faithful to the underlying truth, while hiding that truth from the audience until the final key moment of each play.

In *medea redux*, a young woman confides in the audience about the relationship she had with her male middle school teacher when she was his student. In production, the audience should start off suspecting that the young woman was the victim of child sexual abuse. The young woman speaks to the audience as if they are police officers. She never blames the teacher, nor does she apologize or admit guilt over her actions. Instead, she tries to win over the audience with the story of the relationship they had, and the son she bore from it. As we reach the final twist of the play, she confesses that she and her son, now fifteen years old, met up with his

---

[1]All three contain only Mormon characters. LaBute converted to Mormonism while attending Brigham Young University as an undergraduate, and the first New York production of these scalding plays, originally subtitled 'Latter Day Plays', incited the Mormon church to discipline LaBute with 'disfellowshipment', after which LaBute dropped the subtitle and reduced some of the references to Mormonism. He has since left the Mormon church.

father just that day for the first time since he fled town before the son's birth. Having introduced the son to his father, she then seduces the audience with a quiet, almost innocent description of how she killed her son by pushing his radio into the tub while he was bathing just after the visit. This is a story of a sympathetic sexual abuse victim who confesses that an older man seduced her when she was underage, only to reveal that she took her son's life moments after introducing the father to his son.

In *iphigenia at orem*, the audience should believe they are in a bar, listening to a stranger tell them a tale about his bad luck. The father of an infant girl, the man overreacts when a co-worker, playing a nasty prank on him, tells him that he's about to be fired. In his panic over whether he can continue to provide for his family, he nudges his child underneath a heavy blanket and then falls asleep (or pretends to fall asleep), until the girl has suffocated. As with *medea*, the man never admits his guilt, nor is it clear that he even feels guilt. He appears to believe he's a victim, yet he feels a need to confess to a stranger. This is a story about a man who tries to convince a stranger that he's the victim of the fateful tragic death of his infant daughter, only to reveal that he prompted or directly caused his child's death.

In *a gaggle of saints*, a happy college-age couple tells a story to their (by now) close friends, the audience, of a romantic trip to Manhattan with some friends for a dance. By this point the audience might be suspicious of the couple's motives, which is the main reason I have chosen for this play to be the last one performed – because there are two characters, each addressing the audience separately, the audience will have greater difficulty figuring out who to believe, and who may be guilty of yet another crime. The boyfriend appears to be primarily concerned about his questionable behaviour with a man he and a male friend lured into a men's bathroom in Central Park with the unspoken promise of sex, only to bash the man's head in and steal his ring. The girlfriend, oblivious to the young man's activities, tells the story from her point of view, confiding how her boyfriend gave her a special ring the next morning, one that she proudly displays as a symbol of the young man's love. This is the story of a young couple delighting in their romance, only to reveal that the symbol of their love, a ring, belonged to a gay man whom the young man killed out of either hatred, an unspoken fear of his own sexual preferences, or both.

Period
LaBute clearly set the play in the 1980s, but should the production emphasize that? Or should the action be made universal, like a Greek drama, timeless?

Sound
I would like the transitional sound between plays to abruptly end the action. The music should be driving, primitive (perhaps), drum music, whereas the music pre- and post-show, as well as the music during intermission, should be soothing with creepy undertones, to help emphasize the rollercoaster

of emotions the audience should feel. Listen to the Talking Heads' *Up All Night*, for example.

Set

The set should be simple, intimate, with little or no delineation between the characters and the audience. Each audience member should feel as if he or she is the only person to whom the characters are confessing. The space should be configured to limit the audience to under 50, but if the producers approve, I would love to keep the audience under 25, perhaps for late-night 'special performances'.

Costumes

The costumes need to emphasize only one or two qualities of the characters. The girl in *medea* is poor but still retains some of her precocious sexuality. The man in *iphigenia* is a middle-class, middle management everyman. In *gaggle,* the college-age man and woman are still wearing the clothes from the Mormon dance they attended on the night of the murder – formal wear, upper middle class (they attend Boston College).

A one-paragraph version of this statement, crafted for a fringe festival programme, might look like this:

In the most intimate of settings, a select few audience members sit face to face with three tortured souls as they confess their deepest, darkest secrets. In *medea redux*, a young woman reveals the startling details of her relationship with her middle school teacher during a class trip. In *iphigenia at orem*, a businessman unloads his guilt about the death of his first-born child. In the final duologue, *a gaggle of saints*, a young college couple share the intimate details of their night on the town in New York City and the secret behind the ring the young woman now wears. Neil LaBute has never been more shocking than in this collection of intimate portraits; no audience has ever gotten closer to his characters than in this production of *bash*.

For my university production of Warren Leight's 1999 Tony-Award winning play about jazz musicians, *Side Man*, I sent the following statement to my designers so that they could start their research and begin to develop initial ideas a month or two earlier than would have been possible otherwise, due to final exams and winter break:

Side Man is about Clifford's return to 'the scene', as he puts it, to relive the collective memory of how his parents met, married, and raised him, so that he can finally 'cut the cord' from his parents, move away from home, and start his own life. Over the years depicted in the play, his mother Terry reacts to his father Gene's emotional absence from their marriage by drinking excessively. For his part, Gene finds himself unable to connect with other people except through jazz, while high strung Terry, lonely from nights home alone while Gene plays gigs, gradually deteriorates into hysteria, alcoholism, and suicidal behaviour. Significantly, Terry starts drinking on their wedding night, when her husband's fellow musician and friend Jonesy, a veteran trombone player and heroin addict, advises her that marrying a musician requires her to drink hard liquor. Terry's alcohol problems and Gene's 'slow fog' have pushed Clifford into the position of family caregiver and saviour since childhood. He has become the adult child of an alcoholic mother and a distant father who lives only for jazz.

This play is about putting the past away, about letting go of expectations not only for Clifford, who must finally find the courage to stop being on call for his parents' emergencies, but for Gene and Terry, who must accept that they have to learn to live without him. For these men and women, jazz replaces intimacy, obliterating their relationships with anyone else. The play is a montage of collective memory in a fog of jazz oblivion; a rhythmic journey that moves seamlessly from time to time and place to place until returning to the start of the play (the present day), so that Clifford can find peace with his decision to move on.

Key elements

Rhythm. All transitions among different times, scenes, and spaces must be handled fluidly so that the action moves like a piece of music.

Memory is always partial. We see enough to give us the illusion of a complete picture, but the memory is always incomplete. The show is a montage of incomplete memories.

Time. The play covers over thirty years. To tell the story well, we must make clear the *when and where* of each scene.

Some questions for designers

Set:

How many *acting areas* do we need? How can the space add to the sense of selective and collective memory?

What are the *key textures* in the set?

What contrasts do you see between the two acts? Can we find an arc to how the space changes and develops throughout the play?

Doors seem to be prominent in the script. How many doors do we need? Where would they be most effectively placed?

Where does Terry's aborted suicide attempt take place? Can we create a safe area ten or more feet above stage level for this scene, so that we can create a sense of danger when she steps out of the apartment window?

Costumes:

How can we help express the jazz musicians' differing personalities while still communicating that the musicians play in a big band orchestra together, particularly in the scenes that take place backstage before or after a gig?

How can we suggest or capture the different times and places of the play economically, through costumes?

How can we maintain the *fluidity* of the show throughout costume changes?

How can we help Clifford make the transitions back and forth from role-playing himself at age 10 to present-day adult?

What does Terry wear for her wedding? What does Jonesy wear in jail?

Lights:

How can we capture the '*jazz atmosphere*' of the clubs?

How can we capture the sense of *selective and collective memory*?

How do we light Clifford when he observes memories, so that he floats seamlessly between outside commentator and inside character?

Sound:

How much *underscoring* can we use? I have secured a body mic for each actor, so don't be afraid to underscore frequently. I'd like to meet to discuss cue placement early in the process.

How often should we move away from trumpet-centred jazz? How much do we stay true to period (1950s–80s) in music choices?

Should we use pre-show music? Should we use music during intermission?

How do we create the music for Gene and Terry's Debussy scene, in which Terry plays flute and Gene plays trumpet, given that it's unlikely I will be able to cast actors who actually play their instruments?

I'll need most major sound cues for the first rehearsal.

Props:

How do we handle the few moments during which the script calls for actors to play an instrument?

Since a lot of the action involves re-enacted scenes from Clifford's memory narrated by him, I'd like him to handle all of the on-stage prop changes. We'll need props no later than the second week of rehearsal, so that Clifford has time to learn how to move the props on and off stage.

Everyone:

The characters are all from the Bronx, except for Terry (East Boston) and Clifford (New York City, unsure of borough). I'm not sure about Patsy. Do we need to use *dialects*?

How do we capture the sense that when the men listen to the lost Clifford Brown recording, it's incredibly intimate experience for them?

Starting points for background research:

Jazz, Ken Burns's ten-part documentary and accompanying book have great photographic research. The film is available on Netflix streaming. Should we buy a copy as well?

The Jazz Ear by Ben Ratliff

Adult Children of Alcoholics by Janet T. Woititz

In this particular core action, I raised a lot of practical questions for the designers to consider, and I suggested some reading for everyone in the ensemble. For a director or designer, the core action statement should bring up practical elements that must function well in production. By getting these issues on the table early, you can help everyone avoid decisions that will hamper the flow of the production. Some of these issues may limit what is possible in production, but as an art form, theatre always has limitations. The best theatre takes these limitations as a challenge. I always remind myself that *the limitations of theatre create opportunities for artistic expression.*

In the best of all worlds, I complete my entire script analysis before I write my core action statement. But frequently I find there is not enough time for me to do so, for a number of reasons. A theatre might send a script and ask to meet a few days later to discuss production ideas. A university or college season selection committee might want to discuss two or three possible plays for production, limiting the amount of time available for analysis until one has been selected. With limited time, what can be done to prepare to write a core action statement?

Start with basic script analysis, and focus on the big picture, rather than small moments. Break down the script into units and select evocative unit titles that capture the action. Get a sense of the structure of the play and the journey of its central characters. Figure out the key moment or moments in the play and work backwards through the action to see how the playwright has set up the events and conflict that lead to the climax.[2] Analyse this unit and one or two others – the most significant stops on the journey – for actions and objectives. Isolate two or three elements of playwriting and production that might be central to the shape and texture of the action: plot, structure, character, relationships, time, conflict, environment, spectacle, music, and language. Finally, extract the key words from the unit titles, actions, and objectives, and list them for possible use in the core action statement.

When I teach core action in my Script Analysis class, I ask students to come up with a list of key elements in Paula Vogel's 1998 Pulitzer Prize-winning play, *How I Learned to Drive*. They usually discover most if not all of the elements below:

1. **Structure, time, and memory:** The action is an episodic journey that moves backwards and forwards in time, until the most significant past action – L'il Bit's secret – is revealed. It is L'il Bit's memory play.

2. **Driving lessons:** Vogel has divided the play into a series of driving lessons that gradually reveal how L'il Bit takes control of the direction of her life.

---

[2] I am indebted to David Ball's *Backwards and Forwards* for the idea of moving backwards from the climax in analysing plays. *Backwards and Forwards: A Technical Manual for Reading Plays*, Carbondale, IL: Southern Illinois University Press, 1983.

3. **Relationship**: How do we define the relationship between L'il Bit and Peck? How does it start, and how does it change?

4. **Objectives**: What do these two characters want from each other? Where are they going together? Peck wants to be loved and forgiven. L'il Bit wants to be nurtured, treated as an adult, and perhaps also seeks forgiveness.

5. **Chorus**: How does the chorus function in this play?

6. **Spectacle** (or lack thereof): How do we keep the focus on the two central characters and keep the action moving, without getting bogged down by the scene changes?

7. Most significant **visual moment**: When Peck molests L'il Bit, a chorus member speaks her lines as the actor playing L'il Bit plays the physical action.

8. **Key moments**: L'il Bit's birthday, in which she turns down Peck's proposal, leads to her recovering the repressed memory of Peck molesting her at age 11.

From this initial analysis, I shape these discoveries into a core action statement along these lines:

'Sometimes to tell a secret, you first have to teach a lesson', confides the central character, L'il Bit, at the start of *How I Learned to Drive*. Vogel has structured the play as a series of driving lessons that show how L'il Bit finally takes control of her life in the wake of a long, sexualized relationship during her teens with her older Uncle Peck. These lessons focus primarily on the years 1964–69, from when she first makes a deal with her Uncle Peck to meet with him once a week until her eighteenth birthday, when he drives to meet her in a hotel room in the hope that she will return his love. Only after the story of those years has been fully explored can L'il Bit reveal her secret.

The play moves backwards and forwards in time at first, until gaining a bit of traction and moving more steadily backwards from 1968, when L'il Bit gets her driver's license, to 1964, when Peck and L'il Bit strike a deal for Peck to teach L'il Bit to drive. Three 'Chorus Members', a man, a woman, and a teenage girl, portray all of the other characters in the story, including (most prominently) L'il Bits' mother, grandmother, grandfather, and Peck's wife. The family does little to stop the developing relationship between Peck and L'il Bit, and the family members' boorish and buffoonish ways should make the two central characters seem all the more human and sympathetic to audiences.

Once the deal is struck and we think we understand how the relationship started, the action moves forward to 1969, leading up to their meeting in the hotel on her eighteenth birthday. When L'il Bit rejects Peck's advances, we then go back to the secret – the climactic scene in 1962, when it is revealed that Peck molested L'il Bit at age 11. In this scene, two actresses portray L'il Bit: the actress cast as L'il Bit plays the physical action in the car, while the teenage girl chorus member portrays her vocally. I see L'il Bit's separation of body and voice in this scene as essential to our production, as it represents how L'il Bit feels about herself: 'That was the last day I lived in my body.'

By holding back the secret of what happened when L'il Bit was 11 until the very end, the play makes Peck as sympathetic as possible under the circumstances. While Peck aims to win L'il Bit's love and ultimately seduce her, we see him nurture her as well. Ironically, Peck's lessons ultimately teach L'il Bit how to defend herself from his advances. He simultaneously preys on her and cares for her – a man at war with himself – so that audiences might find it more difficult to despise and dismiss him. In the end, after learning that Peck drank himself to death after L'il Bit rejected his proposal of marriage in the hotel room, she gets into the car and adjusts the rear view mirror so that she can see him for the rest of the ride. Ultimately, she doesn't reject him but realizes that he will always be present in the back of her mind. She has forgiven herself, something Peck was never able to do.

The play is fuelled by the driving lessons, which serve as metaphors for L'il Bit's life lessons, as she learns to drive defensively, handle alcohol responsibly, and make decisions about where their relationship is going and where she draws the line. The production needs to move seamlessly backwards and forwards in time, so I'd suggest a minimalist set. I am not interested in realistic set details, such as a complete automobile. I would prefer a few chairs or benches that help the audience members believe the scene is taking place in a car but allow them to see the actors' entire bodies clearly. I like the idea of the entire play being exactly what it is – a re-enactment and retelling of these events on a stage for an audience. The set should look more like a rehearsal room or an empty stage than a fully realized set. Keep the focus on the actors' bodies, as the audience should focus on the characters' bodies more than their environment. Sound will play an important part in the play, by being an audible but invisible indicator of time period and mood. As L'il Bit never leaves the stage, her costume should, I think, be appropriate for the year in which she is telling the story (present day?), although we can explore the possibility of additional pieces being added to her costume for particular scenes. Keep the fluidity of the action in mind in all design choices.

Delivering the Pitch

If you present your statement in person, how you speak will be just as important as what you say. Depending upon your personal strengths, you may choose to read your statement, memorize it, or reduce it to an outline to guide a more extemporaneous delivery. If you can look up 80 per cent of the time – an invaluable skill acquired through practice – then reading the statement may work well for you. But if you struggle to keep your eyes up and make eye contact, then you might prefer to use an outline. The outline will give your speech structure, but its condensed nature will encourage you to make more consistent eye contact. An outline also helps if you get lost in a thought and forget where you are within your pitch. Finally, some people memorize their statements. In this case, I still recommend bringing an outline with you, just in case you forget your lines or lose your place, which can happen quite easily if nerves get the better of you or when someone asks you a question.

You must make consistent and confident eye contact for a pitch to succeed. Just as we inquire of every character, 'what do they want, and what are they doing to get it', ask the same question of yourself and play the action to achieve your objective – to persuade collaborators or producers that you have something unique to offer so that they will support you. Regardless of which technique you use, rehearse your statement before you give the actual presentation, to get comfortable with the content and flow of the pitch. The more you can internalize the pitch, the more persuasive you can be. Aim to convey not only your interpretation of the play but also your passion for the project as a theatre artist.

AVANT-GARDE

The repertoire of plays produced in North America and the United Kingdom continues to be dominated by plays with linear and causal action: the action proceeds in a series of steps, with one action leading to the next. I have sought to capture the range of plays with strong lines of action in our case studies. *Hedda* and *Streetcar* exemplify how this can work in a predominantly realistic style. *Oedipus* employs a chorus to interrupt the otherwise predominantly linear progression of events. In her episodic play *How I Learned to Drive*, Vogel shifts fluidly back and forth among different time periods in a line of flashbacks that follow the logic of her central character's life lessons, whereas Shakespeare employs episodic structure and verse in the chronological plot of *Twelfth Night*, effectively harnessing more poetic language to several converging plot lines. Yet regardless of the style and dramatic structure of these plays, we can break down the action into playable units and discover how the playwright has used given circumstances, fully developed characterizations, and complex relationships to support the action.

A small but significant body of work – experimental and avant-garde – completely and deliberately rejects the conventions of linear, causal action. Nonetheless, for most of these plays, the skills we have developed throughout this book remain useful; indeed, by looking for the disparities between what we expect from more traditional plays and what avant-garde and experimental plays offer, we can isolate the unique qualities of experimental and avant-garde plays in rehearsal and performance. As a general rule, plays that avoid using particular elements of traditional drama shift their emphasis to other elements and bring increased attention to the missing elements.

Traditional drama depends on the logic created by a clear chain of events to construct sequences that help audiences and readers make sense of the world of the play. Avant-garde and experimental plays, with rare exception, avoid this structural logic, in part because the vast majority of playwrights writing in this vein prefer to create worlds that defy neat and rational explanations. As Julia Listengarten and I explain in the introduction to *Theater of the Avant-Garde, 1890–1950*, 'Maurice Maeterlinck's earliest Symbolist plays, for example, emphasize mood, tone, and atmosphere over causality. The impulse is to avoid offering audiences seemingly rational explanations of behavior that help reassure them of the legitimacy of society's status quo' (4). Such a shift in emphasis, however, can still be understood by analysing the action, as long as we remain aware that we may not be able to make sense of the actions in the ways we have come to expect. Characters may pursue hidden objectives by committing to unusually obscure or counter-intuitive actions; the arc of an avant-garde play, in many cases, will not lead directly to an unambiguous final key moment. Many of the early avant-garde playwrights, such as Wassily Kandinsky, Gertrude Stein, and the Italian Futurists, eliminate causality wholly from most of their plays. Yet from moment to moment, the ensemble can still select actions and commit to them; the actions simply will not fall into a clear line, with one action leading to the next.

Much of the early avant-garde also dispensed with the ubiquitous psychological motivations of realistic drama, sacrificing three-dimensional characters in favour of the ones that are 'illogical, one- or two-dimensional, or exhibit elements of abnormal psychology … or reflect the inner workings of the playwright's psychosis' (4–5). Analysing such characters involves understanding and accepting the playwright's distorted world: the Surrealists' combination of dream and reality, the infantile egotism of Alfred Jarry, and the body parts that populate Tristan Tzara's *The Gas Heart*.

The avant-garde frequently renounces the mainstream morals of the society within which it has been created, whether authoritarian, communist, fascist, or even democratic. By performing dramaturgical research into the playwright's period, we might be able to distinguish the immorality or amorality of the world of the play in contrast to the world of the playwright. Words and actions that seemed taboo to audiences in the playwright's time and place might not have the same impact for a contemporary audience in a different society or nation, but by understanding the playwright's world, we might be able to discover a contemporary parallel. Avant-garde and experimental plays frequently devalue language itself:

> From the macrocosmic challenge to rationality rooted in the gibberish of many Futurist and Dada plays, to the stream-of-consciousness language of Stein and the Surrealists, to the unexpected and unrestrained macrocosmic violence of Artaud, the avant-garde has continually assailed the idea that language can and should convey ideas clearly and logically. (6)

Yet we can still use the terminology and skills of action analysis to describe what the characters are doing to each other, even if the language and intent remain deliberately ambiguous or obscure. Indeed, the lack of meaning of gibberish, for example, makes the ensemble's choice of action even more important. The disconnect between the meaning of the word and a strongly committed action might fuel avant-garde performance – the greater the commitment to an action, the more the ambiguity of meaning fuels yet hinders the audience's efforts to understand it.

In the absence of logic, the other elements of script analysis – tempo, rhythm, key moments, and environment – become indispensible. These elements lend shape and texture to avant-garde theatre, in the absence of easily accessible meaning. They help empower theatre that favours experience over meaning. The experience of an avant-garde performance – oft-times lacking logic, sometimes lacking meaning, occasionally lacking even words – needs to be navigated with a steady artistic hand. Whereas Shakespeare's use of language supported meaning, Stein's circular and repetitive language, for example, contains meaning in its shape, as we might detect in *Doctor Faustus Lights the Lights*:

> I wish (she whispered) I knew why the woods are wild why animals are wild why I am I, why I can cry, I wish I wish I knew, I wish oh how I wish I knew. Once I am in I will never be through the woods are there and I am here and am I here or am I there, oh where oh where is here oh where oh where is there and animals wild animals are everywhere. (*Theater of the Avant-Garde, 1890–1950* 405)

Such language requires the same sensitivity as Shakespeare's verse: we can break up the lines by observing the punctuation and sentence structure and utilizing its repetitions and antitheses. And we might still make choices as to what Stein's characters want and how they go about getting it, even if their language is circular, poetic, and at times, nonsensical.

Other avant-garde plays may be less obscure, particularly those that use more comprehensible language. For example, in his early plays, Harold Pinter used language that might seem familiar and accessible at first. In a play such as *The Birthday Party*, for instance, much of Pinter's dialogue resembles that of a realistic stock play of the period. Pinter's innovation was to take away some of the characters' given circumstances, so that we are never quite sure if people are who they say they are; consequently, we question if they are doing what they seem to be doing. The main character, Stanley, is hiding from something or someone, but we're not sure what or who; every attempt to understand his past simply makes his situation more equivocal. When two men, Goldberg and McCann, come to visit the house in which Stanley has been hiding and offer to help him celebrate his birthday – spoiler: it's *not* his birthday – the most innocent of family rituals becomes one of the most threatening. Only when Goldberg and McCann begin to drive Stanley to the edge of madness does Pinter employ language to pursue unexpected objectives, as the two men tear down his feeble defences by repeatedly and insistently asking him innocuous questions – 'Why did the chicken cross the road?' and 'Which came first, the chicken or the egg?' – until he cracks.

Similarly, in Kenneth Brown's *The Brig*, the warden and his men exploit the rules and required movements of a military prison to reduce its prisoners to animals and mere numbers, and in Naomi Iizuka's *Body Beautiful*, the women, having surrendered so completely to society's pressure to be thin that they have opted for elective surgery to maintain 'ideal' bodies, avenge themselves on the media by eviscerating a TV host through words alone. In each of these plays, the actions are primarily variations on domination and submission, but the playwrights shape the action and render it compelling by varying the characters' levels of aggression and the ritualistic rhythms that help define the world of the play. Text becomes texture – an earthy, gritty substance defined more by the actors' instruments than by a dictionary.

In conclusion, perhaps we have been looking for texture throughout this book: the shape that a play suggests, and that a group of theatre artists interprets by first analysing its action bit by bit, unit by unit, and element by element. A play comes to life when a group of dedicated artists, using a shared language, discovers a collective vision that they then shape by making choices through acting, directing, dramaturgy, and design. I believe that we, as theatre artists, define a play's life and pulse, ultimately, not through thematic statements, but by the shape and texture we find within and beneath its text.

Text = shape = texture. First, we unearth a play's context – the world of the play – looking for hints the playwright provides about given circumstances and environment, supplemented by dramaturgical research. Then, we break down each scene or act into playable units of action, the markers of a play's major structural components, and interpret the actions and objectives by avoiding the obvious, literal, and oft-times superficial meaning of the text in favour of actions that reveal what might lurk beneath the text: its *sub*text. We define the major landmarks of the action, its key moments, while using shifts to navigate its shallower terrain, moment by moment. By exploring tempos and rhythms, we find elements of music in the language, whether it's the harsh brutality of Tennessee Williams's Stanley Kowalski or the seemingly frivolous yet stylish melodies of Oscar Wilde's characters. Finally, we bring all of these elements together into a statement of a play's core action, as we see it: a unique interpretation. And yet always, we must remind ourselves that beneath the art of the playwright, where theatre artists work, lays the true gift of theatre. Each interpretation and production of a play is ephemeral, and after closing night, only a flicker remains in the memories of the audience. From all of our efforts – script analysis, production meetings, and rehearsals – we take away theatre's most important lesson: collaboration. For only by collaborating, using a shared language to create a common vision, do we reach our fullest potential as an ensemble, and only by embracing theatre's essential spirit of collaboration do we have a chance of fully developing the individual skills and talents of each member of an ensemble for his or her future work.

CHAPTER FOUR

Blueprints

GIVEN CIRCUMSTANCES BLUEPRINT

Setting
    Continent, country, city
    Physical area(s)
    Environment
    Climate and light	

Time
    Year, season, time of day.
    Length of time covered
    Logic of time movement	

Class structure
    Classes
    Economic health
    Characters in each class	

Government and laws
    System
    Relevant laws
    Restrictions/freedoms
    Participation/environment	

Social circles
    Family and friends
    Community
    Media
    Restrictions/privileges	

Religion
    Institutions
    Beliefs
    Restrictions/privileges	

Previous action	This is a world in which…
Previous action	This is a world in which…
Previous action	This is a world in which…
Previous action	This is a world in which…
Previous action	This is a world in which…
Previous action	This is a world in which…
Previous action	This is a world in which…

CHARACTER BLUEPRINT

Physical *What does the playwright tell us about the physicality of the character, if anything?*	
Psychological *What is the character's mental state? Are they in any way balanced, neurotic, psychotic, or deluded?*	
Intellectual *In what ways has the character's mind developed (schooling, environment, self-teaching, street smarts)?*	

Social class and job	
Within what class was the character raised, what class are they throughout the play, and how would you describe their job or career path?	
Family and friends	
Where were they born and raised, and how has this shaped their identity? How did their family influence their religious, political, and ethical beliefs? To what degree is the character surrounded by friends and family or isolated?	

RELATIONSHIP BLUEPRINT

Analyse and explain the relationship and status of the character you've selected to the other character in the scene, using the following rubric:

Generic relationship

What is the **type** of relationship? (examples: husband/wife, boss/employee, best friends)

What are the characters' social positions?

How does the location of the scene affect their relationship?

Specific relationship

What is the relationship between the characters at the start of the scene you are examining? For the analysis of the entire play, choose three significant scenes to analyse.

What is the primary subject matter of the scene, and how does that affect the relationship?

STRUCTURE BLUEPRINT

Play title and playwright

Sample unit breakdown: Act 1

Unit	Unit title	Character	Character	Character	Character	Character
I, 1						
I, 2						
I, 3						
I, 4						
I, 5						
I, 6						
I, 7						
I, 8						
I, 9						
I, 10						

ENVIRONMENT BLUEPRINT

Whose space is it?	
How does the environment affect relationships?	
How does the environment define the pattern created by the structure of scenes?	
How does the environment raise the stakes of the action?	

Action Verbs

LOVING WORDS

Accept, Admire

Bless

Calm, Coddle, Comfort, Compliment, Confide

Delight

Enchant, Enlighten, Entertain, Entrance, Envelop

Glorify

Honour

Idolize, Inflame

Liberate, Lull, Lure

Nourish, Nurse

Pacify, Pamper, Pardon, Please, Praise, Protect

Ravish, Redeem, Reform, Regale, Rehabilitate, Relax, Relish, Rescue, Revere, Revive, Romance, Rouse

Satisfy, Save, Seduce, Shield, Soothe

Tease, Thanks, Thaw, Titillate, Transfix, Transform, Treat

Unburden

Validate, Vindicate

Waken, Welcome, Win, Woo, Worship

ENCOURAGING WORDS

Absolve, Acknowledge, Aggrandize, Arouse

Befriend, Boost, Brighten

Cajole, Coax, Compel, Congratulate, Convert, Convince, Correct, Cultivate

Delegate, Designate, Drill

Electrify, Elevate, Empower, Encourage, Energize, Excite, Exhilarate

Focus, Free, Fuel

Greet, Guide

Heal, Help

Ignite, Implore, Improve, Infect, Inflate, Influence, Instruct, Invigorate, Invite

Lecture, Lighten

Organize

Persuade, Pressure, Prod, Prompt, Pursue

Reassure, Recruit, Reinvigorate, Rejuvenate, Reward

Spark, Spur, Steer, Stimulate, Strengthen

Tantalize, Teach, Thrill, Toughen, Train, Tutor

Urge

APPROVING WORDS

Accommodate, Advise, Aid, Alert, Approve, Assure, Authorize

Bolster

Champion, Commend, Confess, Corroborate, Counsel

Defend

Endorse, Entrust

Follow

Guard

Hail

Legitimize, Lift

Maintain, Manage

Obey, Ordain

Pardon, Proclaim

Reinforce, Rule

Stabilize, Steady

Toast

Uphold

MANIPULATING WORDS

Amaze, Amuse, Appease

Bait, Beguile, Bewitch, Blackmail, Brainwash, Bribe

Charm, Coerce, Corrupt

Dazzle

Ensnare, Entice, Entrap, Exploit

Fascinate, Flatter, Force

Hoodwink, Humble, Hurry, Hush, Hypnotize

Judge

Lull

Manipulate, Manoeuver, Mesmerize, Mould

Negate

Outwit, Overcome

Preoccupy, Probe, Programme

Rush

Sabotage, Seduce, Solicit

Tempt, Test

Vilify

UNDERMINING WORDS

Bamboozle, Betray, Bluff

Cheat, Con, Corrupt

Deceive, Delude, Dupe

Entrap

Flatter, Fleece, Foil, Fool

Humour

Kid

Lampoon

Malign, Misdirect, Misguide, Mislead, Mystify

Puzzle

Snare, Swindle

Trick

Undercut, Undermine

PROVOKING WORDS

Abandon, Accost, Agitate, Alarm, Alert, Annoy, Antagonize

Badger, Bedevil, Bewilder, Bother

Challenge, Confound, Confront, Confuse

Daze, Derail, Deride, Disrupt, Distract, Disturb, Dominate

Elude, Engulf

Fluster, Frighten, Frustrate

Goad, Grill

Harangue, Haunt, Heckle, Horrify

Infect, Infuriate, Interrogate, Interrupt, Irritate

Jolt

Menace, Mortify

Nag

Outrage

Panic, Perplex, Pester, Provoke, Puzzle

Query, Question, Quiz

Rattle, Reproach, Repulse, Revile, Ridicule, Rile, Ruffle

Shame, Shock, Sicken, Slight, Snub, Startle, Stifle, Stun, Surprise

Tarnish, Terrify, Terrorize, Threaten, Thwart, Traumatize

Uncover, Undermine, Unhinge, Unnerve, Unsettle, Upset

Vex

DISCOURAGING WORDS

Abandon, Admonish, Alienate, Avoid

Belittle

Censor, Chastise, Chide, Criticize, Curb

Demoralize, Depress, Deter, Disappoint, Disarm, Discourage, Disregard, Dodge

Evade, Exclude

Halt, Hassle, Hinder, Hound

Ignore, Impede, Inhibit, Insult, Irritate, Isolate

Jilt

Mock

Neutralize

Obstruct, Offend, Oppose, Ostracize

Prohibit, Prosecute, Punish

Rebuff, Rebuke, Refuse, Reject, Renounce, Repel, Repress, Resist, Restrain, Restrict

Sadden, Scorn, Shirk, Shun, Sidestep, Silence, Stall, Stop, Suppress

Thwart, Tolerate

HARMING WORDS

Abuse, Accuse, Assail, Assault, Attack

Batter, Berate, Besmear, Blacken, Blame, Browbeat, Brutalize, Bully

Castigate, Chastise, Cheapen, Chide, Criticize, Curse

Deceive, Defame, Degrade, Demean, Denigrate, Denounce, Diminish, Discredit, Disgrace, Disown

Embarrass, Embitter, Endanger, Enrage, Expose

Flail

Harass, Harm, Humiliate, Hurt

Imperil, Imprison, Incapacitate, Incriminate, Indict, Intimidate, Invalidate

Jeer

Maim, Malign, Mimic, Molest

Needle, Neglect, Numb

Offend, Oppress, Outlaw, Overthrow, Overturn, Overwhelm

Paralyze, Patronize, Pester, Prod, Punish

Ravage, Repress, Rob

Sap, Scare, Scold, Slander, Smear, Soil, Subdue

Taunt, Tire, Trash

Violate

Warn

DESTROYING WORDS

Abolish, Annihilate, Avenge

Banish

Conquer

Dehumanize, Destroy, Dethrone, Devastate, Devour

Eliminate, Exterminate

Finish

Nullify

Obliterate, Oust

Persecute

Quell

Ransack, Ravage, Ruin, Rule

Sabotage, Sacrifice, Shatter, Silence, Suppress

Terminate, Torment, Torture

Wreck

Sample Scores

TWELFTH NIGHT
by William Shakespeare

ACT 3. SCENE 1. OLIVIA'S garden

Unit 1a: Corrupter of words

Viola and Feste each serve a master/mistress of equal rank (Orsino and Olivia). Viola is a respectable member of Orsino's entourage. Feste, as a clown, can get away with saying things that others cannot. They are equal but different, and they jockey for status with almost every line.

Viola questions Feste to gain access to Olivia.
    Obstacle: Feste won't give a straight answer.
Feste dazzles Viola for a bribe.
    Obstacle: Now that Viola has successfully passed herself off as a man (Cesario), she's having too much fun with her newfound power to give in quickly.
Rhythm: a duel   Tempo: Fast

    Enter VIOLA [as Cesario] and FESTE [the clown] [with pipe and tabor]

VIOLA
Save thee, friend, and thy music. Dost thou live by thy tabor?

FESTE
No, sir, I live by the church.

VIOLA
Art thou a churchman?

FESTE
No such matter, sir: I do live by the church; for I do live
at my house, and my house doth stand by the church.

VIOLA
So thou mayst say the king lies by a beggar, if a beggar   ⓢ outwits
dwell near him; or the church stands by thy tabor, if thy
tabor stand by the church.

FESTE
You have said, sir. To see this age! A sentence is but a   ⓢ commends
cheveril glove to a good wit. How quickly the wrong side
may be turned outward!

VIOLA
Nay, that's certain; they that dally nicely with words may
quickly make them wanton.

FESTE
I would, therefore, my sister had had no name, sir.   ⓢ teases

VIOLA
Why, man?

FESTE
Why, sir, her name's a word; and to dally with that word   ⓢ shames
might make my sister wanton. But indeed words are very
rascals, since bonds disgraced them.

VIOLA
Thy reason, man?

FESTE
Troth, sir, I can yield you none without words; and words
are grown so false I am loath to prove reason with them.

VIOLA
I warrant, thou art a merry fellow, and carest for nothing.

FESTE   F↓V
Not so, sir, I do care for something: but in my conscience,
sir, I do not care for you; if that be to care for nothing, sir, ⓢ mesmerizes
I would it would make you invisible.

VIOLA
Art not thou the Lady Olivia's fool?

FESTE
No, indeed, sir; the Lady Olivia has no folly: she will keep
no fool, sir, till she be married; and fools are as like husbands
as pilchards are to herrings, the husband's the bigger; I am,
indeed, not her fool, but her corrupter of words.

VIOLA
I saw thee late at the Count Orsino's.

FESTE
Foolery, sir, does walk about the orb like the sun; it shines
everywhere. I would be sorry, sir, but the fool should be
as oft with your master as with my mistress: I think I saw your
wisdom there.

VIOLA
Nay, an thou pass upon me, I'll no more with thee. Hold,   ⓢ **validates**
there's expenses for thee.

FESTE
Now Jove, in his next commodity of hair, send thee a beard!

VIOLA
By my troth, I'll tell thee, I am almost sick for one; though I
would not have it grow on my chin. Is thy lady within?

FESTE
Would not a pair of these have bred, sir?   F↓

VIOLA
Yes, being kept together and put to use.

FESTE
I would play Lord Pandarus of Phrygia, sir, to bring a
Cressida to this Troilus.

VIOLA
I understand you, sir; 'tis well begged.

FESTE
The matter, I hope, is not great, sir, begging but a beggar:
Cressida was a beggar. My lady is within, sir. I will construe to
them whence you come; who you are and what you would are
out of my welkin: I might say element, but the word is overworn.

   Exit

Unit 1b: Wise enough to play the fool

Viola treats the audience as a confidant, because the audience knows her secret. She has slightly higher status here because she feels confident after matching wits with Feste and is not seeking support, as she does in other asides. Status shifts are minor and dependent upon the audience's reactions during any given performance.

Viola instructs the audience so they'll understand the Clown's methods.
   Obstacle: it is difficult to judge whether the audience understands her.
Rhythm: Steady, even   Tempo: Moderate

VIOLA
This fellow's wise enough to play the fool;
And, to do that well, craves a kind of wit:
He must observe their mood on whom he jests,
The quality of persons, and the time;
And, like the haggard, check at every feather
That comes before his eye. This is a practice
As full of labour as a wise man's art:
For folly, that he wisely shows, is fit;
But wise men, folly-fallen, quite taint their wit.

Unit 1c: I am bound to your niece

Toby and Andrew are friends. Andrew is lower status because he is a guest and foolish, but he never seems to realize when Toby makes fun of him. In this short scene, they team up to try to play higher status than Viola, because she is a visitor to Toby's niece Olivia's house. Viola tries to find the correct status adjustment to get to see Olivia.

Viola charms Toby and Andrew to see Olivia.
   Obstacle: The men are suspicious of her.
Andrew challenges Viola to respect him.
   Obstacle: It's obvious that Andrew is a fool.
Toby bamboozles Viola to be in awe.
   Obstacle: Viola is too smart to be taken in by Toby's bluster.
Rhythm: Halting   Tempo: Medium

Enter SIR TOBY BELCH and SIR ANDREW AGUE-CHEEK

SIR TOBY
Save you, gentleman.

VIOLA
And you, sir.

SIR ANDREW

Dieu vous garde, monsieur.

VIOLA

Et vous aussi; votre serviteur.

SIR ANDREW

I hope, sir, you are; and I am yours.

SIR TOBY

Will you encounter the house? My niece is desirous you
should enter, if your trade be to her.

VIOLA

I am bound to your niece, sir: I mean, she is the list of my
voyage.

SIR TOBY

Taste your legs, sir; put them to motion.

VIOLA

My legs do better understand me, sir, than I understand
what you mean by bidding me taste my legs.

SIR TOBY

I mean, to go, sir, to enter.

VIOLA

I will answer you with gait and entrance: but we are
prevented.

Unit 2a: Leave me to my hearing

Maria is Olivia's maid. She follows her mistress's lead when in her presence.
She is good friends with Toby and may be romantically interested in him (they
marry at the end of the play). Viola lowers her status re: Olivia to convince her
to listen to her pleas on Orsino's behalf. Olivia is the highest status in this unit,
because she is a countess and is in her own home.

Viola flatters Olivia so she'll meet privately.
    Obstacle: Olivia is embarrassed that she previously sent Malvolio to Viola
    with a ring.
Olivia orders Maria to close the door and leave them alone.
    Obstacle: Maria is a busybody and wants to know what they are going to talk
    about.
Andrew amuses Toby so that he will think him witty.
    Obstacle: Toby knows Andrew is a fool. Most of the time, he will laugh at
    him, not with him.

Rhythm: Formal and gracious, with interruptions Tempo: Medium

Enter OLIVIA and MARIA

Most excellent accomplished lady, the heavens rain odours on you!

SIR ANDREW
That youth's a rare courtier: 'Rain odours'! well.

VIOLA
My matter hath no voice, lady, but to your own most
pregnant and vouchsafed ear.

SIR ANDREW
'Odours', 'pregnant', and 'vouchsafed': I'll get 'em all
three ready.

OLIVIA
Let the garden door be shut, and leave me to my hearing.

Exeunt SIR TOBY, SIR ANDREW, and MARIA

Unit 2b: Set mine honour at the stake

Olivia starts with much higher status than Viola, because of her rank and the place, her house or palace. But the more she reveals her romantic interest in Viola, the more she lowers her status and raises Viola's. Viola, trying to redirect Olivia's interest towards Orsino, shifts her status freely in a vain attempt to find a way to her goal.

Viola implores Olivia to consider Orsino's love.
    Obstacle: Olivia has fallen for Viola, thinking she is a man (Cesario).
Olivia sabotages Viola to consider her love.
    Obstacle: Viola is a woman, and she is in love with Orsino and therefore
    Olivia's competitor.
Rhythm: Rapidly accelerating, impulsive Tempo: Starts medium, reaches fast,
                                                    settles to slow after key moment

OLIVIA
Give me your hand, sir.

VIOLA
My duty, madam, and most humble service.   V↓

OLIVIA
What is your name?

VIOLA
Cesario is your servant's name, fair princess.

OLIVIA
My servant, sir! 'Twas never merry world,
Since lowly feigning was call'd compliment:
You are servant to the Count Orsino, youth.

VIOLA
And he is yours, and his must needs be yours;
Your servant's servant is your servant, madam.

OLIVIA
For him, I think not on him: for his thoughts,
Would they were blanks rather than fill'd with me!   O↑

VIOLA
Madam, I come to whet your gentle thoughts
On his behalf.

OLIVIA
                O, by your leave, I pray you,
I bade you never speak again of him:
But, would you undertake another suit,   ⑤ seduces O↑V
I had rather hear you to solicit that
Than music from the spheres.

VIOLA
                Dear lady, –

OLIVIA
Give me leave, beseech you: I did send,   ⑤ entraps
After the last enchantment you did here,
A ring in chase of you; so did I abuse
Myself, my servant, and, I fear me, you:
Under your hard construction must I sit;
To force that on you, in a shameful cunning,
Which you knew none of yours. What might you think?   O↓
Have you not set mine honour at the stake,
And baited it with all the unmuzzl'd thoughts
That tyrannous heart can think? To one of your receiving
Enough is shown: a cypress, not a bosom,
Hides my heart: so let me hear you speak.

VIOLA
I pity you.   ⑤ ridicules   V↓O

OLIVIA
            That's a degree to love.

VIOLA
No, not a grise; for 'tis a vulgar proof
That very oft we pity enemies.

OLIVIA
Why, then, methinks 'tis time to smile again:
O world, how apt the poor are to be proud!
If one should be a prey, how much the better
To fall before the lion than the wolf! [Clock strikes]
The clock upbraids me with the waste of time.   ⓢ abandons
Be not afraid, good youth, I will not have you:
And yet, when wit and youth is come to harvest,
Your wife is like to reap a proper man.
There lies your way, due-west.

VIOLA
                    Then westward-ho:
Grace and good disposition 'tend your ladyship!
You'll nothing, madam, to my lord by me?   ⓢ lures

OLIVIA
Stay:
I pr'ythee tell me what thou think'st of me.   ⓢ dares

VIOLA
That you do think you are not what you are.

OLIVIA
If I think so, I think the same of you.

VIOLA
Then think you right; I am not what I am.

OLIVIA
I would you were as I would have you be!   O↑V

VIOLA
Would it be better, madam, than I am,
I wish it might; for now I am your fool.

OLIVIA
O what a deal of scorn looks beautiful   ⓢ confesses
In the contempt and anger of his lip!
A murd'rous guilt shows not itself more soon
Than love that would seem hid: love's night is noon.
Cesario, by the roses of the spring,   ⓢ inflames

By maidhood, honour, truth, and everything,
I love thee so that, maugre all thy pride,
Nor wit, nor reason, can my passion hide.
Do not extort thy reasons from this clause,
For, that I woo, thou therefore hast no cause:
But rather reason thus with reason fetter:
Love sought is good, but given unsought is better.

VIOLA
By innocence I swear, and by my youth,
I have one heart, one bosom, and one truth,
And that no woman has; nor never none
Shall mistress be of it, save I alone.
And so adieu, good madam; never more
Will I my master's tears to you deplore.

OLIVIA
Yet come again: for thou, perhaps, mayst move
That heart, which now abhors, to like his love.

   Exeunt

KEY MOMENT

Ⓢ **mystifies**

Ⓢ **tempts**

THE IMPORTANCE OF BEING EARNEST
by Oscar Wilde

ACT 2. The Garden at Manor House. July.

Unit 1a: A Miss Fairfax has just called

Merriman is the butler at Jack's country estate and as such is the highest ranked among the servants there. Cecily is Jack's young ward, wealthy and entitled. She is polite to Merriman, but holds higher status, despite her relative youth. As a servant, Merriman keeps his presence to a minimum, attempting to be invisible except when called for. As the young lady of the house, Cecily behaves as if she owns the place.

Merriman warns Cecily of Gweldolen's arrival so she'll be on her best behaviour.
    Obstacle: Cecily doesn't like to behave as others tell her to.
Cecily instructs Merriman to bring in Gwendolen so she can satisfy her curiosity about her.
    Obstacle: Merriman is afraid that this won't go well, but he is powerless to stop it.
Rhythm: Formal and regular   Tempo: Medium-slow

Enter MERRIMAN

MERRIMAN   A Miss Fairfax has just called to see Mr. Worthing.
    On very important business, Miss Fairfax states.

CECILY   Isn't Mr. Worthing in his library?

MERRIMAN   Mr. Worthing went over in the direction of the
    Rectory some time ago.

CECILY   Pray ask the lady to come out here; Mr. Worthing is
    sure to be back soon. And you can bring tea.   C ↓ M

MERRIMAN   Yes, Miss [Goes out].

CECILY   Miss Fairfax! I suppose one of the many good
    elderly women who are associated with Uncle Jack in
    some in some of his philanthropic work in London.   ⓢ **chides**
    I don't quite like women who are interested in
    philanthropic work. I think it is so forward of them.

Unit 1b: First impressions of people are never wrong

Cecily and Gwendolen greet each other as friends, but only superficially. They are immediately suspicious of each other's motives. Both are upper class, but because Cecily lives here, she has both the power of it being her territory and the responsibility to entertain Gwendolen that comes with membership in the aristocracy.

Cecily charms Gwendolen so that she'll trust her.
    Obstacle: Gwendolen doesn't trust any woman who is young or attractive; Cecily is both.

Gwendolen flatters Cecily so that she'll respect her.
   Obstacle: Cecily doesn't respect anyone who is older than her or an authority
   figure; Gwendolen is both.
Rhythm: Overly formal, alternating   Tempo: Medium
brief pauses with bursts of excitement

   Enter MERRIMAN

MERRIMAN   Miss Fairfax.

   Enter GWENDOLEN

   Exit MERRIMAN

CECILY [Advancing to meet her]   Pray let me introduce
   myself to you. My name is Cecily Cardew.

GWENDOLEN Cecily Cardew? [Moving to her and shaking
   hands]   What a very sweet name! Something tells me that
   we are going to be great friends. I like you already more
   than I can say. My first impressions of people are never wrong.

CECILY   How nice of you to like me so much after we
   have known each other such a comparatively short time.
   Pray sit down.

GWENDOLEN   [Still standing up] I may call you Cecily,
   may I not?

CECILY   With pleasure!

GWENDOLEN   And you will always call me Gwendolen,
   won't you?

CECILY   If you wish.

GWENDOLEN   Then that is all quite settled, is it not?

CECILY   I hope so [A pause. They both sit down together].

GWENDOLEN   Perhaps this might be a favourable opportunity
   for my mentioning who I am. My father is Lord Bracknell.
   You have never heard of papa, I suppose?

CECILY   I don't think so.

GWENDOLEN   Outside the family circle, papa, I am glad to
   say, is entirely unknown. I think that is quite as it should be.
   The home seems to me to be the proper sphere for the man.   ⑤ **lectures**
   And certainly once a man begins to neglect his domestic duties he
   becomes painfully effeminate, does he not? And I don't like that.

It makes men so very attractive. Cecily, mamma, whose views
on education are remarkably strict, has brought me up to
be extremely short-sighted; it is part of her system; so do
you mind my looking at you through my glasses?

CECILY   Oh! not at all, Gwendolen. I am very fond of being
looked at.

GWENDOLEN [After examining Cecily carefully through
a lorgnette]   You are here on a short visit, I suppose.

CECILY   Oh no! I live here.

GWENDOLEN [Severely]   Really? Your mother, no doubt,
or some female relative of advanced years, resides here also?

CECILY   Oh no! I have no mother, nor, in fact, any relations.

GWENDOLEN   Indeed?

CECILY   My dear guardian, with the assistance of Miss Prism,
has the arduous task of looking after me.

GWENDOLEN   Your guardian?

CECILY   Yes, I am Mr. Worthing's ward.

GWENDOLEN   Oh! It is strange he never mentioned to me
that he had a ward. How secretive of him! He grows more
interesting hourly. I am not sure, however, that the news
inspires me with feelings of unmixed delight [Rising and
going to her]. I am very fond of you, Cecily; I have liked you
ever since I met you! But I am bound to state that now that
I know that you are Mr. Worthing's ward, I cannot help
expressing a wish you were – well, just a little older than
you seem to be – and not quite so very alluring in appearance.
In fact, if I may speak candidly –

CECILY   Pray do! I think that whenever one has anything
unpleasant to say, one should always be quite candid.

GWENDOLEN   Well, to speak with perfect candour,
Cecily, I wish that you were fully forty-two, and more than   Ⓢ **flails**
usually plain for your age. Ernest has a strong upright nature.
He is the very soul of truth and honour. Disloyalty would be
as impossible to him as deception. But even men of the
noblest possible moral character are extremely susceptible
to the influence of the physical charms of others.

Modern, no less than Ancient History, supplies us
with many most painful examples of what I refer to. If
it were not so, indeed, History would be quite unreadable.

CECILY   I beg your pardon, Gwendolen, did you say Ernest?

GWENDOLEN   Yes.

CECILY   Oh, but it is not Mr. Ernest Worthing who
is my guardian. It is his brother – his elder brother.   ⓢ **enlightens**

GWENDOLEN [Sitting down again]   Ernest never
mentioned to me that he had a brother.

CECILY   I am sorry to say they have not been on good terms
for a long time.

GWENDOLEN   Ah! that accounts for it. And now that I think
of it I have never heard any man mention his brother. The
subject seems distasteful to most men. Cecily, you have lifted
a load from my mind. I was growing almost anxious. It would
have been terrible if any cloud had come across a friendship
like ours, would it not? Of course you are quite, quite sure
that it is not Mr. Ernest Worthing who is your guardian?

CECILY   Quite sure [A pause]. In fact, I am going to be his.   ⓢ **dazzles**

GWENDOLEN [Inquiringly]   I beg your pardon?

CECILY [Rather shy and confidingly]   Dearest Gwendolen,
there is no reason why I should make a secret of it to you.
Our little county newspaper is sure to chronicle the fact next
week. Mr. Ernest Worthing and I are engaged to be married.

GWENDOLEN [Quite politely, rising]   My darling Cecily,
I think there must be some slight error. Mr. Ernest   ⓢ **undermines**
Worthing is engaged to me. The announcement will
appear in the *Morning Post* on Saturday at the latest.

CECILY [Very politely, rising]   I am afraid you must be under   G↓C
some misconception. Ernest proposed to me exactly ten
minutes ago [Shows diary].

GWENDOLEN [Examines diary through her lorgnettte
carefully]   It is certainly very curious, for he asked me to
be his wife yesterday afternoon at 5:30. If you would care to
verify the incident, pray do so [Produces diary of her own].
I never travel without my diary. One should always have

something sensational to read in the train. I am so
sorry, dear Cecily, if it is any disappointment to you,
but I am afraid I have the prior claim.   ⓢ **condescends**

CECILY   It would distress me more than I can tell you,
dear Gwendolen, if it caused you any mental or   ⓢ **ridicules**
physical anguish, but I feel bound to point out that
since Ernest proposed to you he clearly has changed
his mind.

GWENDOLEN [Meditatively]   If the poor fellow has been
entrapped into any foolish promise I shall consider it my duty
to rescue him at once, and with a firm hand.

CECILY [Thoughtfully and sadly]   Whatever unfortunate
entanglement my dear boy may have got into, I will never
reproach him with it after we are married.

GWENDOLEN   Do you allude to me, Miss Cardew, as an
entanglement? You are presumptuous. are presumptuous.   G↓C
are presumptuous. On an occasion of this kind it becomes
more than a moral duty to speak one's mind. It becomes
a pleasure.

CECILY   Do you suggest, Miss Fairfax, that I entrapped Ernest   C↑
into an engagement? How dare you? This is no time for
wearing the shallow mask of manners. When I see a spade I call
it a spade.

GWENDOLEN [Satirically]   I am glad to say that I have
never seen a spade. It is obvious that our social spheres have
been widely different.

Unit 2a. From the moment I say you, I distrusted you.

Gwendolen and Cecily are now about to go at each other's throats, but
Merriman's presence requires them to keep up the pretence of civility (servants
must not see the aristocracy behave like animals). Cecily uses her place as
hostess to ruin Gwendolen's tea, which Gwendolen views as sacrilege.

Gwendolen patronizes Cecily to get her to lose her cool.
Cecily degrades Gwendolen to reveal her weakness.
Merriman tempts Cecily to torture Gwendolen.
    Obstacle: Merriman is watching.

> *Enter MERRIMAN, followed by the footman. He carries a salver, table
> cloth, and plate stand. CECILY is about to retort. The presence of the
> servants exercises a restraining influence, under which both girls chafe.*

MERRIMAN   Shall I lay tea here as usual, Miss?

CECILY [Sternly, in a calm voice]   Yes, as usual
     [MERRIMAN begins to clear table and lay cloth.
     A long pause. CECILY and GWENDOLEN glare at
     each other].

GWENDOLEN   Are there many interesting walks in
     the vicinity, Miss Cardew?   ⑤ inquires

CECILY   Oh! yes! a great many. From the top of one of
     the hills quite close one can see five counties.

GWENDOLEN   Five counties! I don't think I should like
     that; I hate crowds.

CECILY [Sweetly]   I suppose that is why you live in town?
     [Gwendolen bites her lip, and beats her foot nervously
     with her parasol]   C↓G

GWENDOLEN [Looking round]   Quite a well-kept garden
     this is, Miss Cardew.

CECILY   So glad you like it, Miss Fairfax.

GWENDOLEN   I had no idea there were any flowers in
     the country.

CECILY   Oh, flowers are as common here, Miss Fairfax,
     as people are in London.   C↓G

GWENDOLEN   Personally I cannot understand how
     anybody manages to exist in the country, if anybody who
     is anybody does. The country always bores me to death.

CECILY   Ah! This is what the newspapers call agricultural
     depression, is it not? I believe the aristocracy are suffering
     very much from it just at present. It is almost an epidemic
     amongst them, I have been told. May I offer you some tea,
     Miss Fairfax?

GWENDOLEN [With elaborate politeness]   Thank you
     [Aside]. Detestable girl! But I require tea!

CECILY [Sweetly]   Sugar?

GWENDOLEN [Superciliously]   No, thank you. Sugar
     is not fashionable any more [Cecily looks angrily   G↓C
     at her, takes up the tongs and puts four lumps of sugar
     into the cup].

CECILY [Severely]   Cake or bread and butter?

GWENDOLEN [In a bored manner]   Bread and butter,
   please. Cake is rarely seen at the best houses nowadays.   G↓C

CECILY [Cuts a very large slice of cake, and puts it on the tray]
   Hand that to Miss Fairfax.

*MERRIMAN does so, and goes out with footman. GWENDOLEN drinks the
tea and makes a grimace. Puts down cup at once, reaches out her hand to
the bread and butter, looks at it, and finds it is cake. Rises in indignation.*

GWENDOLEN   You have filled my tea with lumps of
   sugar, and though I asked most distinctly for bread   Ⓢ **annihilates**
   and butter, you have given me cake. I am known for
   the gentleness of my disposition, and the extraordinary
   sweetness of my nature, but I warn you, Miss Cardew,
   you may go too far.

CECILY [Rising]   To save my poor, innocent, trusting
   boy from the machinations of any other girl there are
   no lengths to which I would not go.   KEY MOMENT

GWENDOLEN   From the moment I saw you I distrusted
   you. I felt that you were false and deceitful. I am never
   deceived in such matters. My first impressions of people
   are invariably right.

CECILY   It seems to me, Miss Fairfax, that I am trespassing
   on your valuable time. No doubt you have many other
   calls of a similar character to make in the neighbourhood.

SELECT BIBLIOGRAPHY

Baker, Annie. *The Flick*. New York: Theatre Communications Group, 2014.

Baker, George Pierce. *Dramatic Technique*. New York: Da Capo Press, 1919.

Ball, David. *Backwards and Forwards: A Technical Manual for Reading Plays*. Carbondale, IL: Southern Illinois University Press, 1983.

Burns, Selena. 'Accusing and Engaging the Audience through Theatreform: Griselda Gambaro's *Information for Foreigners*.' *Platform* 2.1 (Spring 2007): 38–52.

Else, Gerald Frank. Trans. *Aristotle: Poetics*. Ann Arbor: University of Michigan Press, 1967.

Freytag, Gustav and Elias J. MacEwan. *Freytag's Technique of the Drama*: *An Exposition of Dramatic Composition and Art*. Chicago: S.C. Griggs & Company, 1895.

Gainor, J. Ellen, Stanton B. Garner, Jr. and Martin Puchner, eds. *The Norton Anthology of Drama*. 2nd ed. Vol. 1 & 2. New York: W. W. Norton & Company, 2013.

Gambaro, Griselda. *Information for Foreigners: Three Plays*. Translated by Marguerite Feitlowitz. Evanston, IL: Northwestern University Press, 1992.

Gussow, Mel. 'Madness, Murder and Irrationality, in "Woyzeck."' *New York Times*, 6 March 1990: C17.

Gussow, Mel. 'Woyzeck, Antihero, Cannot Outrun His Destiny.' *New York Times*, 7 December 1992.

Healy, Patrick. 'A London Troupe Thrives with Ambitious Free-Range Theater.' *New York Times*, 7 August 2013.

Hodge, Francis and Michael McLain. *Play Directing: Analysis, Communication, and Style*. 7th ed. New York: Routledge, 2016.

Ibsen, Henrik. *Hedda Gabler*. Trans. Michael Meyer. London: Bloomsbury Methuen Drama, 2001.

Jonas, Susan, Geoffrey Proehl, and Michael Lupu, eds. *Dramaturgy in American Theater: A Source Book*. Fort Worth: Harcourt Brace College Publishers, 1997.

Katz, Leon. 'The Complete Dramaturg.' In *Dramaturgy in American Theater: A Source Book*, edited by Susan Jonas, Geoffrey S. Proehl, and Michael Lupu. Fort Worth: Harcourt Brace College, 1997.

Knopf, Robert, ed. *Theater of the Avant-Garde, 1890–1950*. Rev. ed. New Haven: Yale University Press, 2015.

Kresh, Joseph. 'Georg Büchner.' *Dialectics* 7 (1938): 28–30.

Lawson, John Howard. *Theory and Technique of Playwriting*. New York: G.P. Putnam's Sons, 1936.

Pareles, Jon. 'Woyzeck as a Normal Guy Who Gets Jealous.' *New York Times*, 31 October 2002.

Pfister, Manfred. *The Theory and Analysis of Drama*. Cambridge: Cambridge University Press, 1988.

Raby, Peter. *The Cambridge Companion to Oscar Wilde*. Cambridge: Cambridge University Press, 1997.

Reeve, William C. *Georg Büchner*. New York: Ungar, 1979: 122–165.

Richards, David G. 'Criticism to 1945.' In *Georg Büchner's Woyzeck: A History of Its Criticism*, 1–26. Rochester, NY: Camden House, 2001.

Simon, John. *Singularities: Essays on the Theater, 1964–1973*. New York: Random House, 1976: 30–31.

Taylor, John Russell. *The Rise and Fall of the Well-Made Play*. 1967. Reissue ed. London: Routledge, 2015.

Thomas, James Michael. *Script Analysis for Actors, Directors, and Designers*. 5th ed. Boston: Focal Press, 2014.

Vogel, Paula. *How I Learned to Drive*. New York: Dramatists Play Service, 1997.

Wallis, Mick and Simon Shepherd. *Studying Plays*. 3rd ed. London: Bloomsbury, 2010.

INDEX

BIOGRAPHICAL

Robert Knopf is Director of Theatre Studies at the University at Buffalo/SUNY, USA, and directs, writes, and teaches theatre and film. His directing credits include premieres at New York's historic Town Hall, Circle in the Square Downtown, Circle Rep Lab, Paradise Factory, and the Cherry Lane Annex. He served as series dramaturge for National Public Radio's *The Archaeology of Lost Voices*, for which he directed the radio drama *Hidden Dragon*.

Over the past two decades, he has written and edited six books and two second editions. His two-volume set, *Theater of the Avant-Garde, 1890–1950* and *1950–2000* (the latter with Julia Listengarten), is the most comprehensive and best-selling critical anthology of avant-garde theatre in print.

Before coming to the University at Buffalo/SUNY, he served as Director of Graduate Studies and Associate Chair of Theatre at the University of Michigan, Ann Arbor, USA, and Director of the M.F.A. Directing programme at Purdue University. He teaches Script Analysis, Graduate and Advanced Undergraduate Directing, Improvization, and Avant-Garde Performance.